# Los Protestantes

# Los Protestantes

An Introduction to Latino Protestantism
in the United States

JUAN FRANCISCO MARTÍNEZ

 PRAEGER

AN IMPRINT OF ABC-CLIO, LLC
Santa Barbara, California • Denver, Colorado • Oxford, England

**Library of Congress Cataloging-in-Publication Data**

Martínez, Juan Francisco, 1957–
  Los Protestantes : an introduction to Latino Protestantism in the United States / Juan Francisco Martínez.
    p. cm.
  In English.
  Includes bibliographical references and (p.   ) index.
  ISBN 978-0-313-39313-6 (hardcopy : alk. paper) — ISBN 978-0-313-39314-3 (ebook)
  1. Hispanic American Protestants.  I. Title.
  BR563.H57M36   2011
  280'.408968073—dc23      2011019820

ISBN: 978-0-313-39313-6
EISBN: 978-0-313-39314-3

15  14  13  12  11    1  2  3  4  5

This book is also available on the World Wide Web as an eBook.
Visit www.abc-clio.com for details.

Praeger
An Imprint of ABC-CLIO, LLC

ABC-CLIO, LLC
130 Cremona Drive, P.O. Box 1911
Santa Barbara, California 93116-1911

This book is printed on acid-free paper ∞

Manufactured in the United States of America

# Contents

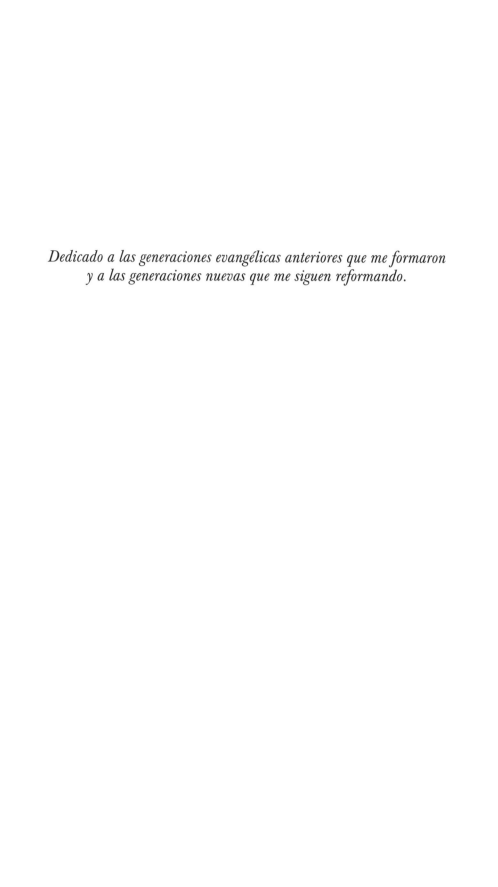

*Dedicado a las generaciones evangélicas anteriores que me formaron*
*y a las generaciones nuevas que me siguen reformando.*

# Introduction

In many ways this book is a family biography. Rafaela García, my great-great-grandmother, became a Protestant believer at the beginning of the 20th century in south Texas. She became a part of a small religious minority, within an ethnic minority (though Latinos have always been the majority in south Texas). Her conversion influenced her daughter, Anita García, and my grandmother, Juanita Cáceres (Guerra, by marriage). Juanita prayed that her children would enter ministry, and she saw my parents become pastors before she died in 1965. Juan and Bertha (Rafaela's great-granddaughter) Martínez have been pastors in small Latino congregations since the early 1960s in south Texas, central California, and now Colorado.[1] I became a pastor in the 1970s and have pastored Latino churches in Texas, California, and Guatemala. That makes me a fifth-generation Latino Protestant, a rare bird in the growing ethno-religious minority of Latino Protestants in the United States.

Though Latino Protestants are a religious minority within an ethnic minority in the United States, we are growing in absolute numbers and as a percentage of the Latino community. Though we are a small part of U.S. Protestantism, we are one of few populations where Protestantism is growing in this country.

The growing Latino community, and the growing Latino Protestant community in particular, is a harbinger of change in the United States. Latinos are now the largest "minority" group in the United States, and they continue to grow, both because of higher-than-average birth rates and because of new immigration, both legal and undocumented. Latinos are a significant part of a changing demographic reality in which it is estimated that "whites" will cease to be the majority of the U.S. population somewhere between 2040 and 2050.

But Latinos are also a reflection of the complex history of the United States in relationship to the Americas. We are the "Harvest of Empire,"[2] a people who originally became a part of the United States as this country expanded into the Southwest by taking over half of Mexico's former territory and into the Caribbean, leaving Puerto Rico as a part of the United States not as a state or a colony, but as a commonwealth (Estado Libre Asociado de Puerto Rico, in Spanish). The United States has also intervened politically, economically, and militarily in various parts of the Americas throughout its history. Latin America is perceived as the United States' backyard. Because of two hundred years of history, the Monroe Doctrine, an extensive border with Mexico, the North American Free Trade Agreement (NAFTA), the status of Puerto Rico, and U.S. economic and political policies, the "Latino issue" will not go away anytime soon.

The Latino issue is also raising questions about the future identity of the United States. Samuel Huntington was convinced that Latinos were a threat to his vision of what the United States should look like in the future.[3] Since the first Latinos became citizens after the takeover of the Southwest in 1848, they have demonstrated a strong commitment to the United States and have contributed in all areas of society. But over the last 160-plus years, they have followed a number of different paths toward participation in U.S. society; some have followed the path of full structural assimilation, but most have integrated in other ways.

Protestant Latinos present a unique situation in this process. Because the vast majority of Latinos are historically Roman Catholic, conversion to Protestantism was assumed to be a sign of assimilating into majority Protestant society. As discussed in chapter 2, a lot of Protestant missionaries among Latinos in the United States assumed that evangelization and Americanization were part and parcel of the same task. The data analyzed in the first and fifth chapters of this book demonstrate that there seems to be a small bit of truth in this hypothesis, though much less than was assumed by many sociologists.

The experience of Latino Protestants has been much more complex. Throughout the 19th century and much of the 20th century, Latina Protestants found themselves doubly isolated. The Catholic majority in the Latino community has often questioned Latino Protestants' ethnic identity commitment because they are Protestants. But Euro-American Protestants have not always received Latino Protestants with open arms because they are Latinos.

Latino Protestant churches often have been a place of ethnic identity maintenance as well, particularly through the formal use of the Spanish language. Generations of Latina young people, like me, not only used Spanish in church but also learned to read and write it because of church participation.

More recent immigrant Latino Protestants have added to the religious diversity because many of them are bringing their own churches and movements and are not connecting to existing U.S. Protestant churches and denominations. Though they share a common theological legacy, there is often very little in common between Latina immigrant churches and their majority culture counterparts.

Yet there are also many Latino Protestants for whom conversion to Protestantism has been a step toward structural assimilation into majority culture. Today many Latina Protestants are in majority-culture Protestant churches and reflect the social and cultural values of the people around them in church. This means that Protestantism has provided a space both for Latino ethnic identity maintenance and for structural assimilation.

This book tells the story of how Latino Protestants got to where they are today. Chapter 1 begins by reviewing three major studies of Latino religious tendencies in the United States and their implications for understanding Latina Protestants in particular. It continues with a description of the diversity of the Latino community, focusing on several areas, including national backgrounds, cultural adaptation, linguistic issues, and ethnic identity maintenance. This first chapter provides a snapshot of Latino Protestants in 2010, when this book was written.

The second chapter begins by describing Protestant missionary efforts among Latinos starting in the 19th-century Southwest after 1848. It reviews how Protestantism took root among U.S. Latinas during the 19th and early 20th centuries. The second part of the chapter focuses on various immigrant waves from Latin America and how these have contributed to the growth and diversification of Latino Protestantism. The last section presents the complex historical relationships between Latino Protestants and Catholics in the United States.

Latino Protestantism is growing. Chapter 3 outlines the various sources of that growth. It describes conversion experiences, Protestant immigration from Latin America, and Latina Protestants in non-Latino churches. This chapter includes a list and a brief description of the major denominations, movements, and organizations within Latino Protestantism.

Chapter 4 describes how Protestantism has developed a unique identity in Latin America and among U.S. Protestant Latinas. It addresses why the common U.S. categories of Protestantism—mainline, evangelical, and

Pentecostal—are often inadequate to describe the complexities of Latino Protestant identity. The chapter includes some of the ways Latino Protestants have attempted to describe themselves.

Many Latinas are part of Protestant churches that do not have a Latino focus. Chapter 5 describes the complex relationship between religious and ethnic identity as expressed by Latino Protestants. The chapter includes a description of the movement of Protestant Latinos between churches and into non-Latino majority churches. It also provides an overview of the types of non-Latino churches that have been most attractive to Latinas.

Latino Protestantism is an ethno-religious identity in the United States. The sixth chapter explores some of the challenges of maintaining an identity that is both Latino and Protestant in the United States. This chapter reviews how Latina Protestants have been understood in scholarly research. The chapter includes the stories and experiences of specific Latina Protestants, reflecting some of the various faces of Latino Protestantism.

The last chapter outlines some of the principal challenges facing Latino Protestants in the United States. It looks at the pressures of cultural adaptation and assimilation, the relationships with Latin American Protestants, Latino Protestants' place in U.S. Protestantism, and scenarios of what Latino Protestants might look like in the future. The chapter concludes with a list of contributions of Latino Protestants to U.S. Protestantism and to the United States in general.

Two terms are commonly used to define the community being studied: Latino and Hispanic. I have chosen to principally use Latino due to personal preferences. But I will also occasionally use Hispanic as fully synonymous with Latino, particularly when those I am citing use that term. Because Latino is a term in Spanish, it has gender. Spanish commonly uses the masculine to refer to both males and females but assumes that the feminine can refer only to females. As with all live languages, Spanish is evolving, and I assume that this issue will eventually find a more equitable solution. At least I very much hope so. Some people have attempted to address the gender issue by using "Latin@" or "Latino(a)" or by repeating "Latina and Latino" whenever they are referring to both male and female. I agree with the challenge they are raising but find these solutions problematic at best. So I attempt to address this issue by using Latino and Latina interchangeably. Unless I specifically refer to females or males, all usages of either Latino or Latina will refer to all. This will probably feel more uncomfortable to Latino males who speak Spanish and are not used to having themselves included in feminine terms. Because Spanish is my first language and one in which I teach and publish, I hope that we will be able to find grammatically acceptable ways to break out of the *machista* tendencies of the language

I love. But until that happens, I want to name the problem and seek ways of addressing it. In this book the solution will be to use Latino and Latina. I apologize to those for whom this is not an acceptable solution, and I am open to other ways of addressing this issue.

There are also other terms that I use throughout the book that should be identified and defined from the beginning. First of all, in the United States there are three broad common categories to define Protestants. *Mainline* refers to those denominations linked historically to the "liberal" side of the liberal-fundamentalist debates of the late 19th and early 20th centuries in this country. Most mainline denominations identify themselves as such, though not all members of mainline denominations would see themselves as theologically liberal. *Evangelical* refers to denominations that come out of the "fundamentalist" side of the debate. A few still prefer the term *fundamentalist,* though most have rejected the term because of the pejorative connotations often associated with it. *Pentecostal* denominations are those that were born in the Pentecostal revival of the early 20th century or that quickly became a part of the revival. Most Pentecostal denominations in the United States also consider themselves evangelicals, though historically, evangelicals have not always been sure that Pentecostals are evangelicals.

There is one term used in Latin America and among U.S. Latina Protestants that is a false cognate and creates occasional confusion. *Evangélico* is the most common term used in Spanish to refer to all (or almost all) Protestants. It is much broader than the English term *evangelical,* though some people treat these terms as synonymous. The nuances of the term and its implications are discussed in chapter 4.

I use the term Euro-American to name the predominant culture and ethnic identity in the United States. Latino, or Hispanic, is the common term to refer to the community being studied. Occasionally, I will use "Hispanic descent" to refer to those who no longer have a Latina self-identity and do not connect with Latino culture in any way. Other terms and concepts are defined within the text itself.

Though Latino Protestantism has been a personal passion for many years, it was Suzanne Staszak-Silva at Praeger Publishers who first proposed this specific project to me. Thank you, Suzanne, for the original idea, and thanks to Michael Wilt, who followed through and made this project a reality. But this book is also the result of mentors, colleagues, and friends who have been studying and writing about various aspects of Latino Protestantism. I am particularly indebted to Justo González, David Maldonado, Paul Barton, Arlene Sánchez-Walsh, and Clifton Holland for all the work they have already done in this area. I also want to thank Susan Wood for editing the manuscript and Arnaldo Soto for checking the footnotes and sources.

But as I stated at the beginning of this introduction, this project is also about the extended family of which I am a part. I am grateful to my ancestors who modeled a way of following Jesus; to my parents, who showed me how service to God and to others is lived out; and to the many pastors and leaders who made me who I am. But I am also grateful for the younger leaders and students who constantly challenge me to rethink the parameters of what it means to be Protestant and Latino. You are all part of this book.

## CHAPTER ONE

# *Protestantes* by the Numbers

Latinos became the largest minority group in the United States sometime during the first decade of the 21st century. Current and projected growth seems to indicate that Latinas will be the largest minority into the foreseeable future. Because of our growth, the community has become an important magnet for studies and analyses. The common question in the background of most studies is, Who are these Latinos, and how are they affecting, or how will they affect, the United States?

The Pew Charitable Trusts has funded many studies on the U.S. Latino community. The Pew Hispanic Center has published research on many aspects of the community, including religious preferences and trends. Its last major study on religion, *Changing Faiths: Latinos and the Transformation of American Religion* (2007), provides a very helpful overview of Latino religious perspectives in general, and Latino Protestantism in particular.[1] This study builds on the work of the 2003 report *Hispanic Churches in American Public Life*.[2] These overviews provide very important demographic information that serves as the framework for a detailed description of Protestantism in the Latino community.

Trinity College of Hartford, Connecticut, also published a longitudinal study on Latina religion, *U.S. Latino Religious Identification, 1990–2008: Growth, Diversity & Transformation*.[3] Broadly speaking, both studies draw similar conclusions about the religious tendencies in the Latino community, though the Trinity study finds more secularization than the Pew research. Each study uses different categories to define Protestants and other non-Catholic expressions in the Latino community. This makes it difficult to compare their conclusions about Latina Protestants. And, as is discussed in chapter 4, the categorizations used by each study present their own difficulties when trying to describe Latino Protestantism. Nonetheless, both studies provide very useful general information about the religious practices and preferences of the community.

## By the Numbers

According to the 2007 Pew study, 68 percent of Latinos are Catholics, 20 percent are Protestants, 3 percent are other Christians (Jehovah's Witnesses, Mormons, Orthodox), 1 percent are part of other religions, and 8 percent define themselves as secular. Of the 20 percent that are Protestant about three-fourths (15% of the total) are part of evangelical or Pentecostal churches, and one-fourth (5% of the total) are part of mainline denominations.[4] The Trinity study asked a slightly different set of questions, so the categories do not exactly match. According to this study, 60 percent are Catholic, 22 percent are other Christians, 1 percent are part of other religions, 12 percent are "None," and 4.5 percent refused to give an answer.[5]

The Pew study uses the common U.S. Protestant categories of evangelical, Pentecostal, and mainline to describe Latina Protestants and separates out the Mormons and Jehovah's Witnesses from the Protestants into an "Other Christian" category. Among non-Catholic Christians, the Trinity study uses the categories Baptist, Christian generic, Pentecostal, and Protestant sects. It separates out Mormons but includes Jehovah's Witnesses in Protestant sects, which also includes Mennonite, Covenant, Churches of Christ, Adventist, and other groups. The "Christian generic" category includes most evangelical Protestants, except those placed in the "sect" category.[6] Since Jehovah's Witnesses do not self-identify as Protestant, and no Protestant group would recognize them as such, these categories make it difficult to use the Trinity study to describe more specific Latino Protestant characteristics in ways that would clearly make sense to most U.S. Protestants or Latino Protestants, in particular. The two studies address religious preferences, and both seek to understand how living in the United States affects Latina religious practices. But because of these significant differences in how they divide up non-Catholic Christians, it is difficult to compare, contrast, or unite the data to develop a larger picture of Latino Protestantism.

Because of the categories it uses, the Pew study is easier to follow for the purposes of this book. The 2007 study correlated the broad Protestant categories of evangelical/Pentecostal[7] and mainline with country of birth, language usage, and generations in the United States. The study presented the following results.

Among evangelicals/Pentecostals, 45 percent were born in the United States, and 55 percent were born in other countries. Within mainline denominations, 65 percent of their Latino members were born in the United States and 35 percent in Latin America.[8] The study did not ask about the length of time immigrants have been in the United States, so it did not distinguish between those who were raised in the United States and those who came as adults.

The Pew survey also asked people to identify themselves by first, second, or third generation in the United States. This question subdivided the U.S.-born portion of the previous question. It found that evangelicals/ Protestants were 55 percent first generation, 23 percent second generation, and 21 percent third generation. Mainline Protestant Latinos were more likely to have been in the United States for several generations. Their breakdown was 35 percent (first), 37 percent (second), and 28 percent (third).[9] Since there have been Latinas in U.S. mainline Protestant churches since the 1850s, one assumes that the third-generation category includes those who have been in the States more than three generations.[10]

The study also divided each of these groups by self-identified country or region of origin.[11] The breakdown for evangelicals/Pentecostals was as follows: Puerto Rico, 16 percent; Mexico, 50 percent; Cuba, 4 percent; Dominican Republic, 1 percent; Central America, 14 percent; South America, 6 percent; and Other, 8 percent. Here the breakdown for Latinos from mainline churches was not significantly different, except for the difference between Mexicans and Central Americans: Puerto Rico, 16 percent; Mexico, 56 percent; Cuba, 6 percent; Dominican Republic, 3 percent; Central America, 6 percent; South America, 4 percent; and Other, 8 percent.[12]

Pew addressed the language question by offering respondents three options: English-dominant, bilingual, and Spanish-dominant. Among evangelicals/ Pentecostals the breakdown was 31 percent English, 32 percent bilingual, and 38 percent Spanish. According to this study Latinos in mainline churches are much more English-dominant, at 45 percent, with 28 percent bilingual and 26 percent Spanish-dominant.[13] These numbers seem to correlate with the previously mentioned statistic according to which mainline churches have a larger percentage of people who have been in the United States at least three generations.

As stated earlier, the Trinity study drew similar broad conclusions related to the total numbers of Catholics and non-Catholics. But their numbers related to nativity, generation in the United States, and language usage often seem to vary a great deal from the Pew results. This may be due to the difference in categories, but given that difference, it is difficult to compare and contrast the two studies. There is one important distinction between the two studies that merits more research; in the area of nativity and generations in the United States, the Trinity study separates out those born in Puerto Rico from those born "abroad" (Latin America).[14] Though they do not draw out any specific conclusions related to religious practices, this distinction will likely be very useful in understanding the complex identity formation of Latinas and of Latino Protestants in particular.

The 2003 Pew study presented some tentative conclusions about the religious tendencies of Latinas that seem to be affirmed by the 2007 Pew study and by the Trinity study:

- The number of Latino Catholics is growing, though not necessarily as a percentage of the Latino population.
- Latino Pentecostalism is growing.
- The number of Latino Catholics who define themselves as charismatic is growing.
- Religious movements from Latin America are growing in the United States.
- Groups such as the Mormons and the Jehovah's Witnesses continue to grow among Latinos.
- There is a religious diversification among those of the second and third generations. A few are draw to mainline churches and others to world religions.
- Latinos are becoming more politically, civically, and socially active.[15]

According to the initial reports of the 2010 Census, there are now about 50,500,000 Latinos in the United States.[16] This means that the number of Latino Protestants is growing. There are now about 7.5 million Latinos that are evangelicals/Protestants, and about 2.5 million are part of mainline denominations. It is also worth noting that according to the Pew study, 54 percent of Latina Catholics identify themselves as charismatic, and 28 percent identify themselves as born-again.[17] So though the vast majority of Latinos self-identify as Catholics, many of them also identify with religious practices that are more commonly identified with evangelicals and Pentecostals.

## Behind These Numbers

These studies point toward several important issues that are discussed throughout the book. On the one hand, the issues of change, diversity, and transformation that are in the titles of both the studies are clearly descriptive of the Latino community in general and of its religious practices in particular. Both Pew and Trinity point to a decrease in the percentage of Latinos who identify as Catholics. Protestants and other non-Catholic groups account for an increasing percentage of religious (or nonreligious) practice in the community. Latinas also reflect the growing tendency in the United States and in Latin America of Christians who identify with independent churches or who downplay or reject traditional denominational labels. But these differences are not uniform among all Latinos. There are clear differences depending on national backgrounds, how Latinas interact with the dominant culture, generational shifts, migration flows, education, and many of the other diversities in the Latino community.

## Countries of Origin

The national background of Latino Protestants roughly parallels the national backgrounds of the Latino population at large with one major exception: the percentage of Protestants from Mexican and Puerto Rican backgrounds. Census figures state that 66 percent of the Latina population is of Mexican background, and 9 percent is of Puerto Rican descent.[18] Yet the Mexican percentage among Latino Protestants is considerably lower, and the Puerto Rican percentage is considerably higher than among the Latino population at large. This is probably because a much larger percentage of the population of Puerto Rico (40%) is Protestant than the population of Mexico (6%).[19] This means that Mexican immigrants are much more likely to be Roman Catholic when they come to the States and that they are most likely to remain Catholic once they are here. Given that Mexicans continue to identify with Catholicism more strongly in Mexico than in any other country of Latin America, it seems likely that people of Mexican descent will continue to be overrepresented among Latino Catholics and underrepresented among Protestants, as a total of the Latino population in the United States. On the other hand, people from Puerto Rico will most likely continue to be overrepresented among Latino Protestants.

The national background categories used by both the Pew and Trinity studies are those commonly used in the United States, but they are problematic because they implicitly assume that all Latinos are immigrants or descendents of recent immigrants. (This is reinforced by the generational categories of the Pew study that go only to the third generation.) They do not provide an option for those who trace their history to the Southwest since the 16th, 17th, or 18th century and whose ancestors went from being Spaniards to Mexicans to Americans in the course of a little more than one generation during the first part of the 19th century.[20] Their history is not one of recent migration, since it was the border that "migrated" over their ancestors, not their ancestors over the border. Since they are not clearly separated out in the study, it is difficult to ascertain how being a part of the United States over 150 years has influenced their religious practices. What

role has Protestantism played in their ethnic and religious identities? Have
they been more or less influenced by Protestantism than Hispanic immigrants from Latin America? Are they more likely to be secularized since
they have been in the States longer than other Latinas?

Given the nature of both studies, it is difficult to account for how the issues of national background affect the regional differences that clearly mark
the religious expressions of the Latino communities in the United States.
The Pew study provides only national statistics. The Trinity study draws
conclusions by U.S. Census divisions. But because Latinos are not evenly
distributed around the United States, it is difficult to compare and contrast
Latino Protestantism across regions from a uniquely Latino perspective.
For example, because of the population base, Latina Protestant worship
in churches of the Southwest tends to have a strong Mexican or Mexican
American influence, with some Central American influence, particularly
in Southern California and other major urban areas. Worship practices in
the East tend to have a more Caribbean flavor in most of the churches,
be it Puerto Rican or Dominican (Northeast) or Cuban (Southeast). Other
regions reflect the migratory patterns of specific Latino communities or
pastors. Does Latino Protestantism have clearly distinguishable practices
in each of the regions where the Latino influence is of a dominant national
background? Do Latina Protestants have a stronger influence on the larger
Protestant church in the United States in those areas where they are a larger
percentage of the population (i.e., Southern California or south Texas)?
Since Puerto Ricans are more likely to be Protestants, does their influence
on U.S. Protestantism look different from the Mexican or Mexican American influence? Neither of these studies allows us to draw any conclusions
related to any of these questions.

## Migratory and Generational Shifts

Both of the studies point to the impact of life in the United States on
Latino religious tendencies. Clearly there is a higher percentage of Protestants (and those who do not identify with any religion) among those who
have lived in the States for generations than among immigrants. The studies recognize that there are several issues involved in this shift, not only the
broader influence of being in the United States.

On the one hand, the Pew research found a higher level of conversions (toward Protestantism or secularism) among those who demonstrated
higher levels of assimilation, such as being born in the United States or
having English-language dominance, higher education, and higher income
levels.[21] The Trinity study pointed in the same direction, finding that in all

non-Catholic categories, Latinas had more education and higher income than their Catholic counterparts.[22]

Nonetheless, the Pew study asked other questions that clearly pointed to a much more complex set of influences. For example, when they broke down the converts by country of origin, they found that people from Puerto Rico were more much more likely to be Protestant converts than Latinos from any other national background (31%, whereas the people from other national backgrounds were around 20% or less).[23] Since the survey did not ask when and where people became converts, it is not clear whether this happened in the United States or in Puerto Rico. So it is not clear how much influence being on the mainland influenced Puerto Ricans' decisions to become Protestants. Since Protestantism is growing in Puerto Rico, would these people have become converts even if they had not migrated to the States? Also, even if they have lived on the mainland for more than one generation, how much of their decision can be attributed to U.S. influence, and how much to religious changes that are occurring in Puerto Rico? This also raises the following question for researchers on both the island and the mainland: to what extent is the shift to Protestantism among Puerto Ricans, and those of Puerto Rican background on the mainland, a function of U.S. influence on the island or vice versa?

Pew researchers also asked Protestant converts about the reasons for conversion and the sources of information about their new religious practices.[24] Their answers were very similar to those one might expect to hear in Latin America. More than 80 percent of respondents said they converted because they were looking for a more direct, personal experience of God. More than 70 percent stated that they first heard about their new church or religious community from family or friends. Since these responses would not likely be different from those given by Protestant converts in Latin America, it is not clear what specific role, if any, being in the States had on the decision to convert. Are Latina immigrants more, or less, exposed to the Protestant message in the United States or in Latin America? Would the answer vary from country to country and state to state, such that people in Puerto Rico might be more exposed to the Protestant message than Latinos in New England, but Latinos in Texas might be more likely to be evangelized by a Protestant than people living in Mexico?

The Pew study also addressed another important, though complex, issue: that of how Protestant converts view the Roman Catholic Church. Again, this series of questions points to a broader issue: the historical role that Catholicism has played in Latin America and among U.S. Latinos. Researchers asked how converts viewed mass, church teachings on divorce, its treatment of women, and its view of immigrants, apparently assuming that these might be reasons for Latinos to leave the Catholic Church.[25] But since these questions are not compared with surveys in Latin America, it is difficult know whether the answers to the first three questions would have been any different among Latin American converts. Another thing that was not clear with this series of questions is why these were the issues the Pew researchers considered important in relationship to the decision to become Protestant. Are these the issues that Latina converts would have raised if the questions related to Roman Catholicism had been more open-ended? The complex relationship between Protestants and Catholics in the Latino community is addressed throughout the book, particularly in chapter 2, but Pew researchers recognized that Protestant converts "left" Catholicism, even though they may not have pointed to all of the principal reasons for this movement.

### Ethnic Identity Maintenance and Religious Practice

One of the most interesting results of the Pew study had to do with the relationship between religious practices and ethnic identity maintenance among Latinos. According to the results of the study,

> the houses of worship most frequented by Latinos have distinctively ethnic characteristics. . . . The growth of the Hispanic population is leading to the emergence of Latino-oriented churches in all the major religious traditions across the country. . . . Foreign-born Latinos are most likely to attend Hispanic-oriented churches and to comprise the largest share of Latinos who worship at such churches. . . . large shares of native-born Latinos as well as those who speak little or no Spanish also report attending churches with ethnic characteristics. . . . Latino-oriented churches, then, are not exclusively a product of either immigration or of residential settlement patterns. . . . the Hispanic population is creating its own distinct forms of religious practice as well as its own religious institutions.[26]

Pew looked for three characteristics in churches or congregations to decide whether they had a clear ethnic identity. These congregations had to have Latino pastors, priests, or other principal religious leaders; services had to be available in Spanish; and most of the people who worshiped together had to be Hispanics. Given these characteristics, Pew found that 66 percent of all Hispanic churchgoers, Catholic or Protestant, attend a church with all three characteristics; 21 percent attend one that has at least two; and 8 percent attend congregations that have at least one characteristic. Only 5 percent of regular church attendees reported going to churches that had none of these characteristics.[27] Churches with all three characteristics were highest among Catholics and evangelicals/Pentecostals, but even

in the smaller group of mainline churches, 48 percent of churchgoers reported attending churches that had all three characteristics.[28] This tendency
declined over generations, but even by the third generation and beyond,
42 percent of churchgoers reported attending churches with all three characteristics, and around 70 percent reported that their churches have Hispanic
pastors or services in Spanish, though the exact percentages of churches
with both among the third generation and beyond were not correlated. The
results among those who identified themselves as English-dominant were
lower, though also significant: 34 percent of the English-dominant attend
a congregation with all three characteristics, and also almost 70 percent
reported they attended churches with two of the characteristics.[29] Specifically, among Latino evangelicals/Pentecostals who attend church weekly,
67 percent attend churches with all three characteristics, and over 80 percent report at least two of the characteristics in their congregations, though
again, the results were not directly correlated for this group.[30]

A separate follow-up survey looked at Catholics and language preference
in relationship to mass. It found that 60 percent of respondents always went
to mass in Spanish and that 12 percent reported that they mostly went to
mass in Spanish. Of those who always go to mass in Spanish, 76 percent are
foreign-born, and 24 percent are U.S.-born (they did not separate this group
out by generations). They also found that among those who always go to
mass in Spanish, 70 percent are Spanish-dominant, 27 percent are bilingual,
and 4 percent are English-dominant.[31] They did not do a similar study of
Protestant linguistic preferences in relationship to worship. But given the
other numbers, the implication seems to be that one could expect similar
types of results among Latino Protestants.

The Pew study does not venture a guess about whether this linguistic tendency will continue over the long term. And since there are no longitudinal
studies on the role of religion and Spanish-language maintenance, it is difficult to compare with the religious practices of previous generations of U.S.
Latinas. But the study does affirm "that ethnic churches are a widespread
and defining attribute of Latino religious practice today."[32]

### Transnationalism and Migration

Neither one of the studies addressed the complex issue of the transnational migratory patterns within the Latina community. Both seemed to
assume a unidirectional aspect to migration and acculturation or at least
focused only on the Latino religious experience north of the border, though
the Pew 2007 study acknowledges that "religious affiliation in Latin America
is very relevant to any examination of Hispanics in the US" and mentions
the growth of Protestantism in Latin America.[33] But given the large numbers

of Latinos who travel north and south on a regular basis, it is important to assess the impact of this movement on religious practices and affiliation both in Latin America and among U.S. Latinas. There is continued religious devotion among Mexican Americans to patron saints and virgins of Mexico. How does this movement reinforce Catholic religious identity even beyond the immigrant generation? How do the people moving in both directions take their faith with them? Do converts remain Protestants if and when they return to Latin America? Earlier generations of Latino converts in the United States became informal missionaries among their relatives and friends when they returned to Latin America—does that tendency continue? How strong is this transnational tendency beyond the immigrant generation, and what religious influences are related to it?[34]

## *Protestantes* within the Larger Latino Community

This demographic overview of Latino Protestantism needs to be framed within the larger reality of the U.S. Latino experience. There are many excellent studies on the Latina experience, so I will not attempt to review or rewrite what others have done. But it is important to provide more background on some of the issues that are addressed in subsequent chapters. In particular, I want to address the various types of diversities in the community and how they impact religious experiences and perspectives.

Though Latinas are referred to as one community, in many ways we are really a group of communities under a common name. There are many ways to think about the diversities reflected in the communities brought together under the umbrella terms Latino or Hispanic. Both the Pew and Trinity studies point to two of the most common diversities: national background and adaptation to majority culture.

National background is probably the easier of the two to describe. It is important to understanding the Latino experience because it helps explain the historical background, the political perspectives, and the various religious practices among various members of the community. Both studies point to it, but neither draws some of the seemingly obvious religious conclusions.

National background potentially tells us about the religious preferences of Latinas before they came to the United States and the religious influences that might have framed their descendents. As mentioned earlier, Puerto Ricans are much more likely than any other Latino group to be Protestants before they come to the mainland. Since they are U.S. citizens, they are free to travel to the 50 states anytime they wish. Also, the two countries in Central America that have sent the most migrants to the United States,

Guatemala and El Salvador, also have high percentages of Protestants, 40 percent and 21 percent, respectively.[35] This means higher migration from these countries would likely increase the percentage of Latino Protestants, even if there were no new conversions in the States.

On the other hand, as mentioned earlier, Mexico has the highest percentage of Catholics of any country in Latin America, though the percentage of Protestants is growing and varies greatly depending on the region of the country. There are parts of Central Mexico today that are less than 1 percent Protestant. This region includes the state of Michoacán, which historically has been one of the states with large migration to the United States and with a significant percentage of transnational or temporary migrants. Mexico has always been the country that sends the most migrants from Latin America, so religious tendencies in Mexico will likely have a strong influence on religious practices among U.S. Latinos. Mexico likely also influences religious practices in the States because many Latinas of Mexican descendent return to Mexico during the Christmas season, which includes important Catholic religious celebrations such as the Day of the Virgin of Guadalupe (December 12), Nochebuena (December 24), and the Day of the Kings (January 6). Traditional *posadas* are part of the celebrations during the Advent season as well. These celebrations are also transnational, practiced by Latinos who might not be able to return to Mexico during the Christmas season.

A third important factor on the religious scene is more recent migration from Cuba and from the southern cone of South America. Cuba has officially been an atheist state and has "significant" percentages of agnostics and atheists. Some of the regions of southern cone also have high percentages of agnostics.[36] Both studies correlated secularization only to the influence of living in the United States. But it is very likely that some of the Latinos who profess no religion in the United States might not have practiced any religion in their countries of origin.

People in Latin America also profess other religions, including other forms of Christianity, such as Mormonism or Jehovah's Witnesses, which have experienced "significant" growth in some Latin American countries. There are also many people who practice religions with an indigenous or African background. In some parts of Latin America, many people's religious practices are a syncretism of Catholicism and indigenous or African background practices. But some of those who practice Santería and similar African-influenced practices would not necessarily identify themselves as religious, though they would consider themselves spiritual. How would people who might call themselves spiritual, but who are not linked to any specific religious expression, be classified in these studies?

Religious practices are changing in Latin America. To what extent are religious tendencies among U.S. Latinos a function of life in the United States, and to what extent are they similar to what is happening in Latin America? For example, even though the United States is a predominantly Protestant country, there are several countries in Latin America that have a larger percentage of Protestants than the percentage of Protestants among U.S. Latinos.[37] There are also countries with higher percentages of atheists or agnostics than among U.S. Latinos.[38] Knowing the national background helps us think about the fact that Latinos are influenced not only by religious tendencies in the United States but also by larger religious movements, particularly what is happening in Latin America.

## Assimilation, Acculturation, Adaptation: How Do Latinos Fit in the United States?

This question has generated numerous studies that have drawn different conclusions about Latinos. In other publications, I have argued that how Latinos became a part of the United States and how they have experienced the process of cultural adaptation is as important for understanding the community today as is the national background of a specific Latina.[39]

In *Harvest of Empire: A History of Latinos in America*,[40] the author, Juan González, used a provocative title to address the complex place of Latinos in the larger history in the United States. The author argues that one cannot understand migratory patterns from Latin America if one ignores U.S. military, political, and economic intervention in the region. U.S. policy in the region has had a direct impact on migration, but because its policies have been different in various countries, Latinas have many different stories to tell about how they became a part of the United States. These fit into various major categories that impact how Latinos interact with majority culture.

It is not easy to draw clear conclusions between how the various Latino groups became a part of the United States and how they view the country. But the differences do seem to mark the American experience. People of Mexican background have the longest relationship, but also one linked to conquest. It is also Mexicans who were at the center of the Bracero program and who have been the most temporary immigrants. Some of the most strident voices of the Chicano movement pointed to the conquest of the Southwest as key to understanding the unequal relationship of Chicanos in the United States. Given the role that Mexican laborers play in the U.S. economic system, Mexicans are the single largest group of noncitizen workers and also the single largest group of people deported from the United States because they do not have legal documentation.

Cuban Americans are much more likely to have a more positive view of the United States. They were received with open arms in the 1960s after Fidel Castro took over Cuba. Subsequent waves of immigrants from the island have been received as political exiles and given support to establish themselves in this country. To this day any Cuban who reaches U.S. shores can anticipate being given refugee status. In contrast, though many Dominicans also came to the United States as political refugees in the 1960s, undocumented Dominicans today are not treated like Cuban immigrants.

Puerto Ricans have the advantage of being U.S. citizens, so they can travel between the island and the mainland at any time. In fact, the initial results from the 2010 census indicate that the population of the island may have decreased since 2000, largely as a result of people leaving for the U.S. mainland. Yet because of the unique status of the island, the majority population often treats them as immigrants when they come to the mainland. Even though legally they are doing something no different from someone moving from Kansas to New York, the fact that they are traveling from Puerto Rico makes them immigrants in popular parlance.

The immigration of Central American immigrants is largely the result of civil wars in which the United States had a fairly direct role. Today many of these immigrants play a very significant role in the economies of their countries of origin, particularly El Salvador and Guatemala. Because of their history and their unique economic role, many Central Americans have received a temporary protected status (TPS), allowing them to continue living and working legally in the States. Currently, three countries in Central America (El Salvador, Nicaragua, and Honduras) qualify for TPS. Guatemala has requested that its nationals also be considered for TPS.[41] TPS does not qualify a person for permanent residency. If the U.S. government removes the TPS status from a country, then those nationals under its protection would lose their legal status and could be subject to deportation. Because these workers send a great deal of money in remittances to their relatives in their countries of origin, in some cases close to 20 percent of a country's GDP,[42] the leaders of these Central America countries regularly asked the United States to extend the TPS designation for their country.

In the midst of these larger groups in the Latino community, there are also smaller populations who often become invisible in the United States. Native peoples from Latin America are usually not distinguished, though Spanish may not be their first language. There are also immigrants (and their descendants) whose ancestors arrived in Latin America only a couple of generations ago from Europe or Asia. Their status is more confused in the United States because of the different ways the United States can categorize people. A few of these people are able to claim citizenship in

European or Asian countries. They usually find it easier to enter the United States on a European Union, Japanese, or Korean passport than to attempt to obtain a U.S. visa on a passport from their country of birth or residence in Latin America.

## Ethnic Identity Maintenance and Interaction with Majority Culture

The Latina experience in the United States is an ongoing story. Several factors keep the experience from becoming a thing of the past, like the immigrant histories of groups from Europe. The unique story described in the previous section presents the historical background that frames the issues. The fact that the United States shares a border and a globally unique borderlands economy with Mexico provides ongoing support for ethnic identity maintenance. It is also supported by the unique relationship with Puerto Rico that allows people to come to the mainland on a regular basis. The size of the community has also created a significant mass media in Spanish, largely financed by multinational media interests in Latin America, that also provides ethnic identity and linguistic maintenance support. Also, the large percentage of Latinas of indigenous or African descent often find that they are not easily allowed to assimilate. All of this makes it unlikely that the Latino experience will ever become exactly like that of the European immigrants of the 19th century.

Nonetheless, there are many Latinos who have structurally assimilated into Euro-American culture. Just as Latinas have become part of the country in many different ways, so too one can distinguish various ways that Latinos identify with Latina culture and interact with majority culture. In the 1970s Catholic sociologist Andrew Greeley did a seminal study of ethnic identity maintenance among "ethnic" Catholics in the United States.[43] His article describes different types of ethnic experiences that he defined as nuclear, fellow-traveler, marginal, alienated, and new ethnic (assimilated into majority culture). I have expanded his categories to describe the various types of Latina experiences. Figure 1.1 attempts to chart the various ways Latinos interact with both Latino and majority cultures. Because it is a drawing on a sheet of paper, it can give the impression that ethnic identity is set and static. The reality is that Latino identity and interaction with Latina culture is in a constant state of flux in this country, and most Latinos, like other minority groups in this country, live a polycentric reality, needing to know how to interact with both minority and majority cultures at all times. But the various categories can help us understand how Latinas address ethnic identity issues and how this impacts religious practices and preferences.[44]

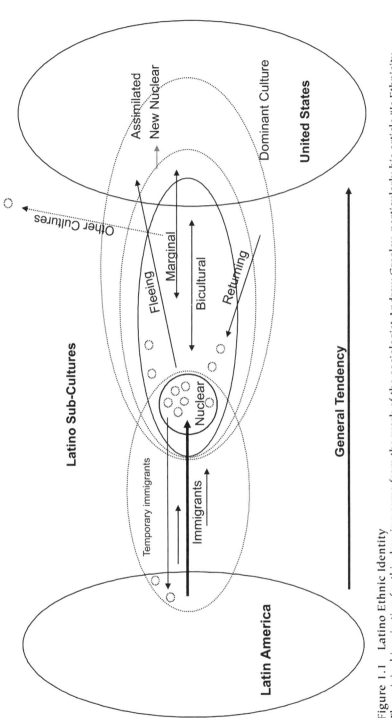

Figure 1.1   Latino Ethnic Identity
The original inspiration for this drawing came from the work of the sociologist Andrew Greeley, particularly his article "Is Ethnicity Un-American?" (New Catholic World, May/June 1976, pp. 106–12). Previous versions of this drawing have been published in *Iglesias Peregrinas en busca de identidad* (Kairós, 2004) and *Walk with the People: Latino Ministry in the United States* (Abingdon, 2008). Adapted by permission.

There is no place where Latino culture stands relatively free of the influences of Euro-American culture or of Latin America. It feels the pull of both, with the pull of U.S. dominant culture being the strongest by far. The public school system, U.S. mass media, and popular dominant culture are always pulling Latinos. But there are also influences that support Latina ethnic identity maintenance, such as constant migration, sharing a border with Mexico, the unique status of Puerto Rico, Spanish-language mass media, and the size of the Latino community. But in the midst of these influences, Latinos are culture creators and continue to develop unique subcultures that draw both from external influences and from the unique experience of being Latino in the United States. How people live this out varies from Latina to Latina and often changes over time.

### Transnational People

Many of the Latin American immigrants who come to work in the United States have the intention of returning to their countries of origin. Their plans are to earn extra income that they hope to invest in their countries of origin, often to build a house or establish a business. Though many end up staying, there are also many who return, either voluntarily or by deportation. But there are also people who move back and forth between the United States and their countries of origin. In earlier years when border enforcement was more lax, there were many people who came to work for short periods of time, such as harvest season, and then would return home, repeating the cycle on a yearly basis. Some undocumented workers continue to do that today, though it is much more difficult now because of stronger border controls. But there are also people who have legal status in the United States who move back and forth on a regular basis. These people have made the movement between the United States and their country of origin a pattern of life and take cultural influences back and forth between countries.

### Nuclear Latinos

In some parts of the United States, Latinos are a very high percentage of the population, such as south Texas, northern New Mexico, areas in central and Southern California, and parts of south Florida. Some people in these areas, usually immigrants, live their lives almost completely within a Latino subculture. Their family, friends, and coworkers are mostly Latinos; they have access to extensive mass media in Spanish; they worship in Spanish; and they live their lives mostly in a Latino environment. Though this is usually seen as a limit to upward mobility in the United States, there are many nuclear Latinos who are living some version of *el sueño Americano* within a predominantly Latino cultural environment. Though most nuclear Latinos are Spanish-dominant, there are also areas where English-dominant or bilingual Latinos live in a similar Latino environment.

### Bicultural

Bicultural Latinos are those who effectively function both in Latino culture and in majority culture. For most it means that their public lives are lived in majority culture, but their private lives are lived in a predominantly Latino environment. Most bicultural Latinos are fully bilingual. Because they are able to function well in both environments, those who know them only in one context might not know of their "other" bicultural identity. Because they usually move between cultural experiences, bicultural Latinos usually live in some level of cultural tension or "cultural schizophrenia."

### Marginal Latinos

There are many Latinos in the United States who clearly identify with things Latino but live their lives very much within majority culture. They enjoy the surface markers of Latino cultures, such as music, food, fiestas, religious traditions, and familial relations, but their values and lifestyles are very much shaped by Euro-American culture.

### Fleeing from Latino Culture

Within all cultural minorities and immigrant groups, there are those who are convinced that the only way to succeed in the United States is to leave behind their own cultural identity. These "alienated" Latinos (to use Greeley's term) may have limited use of English but may refuse to speak Spanish. Many anglicize their names so that they can "fit." This type of person would likely not be interested in anything specifically defined as Latino and would tend to be critical of any attempts to maintain Latino culture in the United States.

### Returning—Looking for Roots

This cultural tendency is often seen among young Latinos who are dealing with their own identity. These are people who take on a stronger Latino identity than the one in which they grew up (and might even question why their parents did not teach them Spanish or raise them "more" Latino). Many young Latinas join Latino clubs in high school or college, work to improve their Spanish, or spend time in Latin America or Spain, all as ways of reinforcing an identity that might have been waning.

### Assimilated—Nuclear Ethnics within Dominant Culture

For these Latinas the term Hispanic or Latino refers only to their ancestral background. They are aware that their ancestors came from the

Spanish-speaking world, but they do not identify with anything Latino. Their attitude toward things Latina tends to look like that of other members of majority culture. Many of them have effectively become "nuclear ethnics" within Euro-American culture.

### Assimilated into Other Cultures

When Latinos out-marry, the common assumption is that they and their spouses are becoming part of Euro-American culture. But that is not always the case, particularly when the marriage is with African Americans. A number of urban Latinas, particularly of African descent, are adopting African American culture, and many are marrying into that community. They are structurally assimilating, but not into majority culture. There are also cases of this happening in relationship with other ethnic minorities, though it is not nearly as common.

Latinos move in and out of these categories, so it is not always easy to place a specific individual in any one of them. But it is important to take this issue into account because there has often been a link between religion and ethnic identity. How Latinos are a part of the United States or how they should "fit" is an ongoing debate. The assumption that Latinos are like earlier European immigrant groups and that they are behaving, or will behave, like those groups seems to be an incomplete explanation of the Latino experience at best. Because of the role religion has had in the adaptation process among earlier immigrants, religion also will likely impact how Latinas participate in U.S. society. Ethnic identity and religious identity are both likely to influence each other in this process of defining how one is both American and Latino.

## Self-Identification: What Do We Call Ourselves?

It was the Census Bureau that began using the term Hispanic to refer to all of the Latina communities. This category was first widely used in the 1970 Census. Subsequent census counts have sought to clarify how they understand the term by including other options under the category Hispanic, be it national background or race. The census also uses the term Latino in the mix. The 2010 census allowed Latinas to mark multiple options to self-identify, though it still left in the "other" option, in case people did not feel included in any of the printed categories.

But in spite of the similarities that fit under a common term, there are also some significant differences between those of us who fit under the umbrella of Hispanic or Latino. Some of us cannot agree on which of the two terms best unifies us. We can make some very impassioned pleas for one or the other of the terms.[45] Others have opted for Hispanic/Latino, or some similar combination, to try to find commonality among us. And there are still those in the Chicano movement who feel that the terms Hispanic and Latino have disempowered those of Mexican background who had named themselves during the civil rights struggles.

Given the fact that ethnic identity is a moving target, it is unclear whether "Latino" or "Hispanic" will continue to be able to include all of those who are currently placed in these categories. Will the undocumented and those "of Hispanic descent" continue to see themselves as part of the same ethnic minority? Or will new terms eventually develop to describe the various communities under the "Latino" umbrella?

## How Do We Want to Fit in the United States?

Given that people in the United States have presented and experimented with several potential ways of bringing together peoples from many backgrounds into one nation, it is not surprising that Latinos reflect the gamut of possibilities. Some Latinas have structurally assimilated into an Anglo conformity model. Others celebrate the contribution we bring to the melting pot. And still others reflect on various versions of cultural pluralism and how Latinos are creating something that is American and Latino. Should we develop and maintain our own institutions, or should we be part of existing structures? This question is closely linked to the religious question, particularly for Protestants. Should Latino Protestants join existing churches in the United States or form their own? How do my views of what "should" happen in the United States parallel or differ from my views about what *my* church should look like?

## The Peculiar Political and Social Perspectives of Latino Protestants

Both the 2003 and the 2007 Pew studies addressed the relationship between religious perspectives and political perspectives. They found that on issues such as abortion, same-sex marriage, or religious influence in politics, most Latino Protestants, particularly evangelicals/Pentecostals, identified with conservative positions. But on issues such as immigration, government-guaranteed health insurance, or a willingness to pay higher taxes for broader government services, most Latinos, including evangelicals/Pentecostals, identified with liberal positions. Both the 2003 and the 2007 studies describe a Protestant community that is theologically more conservative than U.S. Protestantism at large, but also a community that does not define the relationship between faith and politics in the same way that it is commonly defined in the U.S. context. Latino evangelicals/Pentecostals understand that their faith calls them to participate in the political process. But they also understand that their faith calls them to be "conservative" on personal morality issues and "liberal" on issues of social morality, confessing that many of these issues would be resolved "if enough people were brought to Christ."[46]

## *Protestantes:* Growing Communities in the United States

In spite of the different goals and perspectives of the Pew and Trinity studies, both draw many similar conclusions about the Latino Protestant community. Both agree that the number of Latino Protestants in the United States will continue to grow, though it is not clear whether they will continue to grow as a percentage of the overall Latino community. The growth will come from continuing migration and from Catholic converts in the United States. This means that the size and growth of the Latina Protestant community is likely to be influenced by the countries of origin of future migratory flows. Migration from Puerto Rico or Central America will likely increase the number of Protestants, though greater migration from Mexico or from more secularized regions, such as the southern cone of South America, will likely keep the overall percentage from growing.

Assimilation and acculturation will also likely have an influence on the growth patterns. According to the Trinity study, "Americanization . . . leads to both secularization and conservative Christianization [becoming an evangelical or a Pentecostal]."[47] This creates an interesting tension for Latino Protestantism. Is Americanization an inevitable influence that needs to be addressed but cannot be changed? Or should Latina Protestants work to maintain a strong Latino identity among their children as a way of helping them maintain a strong religious identity?

Both studies looked at Latino Protestants within the frame of religious or secularizing influences in the United States. But neither tracked what is happening among Latinas with the impact of Protestant growth and secularization tendencies in Latin America. Until recently, just about all Latino Protestants were linked to U.S.-based churches or denominations. But the growth of Latin American Protestantism has brought new Christian expressions, almost all of which have a Pentecostal or charismatic flavor, to the United States. Some Latin American Protestant immigrants have brought their churches with them. But many of these newer churches also have a strong missionary orientation. Most of their converts in the United States are from within the Latino community, though some of these movements are also evangelizing the larger U.S. population. These movements are not connected to denominations in the United States, so they are often off the radar in discussions of U.S. Protestantism, and most of them are fairly recent implants in the United States. Though these movements are growing, it is not clear what long-term influence they will have on the larger picture of Latino Protestantism.

Globalization, legal and undocumented migration, and transnationalism are also factors that are changing the U.S. Latina religious landscape. Catholics of Mexican background have been returning to Mexican Catholic religious shrines for several generations. More recently, a growing number of mostly Pentecostal churches have members who move north and south on a regular basis. Popular preachers and religious musicians from Latin America are very popular among some Latino Protestants. This is having an influence on the religious practices of churches in both the United States and Latin America. What this will mean for Protestantism in both the United States and Latin America over the long term is still being defined.

Some of the questions that both of these studies hint at, but do not address directly, have to do with Latinos in U.S. Protestant churches and denominations. Clearly, Latinos will become a larger percentage of the U.S. Protestant population. They are becoming part of U.S. Protestant churches in two major ways. Most are joining Latino churches that are part of larger Protestant denominations. But a growing number of Latinas are joining Euro-American churches where they are a minority of the overall membership. Each of these groups is raising a different set of questions for U.S. Protestant structures. In general, these are the same questions being raised in the larger U.S. debate, including, How do Latinos fit? But there are also specific theological, ecclesiological, and missiological questions that Protestants will have to address as the U.S. Protestant Latina population continues to grow in the midst of U.S. Protestantism.

Though the growth of Latino Protestantism is often perceived as recent, because it finally became large enough to be noticed, its roots are in the 19th-century U.S. western expansion into the Southwest and in the Protestant missionary efforts in Latin America and among the "Mexicans" of the Southwest. Latina Protestantism began in the midst of conquest, westward expansion, and Protestant missionary fervor. So we turn there next.

## CHAPTER TWO

# Aren't All Latinos Catholics?

The rapid growth of Protestantism among Latinos and in Latin America is a relatively recent phenomenon. Because of this, many studies of Latinos in the United States have often, implicitly or explicitly, assumed that historically, all Latinos were Catholics, unless they were assimilating into majority culture, and that Latinos have only recently begun converting to Protestantism.[1] Nonetheless, there have been Latino Protestants in the United States from the time of the American takeover of the Southwest from Mexico in 1848. Their continuing growth has been a function of both conversions and new Protestant immigrants from Latin America.

## History of Latino Protestantism

The U.S. Latino Protestant story begins with the Western expansion of Americans across the continent during the 19th century. The first recorded attempt of Protestant evangelization occurred in Mexican Tejas in 1833. Sumner Bacon, a Presbyterian working under the American Bible Society, worked among the Americans who had become Mexican citizens and Catholics so that they could legally settle on Mexican territory. He also distributed Bibles in Spanish, though this was against Mexican law. Though he saw no direct results from his efforts, others followed in his steps during the period of Texan independence (1836–1845).

The early Protestant missionaries were motivated by the Gospel Mandate to preach the gospel to all peoples. But after the U.S. takeover of the Southwest, most of the missionaries also mentioned a sense of responsibility toward the conquered peoples of the region, an American mandate or mission toward the world and toward the conquered peoples in particular. God had opened up the Mexicans to the Protestant message, and they needed to respond. By reaching out to these newly conquered people, they would be able to also reach Mexico with the gospel. Soon after the U.S. takeover of the Southwest, Melinda Rankin, a Presbyterian missionary in south Texas who hoped to work in Mexico, described in military terms the link between the U.S. victory in the Mexican-American War (1846–1848) and the importance of Protestant missionary work in Texas and Mexico:

> Mexico is now open for the dissemination of the Word of life. Its conquest to national power, [*sic*] inspired the martial spirit of American freemen, and shall not the sons of peace and righteousness follow up the victory with those weapons which are mighty through God to the pulling down of strongholds? The work must be done. The honor of American Christianity demands it, and who will lead in advance?[2]

But it was also important that these newly conquered people, who were now U.S. citizens, develop the skills needed to succeed in this country. Specifically, they needed to Americanize, which meant freeing themselves from the "oppression of Romanism," getting an American-style education, and adopting Protestant ethical, moral, economic, and political values. "For many of the Protestant missionaries, the future of the United States as they knew it depended on the success of their efforts."[3]

The first known "Mexican" converts became Protestants in 1850 in New Mexico and Texas. These early converts became the core of small Latino Protestant congregations throughout the Southwest, some of which continue to this day. By the beginning of the 20th century, there were about 150 Latino Protestant congregations in the Southwest, mostly in northern New Mexico and southern Colorado and in Texas, with a few in southern California and southern Arizona. There were also a handful of Spanish-language congregations on the Eastern Seaboard ministering among immigrants from Cuba, Puerto Rico, and Spain. Most of these 19th-century Latino Protestant churches were Methodist or Presbyterian, though there were also a few Baptist and Congregational churches in the Southwest.[4]

The beginning of the 20th century brought major changes to these early congregations. On the one hand, economic upheaval in the Southwest uprooted people in New Mexico and Texas, so many of the early congregations (and some of the communities in which they were located) completely disappeared. By the second decade of the 20th century, several of the early Latino Methodist and Presbyterian churches had closed or had been absorbed into English-language sister congregations. But a few survived, and today there are Latino Protestant churches in the Southwest that are well over 100 years old.

But it was the Pentecostal revival that began in Los Angeles in 1906 that would eventually bring unprecedented Protestant growth in Latin America and among Latinos in the United States. The early records of the Azusa Street revival in Los Angeles state that there were "Mexicans" among the converts and the lay preachers.[5] Some of these new believers were from Latin America, and they returned there, becoming lay missionaries who preached the Pentecostal message in their countries of origin and beyond. But many other "Mexican" converts had been born in the United States or lived there. U.S. "Mexican" Pentecostal converts were part of the principal Pentecostal denominations almost from their origins.

The Azusa Street revival and its aftermath also saw the beginning of the first Latino Protestant denominations in the United States, the Concilio Latinoamericano de Iglesias Cristianas, or CLADIC (1923), and the Apostolic Assembly of the Faith in Christ Jesus (1925). The Assembly is a "oneness" Pentecostal group, one of several Pentecostal denominations that baptize in the name of Jesus and reject the concept of the Trinity. It started forming churches on both sides of the U.S.–Mexican border as early as 1912 and organized itself as a denomination in 1925 in San Bernardino, California. In 1932 its sister denomination organized itself in Mexico. This denomination has historical and theological links to other U.S.-based oneness Pentecostal denominations, but it was not started by any other denomination or missionary agency and has been a U.S. Latino–led and financed denomination from its inception.

Those leading the Azusa Street revival believed that the modern Pentecostal experience would break down racial barriers. During the early revival meetings, people of many ethnic, racial, and linguistic backgrounds worshiped together. But as these new churches started organizing into denominations, the racial divisions in U.S. society started having an impact.

The Apostolic Assembly began its own denomination, in part because the oneness denominations decided to organize along racial lines. A few years after the Assemblies of God was formed, a large group of "Mexicans" left the denomination in 1923 because they were not allowed to take leadership roles in the denominational structure. Evangelist Francisco "El Azteca" Olazábal led these churches into eventually becoming CLADIC. During its formational years this movement included people from Mexican American and Puerto Rican backgrounds. In 1939 Puerto Rican leaders in New York City separated from CLADIC and formed the Assembly of Christian Churches (Asamblea de Iglesias Cristianas, AIC).[6]

When the United States entered World War I, it saw the need for workers on the farm and in the factories to replace the soldiers going to war.

Mexican immigrant workers became one of the sources of labor for the country. Many stayed after the end of the war, and some of them became Protestants. But the Great Depression created another upheaval among Latino Protestants. As the economy became weaker, many Mexicans, and Americans of Mexican descent, were deported to Mexico. This also had a negative impact on the new Latino Protestant congregations. Many Latino Protestant churches lost members, and some disappeared as both pastors and church members were deported.

While Pentecostalism was beginning to take root among many of the "Mexicans" of the Southwest, a different Protestant denomination took root among the "Mexicans" in Texas. The Baptist General Convention of Texas began mission work among the "Mexicans" in the 1880s. A few churches were established during the 19th century, though they began more steady growth during the first part of the 20th century and have continued growing ever since. Today they are by far the largest Latino Protestant denomination in Texas. (The Protestant denominations with the largest Latino memberships are discussed further in chapter 3.)

The Disciples of Christ began missionary work among the Latina population of Texas in 1899. Other Protestant denominations also began work among Latinas during the first part of the 20th century. The Church of the Nazarene began Hispanic ministry in Los Angeles in 1910, the Quakers in 1915, and the Free Methodists in 1917. The New York City Mission Society began its first church among Spanish-speaking immigrants in 1912. During the 1920s the Evangelical Lutheran Church, the Evangelical United Brethren, the Christian and Missionary Alliance, and the Lutheran Church–Missouri Synod all began work among Latinos in various parts of the United States.

In 1926 the Assemblies of God began the Latin American Bible institutes in both Texas and California to train Spanish-speaking leaders for pastoral ministry. From the very beginning, the Assemblies organized the Spanish-language churches it established into a "Latin American" or Spanish-language district, which was subdivided into conferences as the number of churches continued to grow. The Methodists had started this model in the 19th century. Both the Northern Methodists in New Mexico and the Southern Methodists in Texas had organized their Spanish-language congregations into separate districts in the 1870s. Latino Presbyterian churches were organized into a presbytery in Texas in 1908. Other denominations followed this model, and by 1930 the Church of the Nazarene and the Free Methodists also had Spanish-language districts.[7]

In 1930, Robert McLean, the person in charge of the Spanish-Speaking Work in the Southwest department for the Board of National Missions of the Presbyterian Church in the USA, published *The Northern Mexican.*[8] The book includes detailed statistical reports about Latino churches and members from many Protestant denominations. It includes detailed records, including the names of pastors and churches, denominational leaders, schools, and other denominational agencies focused on the Spanish-speaking (see Table 2.1).[9]

This list is incomplete, since it does not include the Seventh-Day Adventists, independent churches, or any Pentecostal denominations or churches. By 1930, there were still not many Latino Pentecostal churches, since most growth would happen after this date. But it provides a snapshot of Latino Protestantism before the expansive growth of the Pentecostal churches. (Samuel Ortegón verified much of the same information in his 1930 master's thesis studying the religious practices of "Mexicans" in Los Angeles.[10])

A second spurt of Protestant missionary efforts among Latinos developed after the end of the Great Depression and as new migration occurred during and after World War II. By 1950 all of the major U.S. Protestant denominations of the period had Spanish-language congregations or other types of ministries among the Latino population.

Table 2.1 Latino Protestant Churches and Members—1930

| Denomination | Churches | Members |
|---|---|---|
| Baptist, Northern | 40 | 3,500 |
| Baptist, Southern | 56 | 3,562 |
| Congregational | 7 | 345 |
| Congregational, S. Calif. | 2 | 125 |
| Disciples | 10 | 805 |
| Free Methodist | 10 | 300 |
| Friends | 2 | 46 |
| Interdenominational | 2 | 164 |
| Lutheran | 3 | 266 |
| Methodist Episcopal | 55 | 4,617 |
| Methodist Episcopal, South | 62 | 5,710 |
| Nazarene | 11 | 415 |
| Presbyterian USA (North) | 60 | 4,185 |
| Presbyterian US (South) | 41 | 2,134 |
| United Brethren | 6 | 425 |
| TOTAL | 367 | 26,599 |

The next published report on the number of Latino Protestants came in 1960. Leo Grebler, Joan Moore, Ralph Guzman, et al. reported the existence of 1,535 Spanish-speaking churches in the United States with an estimated 113,130 adult members (see Table 2.2).[11]

These totals were based on a study by the National Council of Churches, but included only one Pentecostal denomination, the Assemblies of God, and did not include denominations such as the Church of the Nazarene, the Free Methodists, or the Friends, all of which had been a part of the 1930 McLean report (and which had grown in number of churches by 1960). The authors recognized these problems and also the complexities of using denominational reporting. But they used these numbers as a starting point for their discussion of Protestantism among Mexican Americans. Interestingly enough, the authors assumed that these membership numbers represented the whole of the Latino Protestant community and so concluded that "statistically, Protestantism is not important in the Mexican-American population. . . . Mexican-American Protestants are quantitatively as insignificant in Protestantism as Protestantism is generally insignificant to the Mexican Americans."[12]

They drew this conclusion based on two comparisons. First, 113,000 people constituted less than 3 percent of the Mexican American population of the period. Second, this number was insignificant within the total number of Protestant church members in the United States.[13] But if one compares these numbers to the 1930 McLean report, one realizes that

Table 2.2 Latino Protestant Churches and Members—1960

| Denomination | Churches | Members |
|---|---|---|
| American Baptist | 106 | 7,950 |
| Assemblies of God | 392 | 29,054 |
| Church of God (Anderson) | 7 | 465 |
| Congregational–Christian | 7 | 543 |
| Disciples of Christ | 18 | 1,851 |
| Evangelical United Brethren | 14 | 972 |
| Lutheran–Missouri Synod | 7 | 1,245 |
| Methodist Church | 221 | 28,000 |
| Presbyterian US | 38 | 2,842 |
| Presbyterian USA | 94 | 6,604 |
| Seventh-Day Adventist | 68 | 5,000 |
| Southern Baptist | 559 | 28,000 |
| United Lutheran | 4 | 604 |
| TOTAL | 1,535 | 113,130 |

the number of Latino Protestant churches and members had grown by at least 400 percent in 30 years. It is also interesting to note that two of the three largest Latino denominations are the Assemblies of God and the Southern Baptists, which continue to be the largest denominations to this day.

Most of these Latino Protestant congregations were small, and few had full-time pastors. Many, particularly those linked to mainline or evangelical denominations, were dependent on their denominations for financial support, and some of the churches were "ministries" among poor and immigrant Latinos, not churches led by Latinos themselves. Again, it is interesting to note that in the Grebler et al. report, the Assemblies of God Latino congregations are all listed as being self-supporting.[14] Yet by the middle of the 20th century, most of the larger U.S. Protestant denominations had some type of ministry among Latinas.

## The Changing Growth Patterns from 1950 Forward

The 1950s and 1960s saw the beginning of major changes in the growth patterns among Latino Protestants. Mainline denominations, such as the Methodists and Presbyterians, which had been the first to do mission work among Latinas, lost Latino members or slowed in their growth among Latinas. Other denominations, particularly Pentecostals and Baptists, began to grow much more rapidly, completely changing the face of Latino Protestantism in the United States.

When Frederick Whitam wrote a description of New York City Latino (mostly Puerto Rican) Protestants in 1962, he found that about half were members of mainline or evangelical churches, and about half were Pentecostals. But he found that "one of the most important developments in evangelical religion in New York has been the rapid growth of Spanish-speaking Pentecostal congregations." He noted that the Pentecostals were developing their own leaders through Bible institutes and that Puerto Rican pastors led the Latino congregations, whereas many of the English-speaking churches were struggling "to find intelligent and creative approaches to the Spanish-speaking persons in their communities." Another important fact he mentioned in passing is that all the large Latino churches were Pentecostal.[15] This is the first known reference to the relationship between church size and Pentecostalism. To this date, most of the largest Latina Protestant churches are Pentecostal or charismatic.

Because Texas has had Latino Protestant churches since the 19th century, and the number of Latino churches in the state continues to grow, it provides a model of the changing growth patterns among Latina Protestants.

The (Southern) Methodists, Presbyterians, and Baptists all began mission work among Latinos in the state during the 19th century. The (Southern) Methodists were still the largest Protestant group in Texas when McLean reported on Latina Protestantism in 1930. But these three denominations and the Pentecostal denominations that would begin work in the 20th century grew at very different rates. There have been no detailed studies of the reasons for this, though there are at least two major differences between the evangelical/Pentecostal denominations and the mainline denominations that seem to have made an impact in how they expanded in the Latino community.

First, the three denominations made very different decisions about how the Latino churches would relate to the larger denomination and how Latinas would govern their own churches. All of the major denominations established "Latino" districts, conferences, or presbyteries in the state. But each developed a different attitude about their purpose and long-term role. The Tex-Mex Presbytery became a transitional "holding presbytery" for Latino churches until they could become self-supporting and join the existing geographic presbyteries. Because of that goal, the Tex-Mex Presbytery dissolved in 1955 when all of the existing Latino churches became self-supporting.[16] The other denominations all kept or expanded their Latina-oriented judicatories, even as Latinos also joined the "geographical" judicatories. The denominations that have had the most "separate" Latino structures, the Baptists and the Pentecostal denominations, are those that have grown the most since the 1960s. The Presbyterians also have experienced no growth among Latino congregations for many years, and the Methodist growth has been slow in comparison to the evangelical/Pentecostal denominations.

Another important difference has to do with denominational expectations related to the overall costs of developing and maintaining a church. During the 19th century, Methodists had more flexibility than the Presbyterians in relationship to ordination requirements. As a result they had many more Latino pastors. But eventually, both expected their pastors to have a seminary degree as a requirement for ordination. This made it impossible for many Latinos to enter ministry since many did not have the educational background to study at seminary level, many could not study in English, and most could not afford the cost of a seminary education. This also put a burden on local churches, since a seminary-trained pastor had certain "financial" expectations, often dictated by the denomination, which were beyond the financial means of most Latino churches. To this day the assumed costs of developing and maintaining a Latino mainline church are much higher than those of an evangelical/Pentecostal church.

Pentecostal and Baptist churches had much lower ordination expectations. Pastors were trained on the job or went to short-term Bible institutes that usually taught courses in Spanish and with a focus on ministry among Latinos. Ordination was based principally on a sense of God's call and success in ministry. Many of the pastors were bi-vocational, which meant that churches did not have to raise a full-time salary from the very beginning. As the church grew, it could pay its pastor more. Most church planters received limited financial support from their denominations, but many of them were lay leaders who were highly motivated to share the gospel message. The Baptist and Pentecostal models of church and church leadership were much more in reach of working-class, and often Spanish-dominant, Latino communities.

Both Baptists and Pentecostals would also claim that they grew because the Holy Spirit was at work in their churches. These churches preached a conversion message, inviting Latinos to profound change through the work of the Spirit. The change was usually fairly significant, something these Latino converts wanted to share with others, so many were willing to preach the gospel message to their friends and relatives, making whatever sacrifice was necessary to take the gospel to others.

As a result of these differences, Latino Protestantism in Texas looks very different in 2010 than it did in 1910. The Baptists have almost 1,500 Latino congregations in the state, whereas the Assemblies of God have over 400. The Methodists and the Presbyterians each have fewer than 100 Latino congregations in the state. And both Baptists and the Assemblies of God have more Latinos in their "non-Latino" churches than either mainline denomination.[17]

### Acculturation and Latinos in Dominant-Culture Churches

Though most denominations started Spanish-language churches and judicatories, the connection between Latinos and dominant-culture congregations was always somewhat conflictive. During the 19th century, Thomas and Emily Harwood, longtime Methodist missionaries among Latinos in New Mexico, both assumed that Latino-oriented ministry would likely be transitional and lamented when the best and brightest young Latinas joined the English-language congregations.[18] Because all of the early Protestant missionaries assumed that there was a link between Protestant evangelization and Americanization, it was not clear what the missionaries saw on the long-term horizon for Latino congregations.[19]

By the 1950s and 1960s there were growing numbers of Latino Protestants in English-language congregations (more on this in chapter 5). Several of the mainline denominations focused their ministry on helping Latino immigrants acculturate into U.S. society, with the goal that they would eventually fit into English-language congregations, or with the assumption that at least their children would join English-language churches.[20] In some areas Latino churches were "strongly" encouraged to merge with their English-language congregations, and some Latino churches chose to merge because they no longer felt they had a distinctive reason for existence, particularly small congregations in areas where Latinos were a small minority and most in the church spoke English.

In many areas this often meant that as a mainline denomination was closing or merging a Latino church, an evangelical or Pentecostal church was being established to take its place. Some of these new churches were established with members of the closing churches who were not in favor of the move. But many of the new churches were the product of new spiritual experiences, particularly of a Pentecostal bent, or of new Latino migrants into the area.

## Ordination Requirements and the Growth of Certain Types of Latino Protestantism

One of the issues that impacted the growth of Latino Protestant churches, not only in Texas but also throughout the United States, was the educational requirements related to ordination for pastoral ministry. Because many Latinos did not have the ability to study in English or meet the high education requirements and financial cost of seminary study, some of the denominations that required seminary education began Bible institutes in Spanish. Students from mainline denominations who completed these courses of study could become licensed pastors, though in most denominations they could not be fully ordained. A small percentage of Latinos from mainline denominations started going to seminary, but the dropout rate was high. Also, those who graduated from seminaries often found it difficult to work in their own communities of origin. Seminary had not trained them for working among Latinos, and many had been socialized into certain socio-economic assumptions that Latinos churches could not support.

Pentecostal and evangelical churches were already using the Bible institute as their principal means of preparing new pastors for ministry before they began working among Latinos. Many denominations rejected seminaries because they were "theologically suspect." But many of the pastors in these denominations also did not have a great deal of formal education, so the Bible institute was the type of training program that best fit their needs. The Bible institutes also provided another important benefit for many Latinos: they offered courses in Spanish and with a Latino ministry focus. Because the Bible institutes did not have such high educational prerequisites, and because they were considerably cheaper, they became the educational method of choice for most Latino pastors.

In practice this difference between mainline and evangelical and Pentecostal churches meant that the latter were able to prepare many more pastors for ministry, more quickly and much more cheaply. Many of the Bible institutes also had Latino professors and leadership, meaning that Latinas owned and directed the programs. Many of the institutes also allowed pastors already in ministry to study while they continued their pastorates. All of this contributed to a growing number of Latino pastors and leaders who fit well into the working-class communities in which most Latino Protestant churches were located. This meant that there were many more Latino evangelical and Pentecostal pastors available to pastor churches and begin new congregations. So as the number of new Latino churches in mainline denominations began to slow down, the number of evangelical and Pentecostal Latino churches continued to grow, outpacing the churches that had had the most Latino members only a few years before.

### Changing Ministry Focus

The differences between liberals and fundamentalists (later evangelicals) that developed in the late 19th century marked a difference in ministry focus among Latinos in the 1960s and beyond. While evangelicals and Pentecostals were starting more new Latino churches, many mainline churches focused their Latino ministry energies on issues such as civil rights and, later, the farmworkers' movement. These were very important issues for the Latino community, and many Latinas appreciated the support they received from mainline denominations.

But these actions did not attract many Latinos to the mainline churches. In fact, many mainline pastors and leaders encouraged Latinos to remain in the Catholic Church as part of their ecumenical stance. Some also adopted popular Catholic symbols, such as the Virgin of Guadalupe, as part of their support of Latino causes. One can reshape a common quote about Catholics and Pentecostals in Latin America to this situation: Mainline churches opted for Latino civil rights, but Latinos opted for Pentecostalism.[21]

Latino evangelicals and Pentecostals remained largely apolitical, not unlike their counterparts in Latin America. They focused their energies on personal conversion and on church planting. As a result they continued to establish new Latino congregations at a much more rapid pace than their mainline counterparts.

### English-Language Predominantly Latino Churches

Urban gang culture became an important focus of ministry among Pentecostals starting in the 1960s. David Wilkerson's *The Cross and the Switchblade* (1963) introduced many to the needs of urban poor young people in New

York. In Los Angeles, Sonny and Julie Arguinzoni began working with the Latino Assemblies of God to reach a similar audience of mostly Latina youth. In 1967 they decided to organize Victory Outreach as a ministry to work with drug addicts and gang members. Though they have never considered themselves a "Latino" denomination, the vast majority of their converts in Los Angeles have been Latinos. They started preaching mostly in English or "Spanglish." Later they also started churches in Spanish. Victory Outreach now has churches in many countries of the world. But the core leadership is still predominantly Hispanic.

A growing number of Latino churches also began ministries in English or developed a bilingual ministry focus. Some were programs focused on the children, whose instruction in school was in English. But others started churches or worship services that focused on the English-dominant Latinos in their communities. (This is discussed further in chapter 5.)

## Migration Patterns and Latino Protestantism

Migration became a part of life among the Mexicans of the Southwest soon after the U.S. takeover in 1848. Even though the Treaty of Guadalupe-Hidalgo promised U.S. citizenship and respect of property deeds, some Mexicans migrated south, and others established a second home on the Mexican side of the Río Grande River just in case. Movement north and south became part of the pattern of those communities near the new border, particularly in Texas.

During the 19th century and the first part of the 20th century, Latino Protestantism in the Southwest was closely linked to Protestantism in northern Mexico. Some of the early evangelists in Mexico had been converted in the United States. Both the Methodists and the Presbyterians in Texas traced their beginnings to Mexican converts who migrated north: Alejo Hernández and José María Botello, respectively. Also, some of the pastors and missionaries in the Southwest were originally from Mexico. The same Spanish-language Protestant literature was used on both sides of the border. One denomination, the Methodist Episcopal Church, South (Southern Methodist), first organized the border churches into cross-border districts, with pastors assigned churches on both sides of the border at different times during their active ministry. They continued with this model into the first part of the 20th century. Other denominations repeated this pattern in the 20th century.

The back-and-forth pattern changed in the early 20th century because of both push and pull factors. The Mexican Revolution that began in 1910 created an unsettled environment in many parts of Mexico. The United

States' entry into World War I in 1914 created the need for workers. The two events went hand in hand. But the circular pattern returned after 1929 when the Great Depression changed the economic landscape. Mexican labor was no longer welcome, and many were forcibly deported. This migratory cycle exposed Mexicans to Protestantism in the States, and some of the new converts took Bibles and evangelistic tracts back with them when they returned to Mexico.

The cycle repeated itself during World War II. The United States and Mexico created the Bracero program in 1942 to allow temporary workers from Mexico to fill the labor needs left by military personnel.[22] Again, the cycle would close with the deportations of Operation Wetback in the 1950s. Nonetheless, the Bracero program continued until 1964. This cross-border movement provided new opportunities for Protestant evangelization of the Mexican workers. A number of churches and ministries established themselves on the Texas–Mexico border to evangelize those who were living on both sides of the border. Though many of those working on the border saw this location as a bridgehead to work in Mexico, they also established Latino churches on the Texas side.

There were several other migratory flows that augmented the Latino population during this time period. The Northeast, particularly New York City, saw the beginning of significant Puerto Rican migration after World War II. The migratory pattern started before the war but grew significantly after the war ended as new economic opportunities required new labor sources. Puerto Rico had been the focus of significant Protestant missionary work from the time the United States took over the island after the Spanish-American War in 1898. Existing Latino (mostly Puerto Rican) Protestant churches in the Northeast were augmented by new ministries and leaders that came from the island. This migratory pattern created the environment for the growing Protestant ministry described by Whitam in 1962.

During the 1950s and 1960s there was also a significant internal migration of Latinos from south Texas to the West Coast, and lesser numbers into the Midwest. Many people from the region had been migrant workers, following the harvest season from Arizona to Washington. Little by little, some of the migrants began to stay in the regions where they had worked. Protestant churches and denominations established migrant ministries, providing material help and religious services. But there were also many migrant pastors, leaders who often worked alongside their parishioners during the day but led religious services in the evenings and on weekends. New Latino Protestant churches were started in the communities where these migrant communities lived. Pentecostal itinerant preachers who had little formal education but had a strong sense of God's call on their lives started most of these churches.

The Cuban Revolution (1959) created another migratory wave into the United States that also had an impact on Latino Protestantism. Once Fidel Castro took the country toward socialism, many people fled the island and were received as refugees in the United States (and other countries). The people who left did so for political, economic, and religious reasons. Many Protestant leaders left the country, some of them because they were forced, others to avoid persecution or imprisonment. These leaders established churches in Miami and wherever Cuban exiles established themselves. Some of the Protestant churches and denominations from Cuba also established their main offices in the United States, due to the limitations placed on them by the Cuban government.

Changes in U.S. migratory policy and U.S. intervention in Latin America have also affected migration patterns and have impacted the growth of Protestantism. The Immigration and Nationality Act of 1965 began to reflect the reality that future migration would be principally from Latin America. Documented and undocumented temporary migrants, mostly from Mexico and Puerto Rico, had already established the migratory patterns. Family reunification visas allowed people who were part of these patterns to begin bringing their families to the States. The Immigration and Control Act of 1986 legalized those who continued to be a part of these migratory labor flows.

Much of the migratory flow from Latin America during this period had the impact of exposing Latin Americans to the Protestant message. Many churches were involved in the resettlement of Cuban refugees, in helping migrants from the Dominican Republic in the 1960s, and in ministry among migrant workers throughout the period. Civil war in El Salvador, Guatemala, and Nicaragua during the 1970s and 1980s created a new set of issues for Protestant churches. Because these wars were defined within the East–West conflict of the period, liberal and conservative Protestants in the United States tended to respond differently. Liberal Protestants protested against U.S. intervention but also supported the people who fled the violence. They established the sanctuary movement to protect those whose lives were in danger if they returned to their countries of origin, but whom the United States would not recognize as political refugees for political reasons.

On the other hand, most conservative Protestants were strong anticommunists, and so they tended to support the right-wing military governments in Central America. Part of their support went to the Protestant churches of the region. Protestant churches, particularly the Pentecostal and charismatic ones, were in the midst of revival and rapid growth. U.S. Protestant missionary agencies worked alongside these churches, providing financial and logistical support. (Though growth was not as large or as rapid in most other areas, Protestantism also saw significant growth in other parts of Latin

America during this period.) But though Latin American Protestants tended to be anticommunist, the same as the missionaries, they had historically been apolitical and tended to remain so for most of the 1970s and 1980s.

Because of the unsettled political situation in the region, many people emigrated from these countries. Large numbers ended up in the United States. Because of the religious revival happening in Central America at the same time, many of the immigrants were already Protestants, particularly from the growing Pentecostal and charismatic churches of the region. Many joined existing Pentecostal churches or started new churches under existing U.S. Pentecostal denominations, such as the Assemblies of God. But others brought their own new movements with them, such as the Elim Churches of both Guatemala and El Salvador.

The changing attitudes toward migrant labor, mostly from Mexico and Central America, have also created new opportunities and new tensions for Protestants. Many of those workers are undocumented, even though many have lived and worked in the United States for many years. Estimates put the total of undocumented as high as 12,000,000, with the assumption that about 85 percent of them are from Latin America.[23] Because of the weak economy at the time of this book's writing and publication (2010–2011), there is currently a growing anti-immigrant tendency among many in the United States. This attitude is being used to justify laws and actions against anyone who "looks" undocumented—in other words, who looks Latino.

This has created a difficult situation for Latino Protestants, particularly those from evangelical or Pentecostal churches. The Pew study clearly demonstrated that most Latinos, including evangelicals and Pentecostals, favor comprehensive immigration reform. Many Latino churches have significant numbers of undocumented members. This creates a common ethical dilemma in which pastors teach their members to obey the government and to submit to civil authority, while they know that many in the church are undocumented and that most arrived in the States by crossing the border illegally. A common prayer request in many Latino Protestant prayer meetings is for a relative who "is coming tonight" (crossing the border with human smugglers). What does one pray for? That they successfully break the law? That they are caught and treated humanely?

Historically, most Latino Protestant leaders followed the Latin American Protestant model and assumed that they should be apolitical. This began to change both in Latin America and in the United States as the community grew and began being courted by political parties. But for many Latino Protestant leaders, the change became dramatic after December 2005 when Congressman James Sensenbrenner proposed the Border Protection, Anti-terrorism, and Illegal Immigration Control Act of 2005 (HR4437). This bill would have made it a felony to help the undocumented once they are in the States, directly affecting pastors, social workers, medical personnel, and others who regularly interact with the undocumented.

Since most Latino Protestant pastors regularly serve undocumented immigrants, this caused many to decide that they needed to work toward fair and comprehensive immigration reform that included a path for the legalization of the undocumented. This put many of them at odds with the politically conservative leadership of their Protestant denominations. It has also forced many theologically conservative Latino leaders to rethink their understanding of pastoral ministry.

This issue also creates a dilemma for some denominations at the leadership level. There are many undocumented Latino Protestant pastors. Some arrive with ministry credentials from their countries of origin, credentials that normally would be accepted by sister denominations across national boundaries. Should denominations recognize the credentials of undocumented pastors who want to serve in a church in the United States? Should denominations ordain pastors who are undocumented, particularly if they cannot qualify for a religious visa, due to U.S. government restrictions? Should Bible institutes and seminaries train the undocumented for pastoral ministry, particularly those who have been in the United States for many years?

## Protestantism in Latin America and Its Impact on U.S. Latinos

As mentioned in chapter 1, it is impossible to effectively tell the story of Protestantism among U.S. Latinos without weaving in Latin American Protestantism. Protestant missionaries, mostly from the United States, though also from Europe and Canada, had been working in Latin America since the 1830s, about the same time as the first Protestant contacts in the Southwest. Many of the same denominations led Protestant mission efforts in the Southwest after 1848 and missionary expansion into Latin America during the same time period.

Though there were many parallels between Protestant missionary work in Latin America and its outreach to U.S. Latinos, the major difference became one of degree and focus. Missions in Latin America were led by "foreign mission" agencies, and work among U.S. Latinos developed under "home mission" efforts. Early Protestant missionaries in the Southwest wanted Latinas to be treated as a "foreign" mission field, since they were not "Anglos." But Thomas Harwood, one of the early Methodist missionaries, lamented that the Mexicans of New Mexico were too American to be considered part of the foreign missionary efforts, but too foreign to receive strong support from the home mission agencies. The home mission agencies felt that their principal ministry focus should be the "white, English speaking" who were migrating westward and who often had no churches or pastors. Work among non-English speakers or non-Europeans was always secondary to the principal goal.[24]

The foreign mission agencies of the various Protestant denominations did not have the resources to reach all the countries and regions of Latin America. So the various (mainline) Protestant agencies that worked in Latin America during the latter part of the 19th and the first part of the 20th century developed "comity agreements," agreeing to work in different parts of Latin American countries so as not to be in competition with each other. Though they had doctrinal differences, these first denominations decided to coordinate their efforts. This meant that certain strains of Protestantism took root in specific regions of various Latin American countries during the first part of the 20th century.[25]

These comity agreements did not include the second wave of Protestant missionaries who were sent by more evangelical and fundamentalist Protestants. Some of these missionaries were sent under the mission agencies of Protestant denominations. But many went under newly formed "faith mission" agencies[26] that organized the support of a number of churches for a common ministry. Some of the most famous ones developed specific ministries or focused on specific regions. Central America Mission, founded by Cyrus Scofield in 1890, started in Guatemala and became best known for starting the Central American Church, one of the large denominations in Central America, and the largest seminary in the Spanish-speaking world, Seminario Teológico Centroamericano (SETECA), and for its radio broadcasts of the Protestant message. Another famous faith mission that started its work in Guatemala was Wycliffe Bible Translators, started by Cameron Townsend in 1942 to translate the Bible into the languages of the indigenous people of the region.

But it was Pentecostalism that would expand most rapidly in the region during the 20th century. The first missionaries were converts from the Azusa Street revival who returned to Latin America with a Pentecostal experience and a Pentecostal message. The newly formed Pentecostal denominations began sending missionaries to Latin America. But the fastest growth occurred not as a result of missionaries' efforts, but because of converts taking the message to new regions. New revival movements began in the region and expanded the Pentecostal message beyond the regions where U.S. Pentecostal missionaries worked.

Revival movements throughout the continent during the latter half of the 20th century changed the religious landscape of the region. The charismatic movement of the 1960s and 1970s spawned new movements and Pentecostal-like religious fervor among many Roman Catholics. Even as the Catholic Church was losing its hegemonic control over the religious discourse in Latin America (discussed further later in this chapter), Pentecostal and charismatic churches were developing throughout the region. By the 1970s and 1980s these new movements were being influenced by church growth models coming out of Korea during that period. By the last decade of the 20th century, there were large (10,000+) Protestant churches in most of the large cities of Latin America. Some of these new religious movements began to look at the United States, and other parts of the world, as a mission field, particularly as members of their churches began migrating to the United States, Europe, Australia, Japan, and other parts of the world.

Protestant church growth has been uneven in the region. As noted in the first chapter, there is a much larger percentage of Protestants in Central America and Puerto Rico than there is in Mexico. There is also significant variance between countries in each region and between various parts of the larger countries. Guatemala and Puerto Rico have the highest percentage of Protestants of any country in Latin America, and Uruguay has a very low percentage, even though its two large neighbors, Argentina and Brazil, have large and growing Protestant churches. Mexico has a great deal of variation between regions, with a much larger Protestant presence in the southern states than in the central region of the country.[27]

Protestant growth in Latin America has impacted U.S. Latino Protestantism directly and indirectly at several levels. As stated previously, an increasing percentage of Latin American immigrants are Protestants before coming to the United States. Also, some of the Latin America–based churches are sending missionaries into the United States. They are establishing their own churches and ministries in the United States outside of the direct influence and control of U.S. Protestant denominations. Latino Protestants are also influenced indirectly by the preaching and teaching of some of the principal Latin American megachurch pastors, who broadcast their message through television, radio, Internet, and print media. Many of these pastors preach and teach regularly in Latino churches. But many Latino churches also send their pastors and leaders to conferences led by these pastors in Latin America. (More is said about this influence in the next two chapters.)

## Protestant and Catholic Relations in the Latino United States

Many of the "Mexican" communities of the American Southwest were isolated and mostly outside of the direct influence of western migratory patterns during the 19th century. They were now a part of the United States, but many maintained many of their cultural practices throughout most of the 19th century. But the new immigrants from the Eastern Seaboard were increasingly influencing them and changing the economic and political realities of the region. And though Latinos were in the towns or regions where they had been born, they were now considered foreigners in their own land.[28] The new American immigrants were now considered the native people. The "Mexican" communities of the Southwest felt under siege in many areas, including their religious practices. Maintaining a strong Mexican Catholic identity became a way of defending their culture.

Roman Catholicism had been the only legally allowed religion before the arrival of the Americans, and both church and society defended this status. Being a Protestant or even having Protestant literature was a punishable offense. Having a Bible was considered suspect, since the priests were the only ones authorized to interpret Scripture to and for the people. The American takeover brought religious freedom to the region, though Mexican communities continued to try to enforce the previous understanding of religious practice in the areas where they were the majority.

Nonetheless, some of the Mexicans of the Southwest were open to the Protestant message for several different reasons. Some admired the American political and economic system and understood that Protestantism was a core part of its success. Others were looking for religious freedom. But the most common explanation given by the converts was that they had found spiritual life and biblical truth in the Protestant message.

These conversions and the new Protestant congregations established in the Mexican communities created significant tensions. Priests and religious lay leaders worked hard to keep Protestantism out of their communities, and they put a great deal of pressure on those who showed interest in the Protestant message and even more pressure on those who converted. These conversions also created social tensions between the converts and their families and friends. A few returned to the Catholic Church because of this pressure.

But most of the new Protestant converts interpreted the pressure of the Catholic majority as persecution for their faith. Nineteenth- and early 20th-century testimonials often told of the cost converts paid for their commitment to following Jesus Christ. Some of the greatest tensions occurred in the old Hispanic communities of northern New Mexico and southern Colorado. One of the popular Protestant testimonials revolved around getting hold of a Bible, often at great risk or financial sacrifice. All of the stories related the impact that reading the Bible had on the converts' lives and how they were converted to a living faith from a "dead" religious past.[29] Protestant converts told "Bible" stories in which they related the hardships they faced when they decided to obtain and read a Bible, but also the transformation this process brought to their lives.

There were no martyrs in the Southwest, like in Mexico, but there was a great deal of pressure against the Protestants in the Latino communities. During the late 19th century the situation was such that three small communities in northern New Mexico and southern Colorado split up into Catholic and Protestant sections.[30]

Latino Protestants found themselves as a double marginalized community. Because they were Latinos, they were marginalized within U.S. society. But because they were Protestants, they were marginalized in the Latino communities. Majority-culture Protestants were not ready to accept them into their churches or communities, even though they were Protestant converts, so they found themselves on the margins of the U.S. Protestant world and on the margins of their own communities.

This type of situation continued well into the 20th century in those communities that remained predominantly Latino. On a personal note, I remember being marginalized as an *alelulia*[31] while growing up in small predominantly Latino communities in south Texas and central California. Among other things, Catholic children my age were told that we ate babies in our churches, so that they would not want to come to our services, and I was often beaten up for being the son of a *Protestante* pastor in the predominantly Catholic Latino communities of my upbringing.

The relationship between Catholics and Protestants had always been different in Latin America, where Catholics were the majority and had been the only legal religious expression for so long, than in the United States, where Protestants were the majority and where Catholics had been treated as not true Americans through most of the 19th century. The Catholic Church in the United States developed very differently than in Latin America because of their different histories.

After Vatican II, many U.S. Catholics acted as if they were part of one more denomination in this country and not the single largest part of global Christendom, which claims to be "the" Church. The civil rights movement and ecumenical efforts brought Catholics in relationships with mainline Protestants, and the charismatic movement brought a different set of Catholics into contact with Pentecostals and charismatics. But it was not as easy to make this type of change in much of the Latino community. Relationships between Catholic and Protestant Latinos often looked more like the situation in Latin America, where Protestants were still ostracized well into the latter part of the 20th century. And it continued to look the same when Pentecostals began to grow and were increasingly seen as a threat by the Catholic leadership in Latin America.

## Persecution in Latin America

The situation in Latin America was much more difficult for Protestants. Roman Catholicism was the official religion in all of the countries that had been part of the Spanish or Portuguese empires. Non-Catholic religious expressions were either illegal or tolerated only in very limited circumstances. But the forces of reform in these countries were challenging the hegemony of the Catholic Church. Whenever liberal forces had the upper hand, they sought to bring reforms in all areas, including religious freedom. Throughout the 19th century, liberal Latin American leaders allowed, or even invited, Protestant missionaries to enter their countries to provide literacy, free education, medical care, and Protestant evangelization. Some of them used "the Protestant card" as a direct assault on the Catholic hierarchy, and others were more directly interested in what the Protestants could provide. These same leaders also allowed some Protestant immigrants from Europe to settle in parts of the region as part of their immigration policies. There were few converts during the 19th century, but by the end of the century, there were small Protestant congregations in all of the countries of Latin America.

Most of the converts during this period suffered, at some level, for their faith. Their friends and relatives marginalized them, and many were socially ostracized. In many countries their political and civil rights were also limited, by law or by practice. But in almost all of the countries of the region, there were also Protestant martyrs during the late 19th and early 20th centuries. Most of the older Protestant communities in Latin America have testimonies about the people who suffered or died for their faith at the hands of Catholic attackers, often led or inspired by the local priest. Open persecution continued well into the middle of the 20th century in some areas. The situation changed as Protestantism continued to grow in the region and as religious freedom became more prevalent. Yet there are still areas where Protestants are very small minorities and continue to be ostracized. This is particularly the case in some isolated communities in Mexico where Protestants are not allowed to build churches or even allowed to live.[32]

Throughout the 19th and well into the 20th century, most Latin American Protestants assumed that marginalization and persecution were part of the cost of conversion. For many, persecution was proof of faithfulness to the gospel. As Latin American Protestants told their testimonies, they often spoke of the importance of correct biblical knowledge and of suffering as part of the cost of deciding to follow Jesus Christ. One of the best-known Spanish-language Latin American hymns of the mid-20th century, "Hay una senda" (translated as "There Is but One Way"), is the testimony of a convert who suffers for following Jesus. He is walking on a path the world does not know. Friends and relatives from his past now despise him because he gave his life to Jesus. The way of suffering, which is the path God directed him on, will be transformed into the way to heaven.[33] This song is still part of the repertoire of many Latin American and Latino Protestants.

After Vatican II, many things changed in the relationship between Catholics and Protestants throughout the world and in Latin America in particular. The openness represented by the Council created new spaces for interaction and dialogue, particularly with those Protestants who were part of the World Council and/or the Latin American Council of Churches (CLAI by its initials in Spanish).

The deteriorating political and economic situation in many countries, often linked with the Cold War, united some liberal Protestants and Catholics under the common cause of political and socioeconomic change through Liberation theology. The charismatic movement allowed for some interaction between a different set of Catholics and Protestants at the parish level.

But the tensions between many Protestants and Catholics continued at both the official and relational levels. At the local level there are still many places where Catholics continue to persecute and discriminate against Protestants. There are also many Protestants who refer to the pope as the anti-Christ or publicly ridicule popular Catholic devotions toward the saints or the apparitions of the Virgin Mary.

Official Roman Catholic responses have looked different in Latin America, where they are a large majority, than in other parts of the world where Protestants are the majority. Roman Catholic leaders also respond differently to Protestants from more traditional denominations than to those from the new Pentecostal and charismatic churches. Part of this difference reflects the fact that the latter group of churches is growing because Catholics are leaving the church to become part of these congregations. There are many ecumenical types of meetings with Protestants from traditional denominations (that are often not growing very much), but the reaction toward the Pentecostal and neo-Pentecostal groups is much more negative.

For example, the official Catholic stance toward Protestants since Vatican II is that they are "separated brethren." This is the common term used in ecumenical settings. But in Latin America most Pentecostals are seen as a threat to the Catholic Church and are referred to as sects. During the papal reign of John Paul II, he visited Guatemala many more times than any other country in Latin America, per capita. This is largely due to the fact that Protestantism was growing so rapidly in the country. During each of his visits, he made comments about the "sects," their negative impact, and the need to combat them. This has not changed under the new pope.

As late as 2007, the Latin American bishops' conference that met in Apare-cida, Brazil, at which Pope Benedict XVI presided, made several references to the "problems" created by the sects, putting most Pentecostals and new religious movements into the same category.[34]

This conflictive relationship is set in the context of the changing rela-tionship between the Roman Catholic Church and Latin American states and societies. Even as the percentage of Protestants has been growing, the relationship between the Catholic Church and state has been changing. The Roman Catholic Church had been the only legally recognized church during the Spanish and Portuguese colonial periods, and the Inquisition enforced this position. After independence the Church slowly lost power, though it continues to have a great deal of influence in society. Throughout most of the 20th century, countries in Latin America had concordats with the Vati-can that gave the Roman Catholic Church a privileged place in the religious sphere. Most of the concordats with Latin American countries have been modified or repealed, but to this day Peru has a concordat that gives special privileges to the Catholic Church, including subsidies from the government, tax benefits, and control over all religious education in the country.[35]

The changing relationship between church and state is one of several forces creating a new religious landscape in Latin America. The growth of Protestantism has meant that the state has had to recognize that more and more of its citizens are not Catholic. On the other hand, a growing secular-ization meant that many people who called themselves Catholics, or who had been Catholics in the past, no longer felt that the Church had anything to say to society at large. But these changes have also created internal ten-sions among Catholics between those who long to return to the days of Catholic hegemony and those who feel that the Church needs to take a very different role in Latin American societies.

## The Changing Relationship between Catholic and Protestant Latinos

The relationship between U.S. Latino Protestants and Catholics is more complex because it is influenced by the changing relationship between Catholics and Protestants in the United States, but also by the more conflic-tive history in Latin America. But the issue also has some unique aspects in the Latino experience.

Many Latin American Protestant immigrants find it hard to understand the positive relationship that tends to exist between Catholics and Prot-estants in the United States. Their own experience has often been quite negative, and they sometimes feel like their U.S. brothers and sisters do not

validate them. Their experiences in the United States often seem similar to
those in Latin America, particularly when they interact with Catholic relatives or with priests who are recent immigrants from Latin America. So they
often cannot understand that U.S. Catholics may be different from how
they have experienced Catholics in Latin America.

But U.S. Latina Catholics are often also in a complex relationship with the
Catholic Church. When the United States took over the Southwest and the
U.S. Catholic Church took responsibility for the existing Mexican Catholic
churches in the Southwest, many of the new religious leaders looked down
on popular Mexican Catholic practices. The first U.S.-assigned bishop for
Santa Fe, New Mexico, Jean Baptiste Lamy, removed most of the Mexican
priests from the diocese, including the very popular Antonio José Martínez.
It would not be until the middle of the 20th century that there would be a
Latino bishop in the United States, even though Latinas were always the
vast majority in many dioceses in the Southwest. To this day Latinos are
almost 40 percent of the U.S. Catholic population, but they are very underrepresented among priests and bishops.

Many Latina Catholics also feel some of the same "threats" that some
Latin American Catholics feel when they see Latinos leaving the Catholic
Church and becoming Protestants. Some of the literature on ministry to
Latino Catholics warns priests and lay workers to beware of the efforts
of some of the Protestants. Many Latino Catholic leaders find it difficult
to be ecumenical because of this ongoing tension.[36] As in Latin America,
the "threat" comes from the churches that are growing, the evangelicals
and Pentecostals. For the most part mainline Latino Protestantism is not
seen as a threat, so that is where Latino Catholics find it easiest to be
ecumenical.

## Latinos: *Protestantes* and *Católicos* in the United States

Nonetheless, two types of things tend to bring Latina *Protestantes* and
*Católicos* together. On the one hand, the commonality of experience of most
Latinos in U.S. society has meant that both need to address the same issues
at local, regional, and national levels. But the other reason is often much
more personal; during times of celebration or crisis, Protestants and Catholics are often part of the same extended family. This means that priests and
pastors often find themselves needing to work together when pastoral care
is needed.

Latinos from mainline traditions have been working alongside Latina
Catholics for several decades. From the time of the civil rights movement,
one has been able to find Latinos marching together or working together to

address specific issues and needs. This type of relationship has usually been cause-specific, be it local or national. People who already know each other are ready to come together when education, housing, hunger, or immigration create the need for a new response.

Mainline Protestant and Catholic Latinas also find themselves meeting together in local and national ecumenical events. Most urban areas have ecumenical councils that celebrate "Christian unity" through regular meetings and public events. Depending on the region, Latinos interact in these activities, usually sponsored by broader organizations.

Another area of work together has been in the religious academy. Protestants and Catholics have worked together to study the religious practices of the community, but also to train the next generation of religious leaders and professors. Two of the best-known ecumenically driven Latino theologically focused organizations are the Hispanic Summer Program (HSP) and Hispanic Theological Initiative (HTI). Both were started by Latinos working together to address theological education concerns for the community.

HSP provides seminary-level courses for students who are preparing for ministry in the Hispanic community, both Catholic and Protestant. The courses are taught in both Spanish and English, by Latinas, from a Hispanic perspective. Most of the seminaries that are members are from mainline Protestant traditions, though there are also several Catholic institutions and some evangelical seminaries. Students who participate obtain seminary credit, but more importantly, they take courses that help them focus on being pastors and priests in the Latino community.

HTI focuses on the religious academy, providing scholarship and mentoring for Latinas who are earning academic doctorates and who anticipate teaching in seminaries or schools of religion. Because Latinos have been so underrepresented in these institutions, both as students and as professors, the goal of HTI is to support qualified Latinas who have a vocational interest in the field, but who might succeed only if they have sufficient financial support and Latino-oriented mentoring.

Yet in spite of some small areas of common cause, it is clear that some very real differences separate Latino Catholics and Protestants and make it difficult to find common cause beyond specific needs in the community. The differences are theological, structural, and personal. They have very different understandings of what it means to be a Christian, their religious organizations call them to very different actions, and both have often experienced each other in the fairly negative situations that have already been described.

Yet as Latinos continue to grow in this country, they will need to find common cause particularly between evangelicals/Pentecostals and Catholics.

Immigration reform, the rights of minority peoples, and the place of Latinas in U.S. society are obvious places where both need to find ways to work together. But these two groups also share a common concern about values and ethics and the role of faith both privately and in larger society. The Pew study demonstrated that the groups often have similar perspectives, even though they often find it difficult to work together on them.

Latino leaders, both Catholic and Protestant, also find themselves in the midst of the challenges of globalization, because many have transnational ministries. The networks of service cross national borders and challenge modern understanding of the nation-state. Latin Americans/Latinos are crossing all types of borders, and they are taking their faith with them. The familial and social networks of which they are a part cross the Protestant–Catholic divide. Christian leaders, both Catholic and Protestant, have to find ways to keep up and to support them as they walk toward the future.

## CHAPTER THREE

# Streams of Latino Protestantism

Latino Protestantism began with the efforts of U.S. Protestant missionaries in the 19th-century Southwest. From the very beginning of the missionary enterprise, Protestant missionaries and Latino Protestants have interacted with Protestants in Latin America, be it through official missionary efforts or through the movement of peoples north and south. All of this has happened in the midst of the complex political and economic relationship between the United States and Latin America. The encounter between Euro-American Protestants and Latino Catholics in the 19th-century Southwest happened in the midst of the unease that many U.S. Protestants felt with the European Catholic migration to the United States and changes in the hegemony of Roman Catholicism in Latin America. In addition, the Pentecostal revival began in the Southwest and became a crucial player in the religious environment, particularly in Latin America and among Latinos.

The growth of Latino Protestantism, reflective of the changing religious commitments of Latinos, has taken place in this context of rapid political and religious change. During the 20th century there were several attempts to document this growth, by reporting on the number of Latino Protestant adult church members, usually based on denominational statistics. Some used that data to draw tentative conclusions about the overall size of the Latina Protestant community, though most were missionaries or mission executives, and their interest was to report on the number of Latino converts. Because these efforts depended on denominational reports, they were affected by the different ways denominations dealt with statistics. Some denominations kept fairly detailed records, whereas others had irregular record-keeping. Many of the fastest-growing churches, denominations, and movements in the Latino community (i.e., Pentecostal and charismatic churches) have been among the latter. Nonetheless, all studies demonstrated that Latino Protestantism has been growing, though the rate of growth has not always been clear.

## Where Are the New Latina Protestants Coming From?

Conversions have always been the principal source of growth among Latino Protestants. During the early years, missionaries were at the center of that process. They gave away Bibles and gospel tracts. They preached and led Bible studies in homes. They called Latinos to accept Jesus Christ as Lord and Savior. They baptized the new converts and discipled them in their new faith commitment. They organized these new believers into Protestant church communities.

In some of the early Protestant congregations, this process remained principally in the hands of the missionaries. The converts were also encouraged to preach, evangelize, and invite others to Protestant faith. But the implicit, and sometimes explicit, assumption was that most Latinos would never be able to be as effective as the Anglo missionaries because of their culture, lack of education, or lack of adequate resources. As a result, many Latino Protestant churches remained under the leadership or supervision of Anglos for many years.

But some of the Latinos had such profound conversion experiences that they shared their experience, even though they did not have all the tools available to the missionary. During the early years, most Latino converts of this type worked under Anglo leaders. Some denominations had fewer requirements for pastoral leadership, so Latinos from those churches were encouraged to preach, evangelize, and establish churches with the tools they had. But others assumed that it would take a lot of effort on the part of the Latinos to ever be able to effectively share the Protestant message.

The Pentecostal revival changed all of that. The basic message of Pentecostalism was that the Spirit of God worked in the lives of all people and that all people could preach under the power of the Holy Spirit. Anglo culture, education, and resources might be useful—or they might even be a hindrance. The key was to invite others to experience God the way they had experienced God.

This radically changed the missionary efforts. While many missionaries from Protestant denominations were working to train Latinos in an Anglo model, Pentecostal converts went everywhere even if they did not have what were considered the adequate tools for the task. Poor, working-class Latinas, with a limited education, who might not speak English, could be used by the Holy Spirit to call others like themselves to faith and establish churches among these converts. Their churches would not look like the Anglo churches, but they would look like themselves. This change put the evangelistic task in the hands of the converts and created a different reality. But because these new churches were often not under the direct supervision of an existing Protestant mission agency, they did not get counted in some of the reports of Protestantism among Latinos.

Obviously, most Latino converts used to be Roman Catholics. This is the reason for many of the tensions described in chapter 2. Catholics do not see Protestant missionary work as evangelization but as proselytism. As stated in the last chapter, Catholics in the United States sometimes also use the term "sect," like their Latin American counterparts, to describe Protestant ministry efforts among Latinas.[1] In the past, many Protestants took a polemical approach, stating that the Catholic Church taught false doctrine and that people need to hear the biblical message without the control of the Church. But today most Protestant converts would likely state that they had not found spiritual life in the Catholic Church, which is why they were attracted to the Protestant message.

A second important source of Latino Protestant growth is immigration. In earlier years, new immigrants were seen only as more potential converts. But as Latin American Protestantism grew, more and more of the immigrants were already Protestants. Most joined the ranks of existing churches. Sometimes denominations chose to import already trained pastors from Latin America for Latino churches here. But a growing number of immigrants are bringing their faith with them, not unlike earlier European immigrants. Many are starting new churches under existing denominations, churches that reflect their national background. But some are bringing their denominations and movements or starting new ones when they establish themselves here.

Immigration and conversion growth are closely linked at several levels. On the one hand, people are often open to religious change when they are in the midst of other changes. But immigration can also be the space for conversion that might have happened in the country of origin, given more time. In addition, there is also a small but growing group of Latin American immigrants who see migration as part of a mission pattern, not unlike the growth of the early church in the Roman Empire. From this perspective, migration is a key component in Protestant evangelization because the migrants are taking their faith with them and sharing it in their host country. Migrants do not merely adapt to their new environment; they also influence it.

A third source of Protestant growth is the birth rate among Latino Protestants. A growing number of Latinas are growing up in Protestant churches. Most Latino Protestant churches preach that believers must have an individual experience of conversion and be baptized when they are old enough to make their own confession of faith. So these churches do not count their children as members until they have a conversion experience. But as the Latino population continues to grow, second-generation conversions will become a more important part of Latino Protestantism.

Of course there are also sources of losses for Latino Protestant churches. Some Latino Protestants leave Latino churches and become part of majority-culture Protestant churches (see chapter 5). Others return to Catholicism or live between Protestantism and Catholicism. Marginal Christian groups such as the Jehovah's Witnesses or Mormons also attract some Latino Protestants. A few join other world religions. There are also those who drop out of organized religion, temporarily or permanently, and those who become secularized.

Yet current trends seem to indicate that Latina Protestantism will continue to grow numerically into the foreseeable future. Whether it will also grow as a percentage of the overall Latino community is yet to be seen. It is also yet to be seen what impact Latino Protestantism will have on U.S. Protestantism and on U.S. society in general.

## Previous Studies of the Growth of Latino Protestantism

Much of the earlier interest in the growth of Latino Protestantism came from Protestant missionaries or mission leaders. Most of the studies done by mission leaders sought to demonstrate the success of the missionary enterprise or to address some of the challenges faced in ministry among Latinas. As the community has grown, Latino Protestants have been interested in knowing who they are, how many churches and members they have, and where they are located. Most of the studies have collected statistical data, numbers of churches and members, locations of congregations, names of pastors, and similar information.

All of the studies quoted in the last chapter and most of the ones used in this chapter began with the statistical data provided by the denominations and then often followed up with direct observation and interviews with pastors and leaders. Neither McLean nor Whitam attempted to define the size of the overall Protestant community, nor did they attempt to ascertain what percentage of the Latina population these Protestants represented. Grebler et al. assumed that the membership numbers equaled the total size of the community and concluded that Latino Protestantism was insignificant.

Clifton Holland also used denominational data in his extensive 1974 study *The Religious Dimension of Hispanic Los Angeles: A Protestant Case Study.* He began with a general background of the Latina population in Southern

California. He then worked with denominational officials to develop a directory of all the Hispanic Protestant churches in the region. Finally, he contacted all of the churches by mail and did field research, confirming the existence of the churches and interviewing pastors. He was able to identify 227 Latino Protestant churches in Los Angeles and Orange counties, with 209 of those congregations in Los Angeles country, with a total of 14,930 members in 1972. Of these, 80 churches, with 5,005 members, were Pentecostal, and the rest were from other denominations.[2] It is likely that the Pentecostal numbers were low because another directory developed in 1986 using the same methodology found that a much higher percentage of the churches were Pentecostal. The "Directory of Hispanic Protestant Churches in Southern California," covering the nine-county area of greater Southern California, identified a total of 1,048 churches, of which 687 were in Los Angeles County. The two largest denominations in that report were the Assemblies of God (124 churches) and the Apostolic Assembly (108 churches).[3] An update of the directory in 1995 confirmed that of the 1,626 churches identified, only 2 denominations had more than 100 churches: the Assemblies of God (148) and the Apostolic Assembly (131).[4]

Holland has worked with others to develop similar directories in other parts of the United States. He worked with Ildefonso Ortiz in the Miami-Dade area in 1986, finding 222 Hispanic churches. In 1988 a directory in the Bay Area of California identified 157 Latina churches. In 1993 Holland worked with the Hispanic Association for Bilingual-Bicultural Ministries (HABBM) to develop a national directory. He was able to identify 6,837 churches, though he estimated that there were probably more than 10,000 Latino churches and missions in the United States at that time.[5] He is currently working to develop a new updated national directory of Hispanic churches in the United States.

Andrew Greeley[6] and Larry Hunt[7] both did studies during the 1990s of the growth of Protestantism among Latinos by studying data from the General Social Survey. Greeley analyzed data from 1972 to 1988, and Hunt studied data from 1972 to 1996. Both studies sought to understand the growth of the non-Catholic population among Latinos. Using statistical analysis of data collected by others, Greeley concluded that about 70 percent of Latinos were Catholics, 22 percent Protestants, and 8 percent other, with a "defection rate" of about 8 percent from Catholicism to Protestantism, particularly to what he called fundamentalist Protestantism (roughly equivalent to evangelicals and Pentecostals together). Greeley concluded that there was a certain upward socioeconomic mobility among these Protestants and concluded that the Catholic Church had failed to "provide community and respectability for the upwardly mobile Hispanic American."[8]

One potential problem that Greeley acknowledged, but did not address directly, was that there was a potential problem with the GSS data, since it surveyed only English speakers.

Hunt decided to test Greeley's conclusions: was Protestantism in fact providing a safe space of Hispanic upward mobility and loss of ethnic identity? He cross-referenced the GSS data with the 1984 National Alcohol Survey that oversampled the Latino community and allowed Latinos to respond in English or Spanish. Once he correlated that data from the two surveys, Hunt concluded that the "defection" rate was not as strong as Greeley had concluded. He also concluded that there was only upward mobility and less ethnic identity among some mainline Latino Protestants. Many "fundamentalists" actually had a stronger ethnic identity than many Latino Catholics. He concluded that "future research should explore the issues raised by the complex intersections of faith, status, and identity that increasingly define the diversity of Hispanic communities in the United States."[9]

The next major studies of Latino religious practices were the Trinity study and the two Pew studies discussed in chapter 1. They were significantly different from Greeley and Hunt's works since they performed their own surveys that served as the basis for their analysis and conclusions.

## The Major Latino Protestant Denominations Today

As part of the Pew study *Hispanic Churches and American Public Life* (2003), the researchers attempted to ascertain the number of Latinos in various non-Catholic Christian organizations, including Protestant denominations and groups such as the Jehovah's Witness and the Mormons. The initial results of that effort were reported during the public presentation of the study, but they were not published in the final report. The broad conclusions from that oral report are helpful in understanding the size and impact of non-Catholic groups within the Latina community.

First of all, according to the 2003 initial report, two "marginal" Christian movements, Jehovah's Witnesses and the Mormons, have a sizable presence in the Latino community. They have more Latina members than many Protestant denominations. Though they are outside the scope of this study, it is interesting to note how attractive they are as a non-Catholic alternative.[10]

A second important observation has to do with membership distribution. Both the 2003 and 2007 studies point out that the largest Latino Protestant denominations are either Pentecostal or evangelical. Of the five largest Protestant denominations in the United States, Southern Baptist, United Methodist, Evangelical Lutheran, Church of God in Christ, and the Presbyterian Church (USA), only the first has a sizable Latino presence. All of the largest

Latino denominations are Pentecostal or evangelical, and all of the Latino mainline Protestant denominations together do not have as much of a presence in the community as any one of the largest evangelical or Pentecostal denominations.

The Pew results also fit with the statistical studies done by Cliffton Holland on the distribution of Latino Protestants. Holland has developed a tentative list (as of the beginning of 2011) of the denominations with the highest reported numbers of Latina congregations and the adult membership listed for these churches. The self-reporting of denominations is very uneven because some keep very "tight" statistics, whereas others are somewhat lax in their membership reports. But even with that caveat, self-reporting is very helpful in determining which denominations have the largest numbers of Latino churches and members.[11]

The following is a brief history and description of the denominations with the largest number of Latino churches (a minimum of 200 congregations), based on Holland's latest reporting and denominational self-reporting, in approximate order of size (there are several denominations that report similar numbers of churches and members). Since most denominations do not report on total number of Latino members, whether or not they are in a Latino church, this reporting clearly does not account for all Latina Protestant church members. But it is generally in line with the Pew studies in that the top five denominations are all evangelical or Pentecostal and in that only a couple (or three, depending on how one counts the Episcopal Church) of the mainline denominations are in the top 10. It is possible that the top Latino mainline denominations, United Methodist, American Baptist, Presbyterian Church USA, and Disciples of Christ, might be higher on the list if Latino church members in non-Latino churches were taken into account. But overall, this ranking seems to reflect current reality among Latino Protestants.

### Assemblies of God

The Assemblies of God (AG) is the largest Pentecostal denomination in the United States. It also has the largest Latino presence of any Protestant denomination and is the U.S. denomination with the largest percentage of Latinos. In 2009 it reported having almost 600,000 Latinos adherents, a little over 20 percent of all the AG adherents in the United States.[12] More recent reporting indicates that Latinas may be almost 25 percent of the total membership. This sets the contrast between U.S. Protestants, in general, and Latina Protestants, since the Assemblies of God is not even among the five largest denominations in the United States. The Latina presence is particularly important to the denomination since most of its growth is coming from Latino churches and Latino converts.[13]

"Mexicans" have been a part of the denomination almost since the Assemblies of God organized in 1914. The key players in the early years were Henry Ball, Francisco "El Azteca" Olazábal, Alice Luce, and Demetrio Bazán. Henry Ball began preaching in Texas through a translator and in 1918 formed the Latin District Council of the Assemblies of God to begin Latino churches. Olazábal had a Pentecostal experience in 1917 and by 1918 was preaching in Texas. One of the early converts was Demetrio Bazán, who worked alongside Olazábal. El Azteca began preaching among Latinos throughout the United States and Puerto Rico and saw many converts. He worked alongside Ball, but in 1923 he left the denomination because he felt that the "gringos" wanted to control everything and would not allow Latinos to choose their own leaders. Many Latinos left the denomination with Olazábal to form CLADIC in 1923 (see chapter 2 for more details), though eventually Olazábal and many of those who had left returned to the denomination. Alice Luce had been an Episcopal missionary. When she had a Pentecostal experience, she felt called to work among the Mexicans of the United States. In 1926 she started the Berean Bible Institute in San Diego, California, which would later become the Latin American Bible Institute (LABI) of La Puente, California. That same year she worked with Henry Ball to start the Latin American Bible Institute of San Antonio, Texas.

The first Latin American district of the Assemblies of God was formed in 1918 under the leadership of Henry Ball. This district expanded throughout the United States under the leadership of Ball and then in 1937 with Bazán as the new superintendent. Under his leadership the district organized four conferences with full-time leadership to guide the expanding work of the Latin American district. In 1971 the conferences were reorganized as four Latin American districts, which later expanded to become the current eight districts.

Most of the Latino growth has occurred in the last 35 years. At the 1956 convention of the Latin American district, the statistical report stated that there were 321 Latino churches with 19,490 members. The 1977 report of the General Secretary states that that there were 481 churches with 36,000 members, a growth of about 50 percent in 21 years. But the 2002 report stated that there were 1,758 churches, an increase of 365 percent in 25 years.[14] That rate of growth will not likely be repeated, but the Latino Assemblies of God continues to grow at a rapid rate.

In 2009 the Assemblies of God reported having eight Spanish-language districts, including one in Puerto Rico. Because of their growth and/or their geographic size, several of the districts had recently been split or were in process of dividing into two. These districts reported having 1,935 churches and 250,000 members. There are also a number of Latino churches in what the AG calls its geographic (i.e., Euro-American) districts, though it did not report how many were in each district. Outside of the clearly identified Latino churches, there are also a growing number of Latina members in AG churches who do not identify themselves as Latino.

Since Latinos are a growing part of the AG, the leadership issue raised by Olazábal in the 1920s continues to resonate. No other U.S. Protestant denomination has such a high percentage of Latinas, so it has to address issues related to Latino participation in key leadership roles that other denominations still do not have to address. It also have has to address the role of language and culture in how the denomination views its own future. As it continues growing, it is likely that Olazábal's concerns will continue to be a prophetic word within the denomination.

### Baptist General Convention of Texas and the Southern Baptist Convention

The Baptist General Convention of Texas established the first churches among the Mexicans in Texas in the 1880s in conjunction with their missionary work in northern Mexico. Several associations in central and southern Texas established churches, and the state convention also funded some projects. In 1910, 24 Mexican Baptist churches met in San Antonio and organized themselves as the Mexican Baptist Convention of Texas. During these early years, Anglos and Mexicans worked together, though Anglos often initiated the work. But the goal was to establish Mexican Baptist churches, not to bring Mexicans into English-language congregations.

As the number of churches grew, the Mexican Baptist Convention, in conjunction with Anglo associations and the state convention, established several strategic ministry institutions. They established the Mexican Bible Institute in 1925, the Mexican Baptist Children's Home in 1944, the Valley Baptist Academy in 1946, and the Mexican Baptist Bible Institute (now Baptist University of the Américas) in 1947.

In 1964 the Mexican Baptist Convention formally united with the Baptist General Convention of Texas (BGCT). In 1990 the Convention decided to change its name to the Hispanic Baptist Convention of Texas (HBC) in recognition of the growing number of members from other national backgrounds in the churches of the state. Over the years the HBC and the BGCT have integrated ministries and statewide institutions. The number of Latino Baptist churches in the state continues to grow, and today there almost 1,500 Latino Baptist churches in Texas.[15]

Because of doctrinal tensions within the Southern Baptist Convention beginning in 1979, the Baptist General Convention of Texas became one of two state conventions to reject the fundamentalist direction of the national convention. The fundamentalists in Texas started a second convention in Texas, the Southern Baptist Convention of Texas. A few Latino churches joined this new convention. The moderate Baptists formed the Cooperative Baptist Fellowship. Most Latino Baptist churches in Texas remained with the Baptist General Convention. Today some of the Latino churches relate to the Southern Baptist Convention, and others relate to the Cooperative Baptist Fellowship, but the vast majority relate to the Baptist General Convention of Texas. Though the doctrinal divisions remain, the lines between the groups are not nearly as pronounced as they once were.[16]

Other state conventions or local associations slowly expanded beyond Texas, first to California and then into the Southeast. By 1960 they reported 559 congregations and 28,000 members, according to the estimate of a denominational official.[17] Most of these congregations were in Texas, though there were a few Latino churches in other parts of the Southwest and the Southeast.

Most of the growth outside of Texas has been fairly recent. Up to 1993 the Southern Baptists were reporting fewer than 1,000 Latino congregations. That changed in 1994, and since then the number of churches and church-type missions has continued to grow rapidly, particularly in the South. For example, there are currently more than 130 Latino congregations in North Carolina. According to a 2009 report, Southern Baptists have 1,505 Latino churches and 1,733 church-type missions, with a total of 204,000 members.[18] The vast majority of the established churches are in Texas, and most of the church-type missions are located in areas where Latino migration is much more recent.

Southern Baptists have several national projects focused on the Latino community, particularly in the areas of ethnic ministries and publications for evangelism and Christian formation. But Latino Southern Baptists have not developed strong national links. There have been two efforts to develop a National Hispanic organization, one in 1987 and another in 2005. But most Latino Southern Baptists are linked together only through local associations or state conventions.[19]

Currently, there are two very different types of Latino Southern Baptists. There are those such as the Hispanic Baptist Convention of Texas that have a multigenerational Baptist identity. But most of the new congregations are church-type missions that have not yet developed a strong presence in their associations or conventions. Since many of the church members are migrant workers, it may be a while before some of them take root.

The Hispanic Baptist Convention of Texas is the largest Latino Baptist convention in the United States and the single largest statewide entity of Latino Protestants in the United States. It has a solid statewide infrastructure

and a small university, the Baptist University of the Américas, which is one
of the Baptist universities in the state. Though many of the congregations
are small, it has a number of large churches in the major urban areas of the
state. The HBC has a large multigenerational and diverse Latino presence.
Some of the *tejanos* trace their roots to the Spanish or Mexican periods and
are third- or fourth-generation Baptists. But Texas also has a historical and
economic link to northern Mexico and draws many immigrants from there
and from other parts of Latin America. Latino Baptists in Texas feel they
are particularly well situated to reach into the diverse Latino population
because the HBC has Spanish-language, bilingual, and English-language
congregations, and the BGCT has intentionally multicultural congregations
and Euro-American churches, providing churches that reach across the ethnic identity spectrum of the Latino community.[20]

Because the single largest group of Baptist churches is part of a state convention that has maintained a moderate/conservative stance within the Southern Baptist Convention, it is yet to be seen whether Latino Baptists nationally
will follow the same trend as the national convention or whether they will be
able to work well together, particularly since many of the newer churches are
in state conventions that have taken a strongly conservative stance.

### Seventh-Day Adventists

The Seventh-Day Adventists began their first Latino congregation in
Sánchez, Arizona, in 1899. One of the first people baptized was Marcial
Serna, who had been a Latino Methodist pastor in Tucson but converted to
Adventism. He convinced most of his congregation to become Adventist,
and by 1901 the formerly Methodist building became a Latino Adventist
church, the oldest Latino Adventist congregation still in existence. Serna
also convinced three other Latino Methodist pastors to become Adventists.

During the first two decades of the 20th century, the Adventists also
began Latino churches in New Mexico and California. By 1920 there were
a total 471 Latino members. That year they established their first school for
training Latino leaders in Phoenix, Arizona. As they started new churches
in Texas, Illinois, and New York, they expanded their training programs
and started their first Hispanic American Seminary in 1942 in Albuquerque, New Mexico. During its 10-year existence it would receive students
from several states and from Mexico, Puerto Rico, Cuba, and Colombia.
The Adventists continued to slowly expand into other areas where there
was a Latino population. By 1960 they reported having 68 Latino congregations with a total of about 5,000 adult members.[21]

Colporteurs have always been an important means for evangelization
among the Adventists. The first Latino pastor, Marcial Serna, became an

Adventist because of the work of young colporteurs who did not speak Spanish. Adventists have been distributing books in Spanish since 1909. Because of the importance given to healthy living as part of their understanding of what it means to be a Christian, their books are either about Christian faith or about health and diet. They have also had extensive radio and television programming in Spanish in both the United States and Latin America. Through this programming they have had an influence on the larger Spanish-language Protestant world.[22]

The Seventh-Day Adventists have always valued education, so they have established many schools and universities. Because of the link between Latino ministry in the United States and ministry in Latin America, one of the educational institutions that has been very influential among U.S. Latino Adventists has been the Universidad de Montemorelos in Mexico. They have also developed the Seminario Teológico Adventista Interamericano in Mayagüez, Puerto Rico. Many U.S. Latino pastors completed their seminary degree in Montemorelos, and the seminary in Puerto Rico will be the basis for the Adventists to offer theological education throughout the Spanish-speaking world.

The Adventists have eight geographic districts in the United States, which they call unions. Each has a Hispanic coordinator, and several have more than one coordinator. The Latino churches started in the Southwest and have their largest presence there. But there are Latino Adventist churches throughout the United States. Today one in nine of all Adventists in the United States is a Latina, close to the same percentage as the Latino population in the United States. As of 2009, there are 167,000 adult Latino church members in 1,077 churches.[23]

One of the interesting aspects of Latino Adventist leadership has been that many Latino pastors serve, or have served, in both Spanish- and English-language congregations. Adventists are very proud of the fact that their first Latino pastor, Marcial Serna, was bilingual and pastored congregations in both languages. Latino pastors are expected to be bilingual and to be able to minister effectively in both languages. Theological education usually includes the requirement that graduates be able to communicate effectively in both Spanish and English.

The Seventh-Day Adventists denomination is unique among the Protestant denominations in that it is the only one that has done an extensive study of its Latina members. *Avance: A Vision for a New Mañana* was an extensive survey that "focused on the unique needs and challenges facing the Hispanic Adventist community in North America."[24] It studied the role of Adventist institutions and their impact on the faith of Latino members in the context of socioeconomic mobility and acculturation. The study drew several important conclusions about Latina Adventists. One is that Adventists need to understand and respond to the impact of acculturation on Latino youth. Both Latina and Euro-American churches need to take into account the fluid reality in which these young people are defining their faith and to make sure that their church structures can respond effectively. They also noted that Latino Adventists tend to have a more legalistic view of Christian life and that the church needs to address how they understand the gospel. The authors of the study state that Adventist churches can best address these issues through education, making Adventist education more accessible to Latinos and making sure Adventist schools specifically address the needs and challenges of the Latino community.[25]

### Church of God (Cleveland, Tennessee)

The Church of God established its first Latino congregation in 1911 in Ratón, New Mexico. During the 1940s work among the Spanish-speaking was divided into two major sections, with work west of the Mississippi based in San Antonio and work in the east based in New York. In May 1946 the denomination established the Office of Superintendent for Latin America and placed the Latino churches in the United States under its supervision.

The denomination established Instituto Bíblico Preparativo (IPI), its first Bible Institute in Spanish, in 1947 in San Antonio under the leadership of Bessy (Vessie) Hargrave. It established another program in Houston in 1975. The Church of God Bible colleges have also played an important role in preparing Latina pastors. Several of them have programs focused on the Latino community.

Another important program established by Hargrave was the Editorial Evangélica (1946). It produced a magazine, Sunday school materials, and other resources for the churches. This publishing house was merged with the Department of Hispanic Ministries in the 1990s.

In 1998 the Church of God formed the Department of Hispanic Ministries and named a national director. Nonetheless, the Latino churches have a strong ongoing relationship with Latin America. Leaders from both areas regularly serve in the north and the south.

Currently, the Church of God has about 1,000 Latino churches and 60,000 adult members. Most of the Latino churches are part of one of the eight Hispanic regions of the denomination. A few of the congregations work under a Euro-American church or an English-language overseer. There are also an unspecified number of new church planting projects under the latter model that are not clearly reported. The eight Hispanic regions have their own Bible institute programs and are committed to establishing 1,000 new Latina congregations by 2020.[26]

### Apostolic Assembly of the Faith in Christ Jesus

The Apostolic Assembly was born in the midst of the tensions related to the "proper" baptismal formula among the early preachers from the Azusa Street revival. Most Pentecostals baptized in the name of Father, Son, and Holy Spirit, but a significant minority baptized in the name of Jesus, including one of the key leaders, Charles Parham. One of the first "Mexican" preachers to come out of the revival, Juan Navarro Martínez, baptized converts in the name of Jesus. In 1912 he baptized Francisco Llorente, who would later become the first president of the Apostolic Assembly. Under Llorente's ministry many people were converted in both the United States and Mexico. The Mexican Revolution caused people to move north and south across the border. As they did, they were exposed to the preaching of these evangelists, and many also became lay evangelists as they returned to Mexico.

In 1925 the congregations that had been established in this movement organized themselves as the Iglesia de la Fe Apostólica Pentecostés. This became the first Latino Protestant denomination in the United States that had no historical link to a U.S. denomination. During the early years, they were a "borderlands" group of churches, without a clear line of demarcation between the churches in the United States and Mexico. In 1932 a sister denomination in Mexico organized itself as separate entity.

The Assembly established churches throughout the Southwest, where the Mexican American and Mexican populations were largest. In particular, it established a large number of churches in California and Texas. In 1940 it established the Colegio Bíblico Apostólico Nacional (CBAN), a national program of regional Bible institutes to train pastors and key lay leaders. Bible institutes have continued to be the principal model of leadership development, though a growing number of their key leaders are seminary graduates.

As the Assembly grew, it established churches in areas beyond the Southwest, though its core membership remains in California and Texas. Most of its members are Mexican Americans or Mexican immigrants, as is most of its national leadership. It has also worked alongside its sister denomination in Mexico to establish Apostolic churches in many parts of Latin America and in Europe. Apostolic immigrants from Central America are broadening the membership base of the denomination. In 2004 the Apostolic Assembly reported having 700 churches with 52,000 adult members in 44 states. These churches are divided into 27 districts. It also has 600 churches with 31,000 members in 19 different countries.[27]

The Apostolic Assembly was born among working-class "Mexicans" of the Southwest. Its early leaders were all Spanish-dominant. It grew among migrant workers and the urban poor. But over the years many of its members have become well educated, in English. At times there have been tensions between the Spanish-dominant and English-dominant members. Like the other oneness Pentecostal denomination, it has historically taken a sectarian view of its participation in society. Now it is working to redefine itself beyond its working-class Mexican American roots to reach out to the larger Latina community and beyond.

The cultural changes between the Apostolic Assembly (U.S.) and the Apostolic Church (Mexico) have also created some unique tensions between these sister denominations. They started as one group and divided into two with the commitment that they would work with each other if and when members of each crossed the border. But migratory patterns across the U.S.–Mexican border created new types of relationships, and eventually both started sister denominations in the other country. Both denominations continue to work together on mission efforts beyond the United States and Mexico. But their relations in the United States and Mexico are a bit more conflictive. Currently, the Apostolic Church of the Faith Christ Jesus (Mexico) reports having six districts, with a total of 209 churches and more than 8,000 adult members in the United States.[28] There are also an unknown number of independent Latino churches in the United States that have split from either the U.S. or the Mexican denominations but that also call themselves Apostolic churches and that share the same historical and theological background.

### United Methodist Church

At the time of the U.S. takeover of the Southwest, the major white Methodist denominations were divided into southern and northern denominations. The Methodist Episcopal Church, South, had some Latino converts in Texas during the 1850s. But it did not begin formal missionary work until after the Civil War (1870). Throughout the 19th century it established churches on both sides of the border and in Arizona. By 1900 the Southern Methodists had developed three district conferences that crossed the U.S.–Mexican border.

About the same time, the Methodist Episcopal Church (North) began work in New Mexico. It worked during the 1850s and saw the conversion of an ex-Roman Catholic priest, Benigno Cárdenas, from New Mexico. Those efforts ended with the beginning of the Civil War. The Methodists restarted their work in New Mexico in 1870, largely under the leadership of Thomas and Emily Harwood, who were missionaries in the region for more than 40 years. By 1900 the New Mexico Spanish District of the Methodist Episcopal Church had congregations in New Mexico, Texas, Arizona, and Colorado and had mission contacts in California.

The changing economic situation in the Southwest adversely affected the communities in which the Methodist congregations, both North and South, were located. By the second decade of the 20th century, some of the congregations had disappeared. But in 1930 Methodists, both Northern and Southern, reported having 117 churches and constituted 39 percent of the Latino Protestants reported by Frank McLean.[29] This report included the new congregations that were forming in other parts of the United States. By 1960 the Methodists reported having 221 Latino churches with about 28,000 members.[30]

Methodists in Florida began ministering to Cuban immigrants in the late 19th century. In 1913 a "Cuban-Spanish Mission" was reported with five congregations. The number of churches grew and shrank depending on migration from Cuba. The congregations in the area grew after 1959 with the new Cuban exiles, including some who had been Methodists in Cuba.

Methodists in the Northeast had a similar beginning, but among Puerto Rican immigrants. The first congregation was formed in 1893, but the second one did not begin until 1920. Ministry did not develop strongly until the 1960s. A similar pattern developed in Chicago where the first Latino Methodist congregation was started in 1926. The churches grew as new immigrants came into the area. Ministry in other parts of the United States has had a slower beginning, usually linked to new Latino immigrants into the area.[31]

Methodists have always found it important to produce written materials for Spanish-speaking churches. Tracts, Sunday school materials, denominational newspapers or magazines, hymnals, and other materials were already being translated into Spanish in the late 19th century. They have continued that commitment to producing Spanish and bilingual materials for the life of the church.

In 1939 the two major streams of Latino Methodism came together when the Methodist Episcopal Church and the Methodist Episcopal Church, South, reunited. New areas of ministry developed under the new denomination. Other likeminded denominations joined with the Methodists to form the United Methodist Church (UMC) in 1968, though most of those other denominations did not have a significant Latino ministry and so did not add many new Latinos to the Methodist community.

In 1970 Latinos in the UMC began Metodistas Asociados Representando la Causa de los Hispano-Americanos (MARCHA) as a caucus of Latinos within the denomination working to develop initiatives in the Latino community. MARCHA has been at the forefront of initiatives related to Latino ministry and theology within the UMC. One of the first things MARCHA pushed for was theological education for ministry in the Latino community.

The Perkins School of Theological established its Mexican American Center in 1974 to prepare pastors to serve in the Spanish-speaking context and in Latino culture. It offers a Certificate in Hispanic Studies, provides support for Latino seminary students, and has a program to prepare lay leaders to be a part of the National Plan for Hispanic/Latino Ministry. The Center publishes *Apuntes,* a journal of theology from a Latino perspective.

In 2008 the General Conference of the UMC approved the National Plan for Hispanic/Latino Ministry. It committed the UMC to charter 75 new Latino churches from 2009 to 2012 and to form 500 new faith communities. Currently the UMC reports having 673 Latino churches with their own building and about another 150 congregations that work under a Euro-American church. They have about 63,000 members in those churches.[32]

The United Methodist Church has the largest number of Latino members of any mainline denomination, by far. It has a strong initiative to start new churches and a strong program in Spanish to train new lay pastors and leaders. It may be the denomination that provides a model for successful Latino ministry among mainline churches.

### Church of the Nazarene

Maye McReynolds began preaching to the Mexicans of Los Angeles in 1903. In 1906 the group she organized became the First Mexican Church of the Nazarene. One of the early converts, Santos Elizondo, returned to her native El Paso, Texas, and helped found a church there in 1907.

In 1930 the foreign mission board of the denomination formed the Pacific Southwest Mexican District with five organized churches in Southern California and northern Mexico. As ministry grew in the Southwest and northern Mexico, it became increasingly difficult to supervise the work from Los Angeles. So in 1942 the district was divided into two. A third locus of ministry developed on the Eastern Seaboard in 1952 when Rosita Iglesias established a church in Stamford, Connecticut. A third Hispanic district was formed on the East Coast in 1958.

The Nazarenes established the Hispano-American Seminary in San Antonio, Texas, in 1946 to train Latino pastors and leaders. It functioned until 1980. After that date the denomination often imported pastors trained in Latin America. In 2003 it developed a program of intensive courses for pastors called Educación Nazarena Teológica Especializada.

The immigrant waves of the 1980s and 1990s created a new interest in ministry among Latinos. Existing Anglo districts began new churches and ministries focused on the Latina community. In 2001 the Church of the Nazarene established the Office of Hispanic Ministries for the United States and Canada to oversee all work in the Latino community. Currently, there are 435 Latino Church of the Nazarene congregations. Eighty of them are part of the three Hispanic districts, and the rest are part of geographic Euro-American districts. The Office of Hispanic Ministries oversees new projects and serves as the link between Latino churches.[33]

The Nazarenes started Hispanic ministry using the model of establishing Hispanic districts, but most of the Latino churches today are not part of those districts. At one point the denomination considered absorbing the districts into the existing geographic districts, but the Hispanic districts opposed that move. This has created a potentially awkward situation in which most of the Latino churches are not connected to the Hispanic districts. It is yet to be seen whether this is a workable model or whether it will create other tensions between the "old" churches of the Hispanic districts and the "new" churches that are in the geographic districts.

### United Pentecostal Church (UPC)

The United Pentecostal Church (UPC) is the largest oneness Pentecostal church in the United States. It started in 1945 when the Pentecostal Assemblies of Jesus Christ and the Pentecostal Church Inc. decided to form one denomination. For many years the UPC and the Apostolic Assembly of the Faith in Christ Jesus sent delegates to each other's national conventions. Because of the major cultural differences between them, they had a tacit agreement that they would send any Latino converts to the Apostolic Assembly and that the Assembly would send any Anglo converts to the UPC. Over time this understanding faded, and the UPC decided that it should start its own Latino congregations.[34]

The UPC began Spanish-language ministries in 1978 in New York when a group of Spanish-speaking Apostolics met with leaders of the UPC. Home missions named a coordinator for Spanish ministries, and new churches were established. Currently the UPC has a Spanish Evangelism Ministries office that coordinates the work in the United States and Canada. It has 350 Spanish-language congregations and a number of church planting projects linked to existing English-language congregations, with the largest church being in Los Angeles.[35]

The UPC has sent missionaries to several countries around the world. One of the most successful efforts was in Colombia, where the United Pentecostal Church of Colombia has been one of the largest denominations in that country. Years ago there were some tensions when the Colombian denomination became independent of the U.S. body. One of the results of that history is that when some Colombian UPC members migrated to the United States, they did not join the U.S. body but created their own denomination with links to the Colombian body. Today the Iglesia Pentecostal Unida Latinoamericana has 84 congregations in the United States.[36]

The splits within oneness Pentecostalism also resulted in another denomination started by Latinos in Houston in 1971. The Iglesia Pentecostal Unida Hispana, Inc. reports 100 churches in the United States and Canada.[37]

Ethnically based denominations are part of the religious history of the United States, as are the historically African American denominations, many of which were formed because African Americans found no space in the existing Anglo denominations. Oneness Pentecostalism organized itself into ethnically distinct groups almost from its very beginning. The implicit assumption was that each group would minister in very different communities. But as these denominations have expanded, they have found that the exclusive areas of ministry no longer exist. Their missionary expansion, along with the transnational reality of the Latino experience, has also created new entities that no longer fit under the old agreements. It is yet to be seen how these groups will interact in the future or whether their transnational members will create even other entities to respond to the changing realities.

### Episcopal Church USA

The Episcopal Church reports around 400 parishes that have some ministry in Spanish. This number cannot be easily compared with that of the other denominations since this number does not mean that it ahs 400 churches that are predominantly Latino. Since its ecclesiology is similar to that of the Roman Catholic Church, this means that it has some 400 parishes that minister to the Latino community, in some way or other. The denomination's reporting information is not very clear, other than to show that it has not done a very good job of working among Latinos since it began to focus on the community around 40 years ago.[38]

In reaching out to Latinas, the Episcopal Church faces a number of challenges that complicate its task. First is the traditional evangelical versus Anglo-Catholic tension within Anglicanism. Because of the Roman Catholic hegemony in Latin America, Anglicans have tended toward the evangelical wing, focusing on their differences with the Roman Church. In the United States, some parishes have gone in the completely opposite direction, adopting Latino Catholic practices, such as veneration of the Virgin of Guadalupe. This has often created tensions with people who have an Anglican tradition from Latin America. Some Latino Catholics attend Episcopal masses without a sense of a clear difference between the Episcopal and Roman Catholic churches.

The other potential challenge has to do with the Episcopal stance on homosexuality. The position has been attractive to a few Latino Catholics who want the Roman church to take a more liberal stance on the issue. But it is not likely to be very attractive to the vast majority of practicing Catholics. The Episcopal stance has been strongly rejected by most Anglicans in Latin

America, so it is not likely to attract Latin American Anglican immigrants. It is yet to be seen how other Latinas will respond, particularly if it becomes a prominent issue in any particular parish or diocese.

### Presbyterian Church USA

Because the principal Presbyterian denomination split due to the issue of slavery, like the Baptists and the Methodists, Latino Presbyterian mission work has two points of origin. Northern Presbyterians began work in Las Vegas, New Mexico, in 1870. They established churches and parochial schools in many small communities in northern New Mexico and southern Colorado. During the early years they drew a number of *Penitentes* who were disenchanted with the Catholic Church under U.S. jurisdiction. One of the most famous lay leaders was Vicente Romero, son of Antonio José Martínez, a New Mexican priest who was removed from the priesthood by Bishop Jean Pierre Lamy, who was assigned to Santa Fe, New Mexico, by the U.S. Catholic Church after the U.S. takeover of the Southwest.

The Presbyterian Church USA (PCUSA) established the first program for formal theological education of Latino leaders in 1890. The Presbyterian College of the Southwest in Del Norte, Colorado, had been established to provide Christian higher education in the area in 1884. One of the Presbyterian missionaries persuaded the institution to develop a Spanish-language program to train pastors and evangelists. The college closed in 1901 because of financial difficulties. But it prepared a generation of pastors and leaders who would influence Latino Presbyterian work in the Southwest well into the middle of the 20th century.

Southern Presbyterian (Presbyterian Church US–PCUS) work in Texas began under the leadership of a lay pastor from Mexico. José María Botello, from Matamoros, Tamaulipas, helped establish a church across the Rio Grande River in Brownsville, Texas, in 1877. Because of its ties to Mexico, it was a part of the Mexican Presbytery of Tamaulipas. Botello also evangelized in the San Marcos area in 1885 and brought together a group of converts who organized themselves as a church in 1887. Walter Scott, who was born in Mexico but raised in Texas, became the pastor of this group and later a key leader in Mexican Presbyterian work. Henry Pratt, best known for his translation of the Bible into Spanish (*Versión Moderna*) joined the work in 1896 and helped start several churches. He also developed a program of study for Mexican pastors.[39]

In 1908, 17 Mexican churches organized themselves into the Tex-Mex Presbytery. New Latino churches were started over the next few years, but they grew slowly, and most were weak financially. Most of the pastors did not have the same level of education as their Anglo counterparts, and many buildings were in disrepair. The Synod of Texas decided to dissolve the Presbytery in 1955 and have the 38 churches join existing geographic presbyteries. In 1960, the Presbyterian Church US reported having 38 Latino churches with 2,842 members.[40]

Northern Presbyterian work in California began in the 1880s. The early work began to stagnate until the Mexican Revolution (1910–1921) created a flow of Mexican immigrants into the area, particularly Los Angeles. The national Board of Home Missions developed a Spanish-Speaking Department to expand the work into new areas. These efforts reached their first high water mark in 1940, reporting 62 churches and 4,068 members. Many of the congregations were small, and some would close during the next couple of decades. Much of the Home Missions effort during this period went to establishing schools, hospitals, and community service programs in predominantly Latino communities.[41] Toward the end of this period, the synods of Arizona and Colorado worked to integrate Anglo and Mexican Americans at the congregational level. As a result, some of the Latino congregations in these states disappeared. But growth continued in other areas. By 1960 the Presbyterian Church USA reported having 94 Latino churches with 6,604 members.[42]

Both northern and southern Presbyterians faced the impact of the changes that occurred in the 1960s. As Latinos struggled to gain a voice within the larger denominations, they formed a Hispanic Caucus that was a key voice in bringing changes in how Presbyterians did mission among Latinos and in Latin America. They worked to see Hispanic ministries be a part of presbyteries throughout the United States.

The union of the PCUSA and the PCUS in 1983 brought together the two principal streams of Latino Presbyterianism. In 1984 the united denomination approved a document titled *Hispanic Ministries in the Southwest; Directions for the Future* that helped frame how Presbyterians work in the Latino community. This statement was followed by *The Strategy for Ministry with the Hispanic/Latino Constituencies in the Presbyterian Church (USA)* that has guided Latino ministry since 2002.[43] The Hispanic Caucus was also crucial in helping take strong stances in favor of the sanctuary movement and in a pro-immigration reform statement by the denomination. A number of organizations support the work of the PCUSA in the Latino community through a national director for Hispanic/Latino-a Congregational Support.

Presbyterians from Puerto Rico are closely linked to the work among Latinos. The Synod of Puerto Rico is part of the PCUSA, so it has significant influence. Some of the larger Spanish-language congregations in the PCUSA are on the island. Many Latino Presbyterian leaders were formed in Puerto Rico, including most of the Latinos who have served as professors in Presbyterian seminaries. The recent emigration from Puerto Rico has also created the basis for new church development in the Latina community.

The 2010 directory of Hispanic Presbyterian congregations reports 338 established churches and missions, 76 of which are in Puerto Rico. This does not count new church plants that are still under an existing church or presbytery. They report over 40,000 members. According to the report in the directory, 66 percent of these churches have a regular attendance of 15–100 people in their principal worship service.[44]

The Presbyterians have a long history in the Latina community. But they also have a very conflictive history. The overt efforts at Americanization and then integration created many tensions between Anglos and Latinos. There are still Latina Presbyterians (or former Presbyterians) who remember that history and lament the actions taken. But the growing Latina community also raises new types of questions. How do Latinos grow in the midst of a mainline denomination that is shrinking? How does only one Latino church function in a presbytery? The denomination also has to address the advantages and challenges of having many trained pastors and leaders in Puerto Rico take leadership positions among U.S. Latinos. Latino Presbyterians have a rich legacy in the Southwest and in Puerto Rico, but also some important challenges as they look toward the future.

### American Baptist Churches

The American (Northern) Baptist church was the first denomination to see Latina converts and to establish Latino churches after the U.S. takeover of the Southwest. Pastor Hiram Read and his wife were on their way to California and ended up staying in Santa Fe in 1849. During the 1850s the Baptists established several congregations and were the only Protestant witnesses among the Spanish-speaking. But the missionaries left before the Civil War, and after the war they did not return. The Latino congregations and pastors ended up working with the Methodists, though several of the leaders continued to consider themselves Baptists and rejoined the Baptists in the early 20th century when they began permanent work in the region.

The first permanent American Baptist mission work among Latinas began in California in 1901 and New York in 1920. In the latter case the church planters included converts from Puerto Rico, where the American Baptists had begun missionary work in 1899. They also established churches in the Midwest in the 1930s and 1940s and in the Southeast. By 1960 the American Baptists reported having 106 Latino churches with 7,950 members.[45]

The American Baptists established the Hispanic American Theological Seminary in 1921 in Los Angeles to prepare pastors for ministry. It was one of the early efforts to establish formal theological education in Spanish in the United States. The seminary closed in 1964 due to financial difficulties, but it was influential in preparing generations of pastors for Latino Baptist congregations throughout the Southwest. A second attempt at establishing a seminary lasted from 1978 to 1988. Currently the denomination has the American Baptist Theological Center at Fuller Theological Seminary, which works with both LaVerne University, to prepare people at the undergraduate level, and Fuller, for seminary-level formation of its pastors and leaders in Southern California.

The denomination established a director of Hispanic ministries in 1948, and the position continues to this day. It works with churches across the United States and Puerto Rico. In 1991 the Latino churches established Visión 2001 with goal of establishing 100 new Latina congregations. From 1995 to 1999, 40 percent of all new American Baptist church planting projects were among Latinos. This first effort led to another called Nueva Vida 2010 with the goal of establishing 200 new Latino churches.

Currently the American Baptist denomination has 377 Latino churches and 39,714 Latino adult members.[46] This total includes 123 congregations in Puerto Rico, since the island is part of the national structure of the denomination. There is a solid American Baptist denominational structure on the island, which provides a "natural" source of potential new members in areas where Puerto Ricans are migrating to the mainland. Because the Baptist churches of Puerto Rico are among the co-owners of the Seminario Evangélico, they also have access to a number of seminary-trained pastors from the island.

The American Baptist Convention is unique among U.S. Protestant denominations in that its two largest ethnic groups, Euro-Americans and African Americans, are about the same size and together constitute about 90 percent of the denomination. This balance is unknown in any other U.S. denomination. Latinos constitute about 3 percent of the total number of members.

American Baptist Latinos face the same challenges that confront Latinos in other mainline denominations. They have a long history with the denomination, but they have never been a sizable part of it. The denomination has been declining in size, even as it has developed a strategy for expanding substantially with the Latina community.

The denomination also has the opportunities and challenges faced by denominations such as the Presbyterian Church USA (and the Disciples of Christ). Because it has a strong presence in Puerto Rico and because the island is part of the U.S. structure, it has access to well-prepared pastors and leaders without making a major investment in preparing Latino leaders here. But that opportunity also creates the potential tension that

Puerto Ricans tend to be overrepresented in the Latino leadership of the denomination.

### International Church of the Foursquare Gospel

Soon after Aimee Semple McPherson, the founder of the Church of the Foursquare Gospel, started Angelus Temple in 1923, she began showing interest in the Mexican community of Los Angeles. Sunday school classes were started in Spanish by 1925. One of the influences on her vision was the preaching of the "Aztec" Francisco Olazábal. The church started programs in Spanish in 1927. Among the people who preached in Spanish was a young Mexican who later became the famous actor Anthony Quinn.

Later, Antonio Gamboa, who had worked with Olazábal, founded the McPherson Mexican Mission (later called "El Buen Pastor"). In 1929 the church named A. M. López as the "Pastor in Charge of the Mexican Work in the Southern District" in Texas. Graduates of the denomination's LIFE Bible Institute, which offered Spanish-language courses, supported the early work. During the 1930s churches were established throughout Southern California and in the western United States. By the time McPherson died in 1944, the Foursquare Church had 63 Spanish-speaking congregations.

In 1966 Angelus Temple reestablished a ministry in Spanish, and by the 1980s the Spanish-language congregation had become the basis for a new generation of work among Latinas in Southern California. One of the key pieces of that effort related to the training of pastors and leaders. In 1986 the Angelus Temple established the Angelus Bible Institute in Los Angeles, California, offering course options in Spanish and English.

This denomination has gone through two major growth spurts in the Latina community. It had significant growth in the 1930s and 1940s. After that most of its growth among Latinos has happened in the last couple of decades. Currently the denomination reports having 250 Latino churches, which are organized into five districts. Most of the churches are in the Southwest. Rev. Jim Tolle, pastor of Iglesia en el Camino, the largest Latino Protestant church in Los Angeles (about 10,000 in worship services), and Church on the Way, is in charge of the Office of Hispanic Ministries, started in 2008.[47]

### Church of God of Prophecy

The Church of God of Prophecy is part of the Pentecostal Holiness tradition. It split from the larger Church of God (Cleveland) in 1923 over issues of governance and finances. Both denominations are based in Cleveland, Tennessee.

The first Latino congregations that would later become a part of the denomination started in a series of revival meetings in communities around

Riverside, California, starting in 1933. Pastors Eduardo Rodríguez and José Jiménez established several congregations and in 1935 organized them into the Movimiento Libre Pentecostal. Leaders from this group interacted with pastors from the Church of God and participated in activities together. In 1945 the leadership of the Church of God of Prophecy participated in a convention of this group of churches and officially invited them to become a part of the denomination.[48]

In 1964 the Latino churches were organized as a separate district so that they would have more freedom to administrate their own work. They have developed slowly, and most of the churches are on the West Coast. Currently the denomination has 230 Latino churches, mostly small. Most of the congregations have 50–60 members, though the denomination does not have exact membership numbers for the Latina congregations. In 2010 the denomination decided to name a Latino to become bishop of both the English- and Spanish-language districts in California.[49]

### Concilio Latinoamericano de la Iglesia de Dios Pentecostal de Nueva York (CLANY)

The Concilio Latinoamericano de la Iglesia de Dios Pentecostal began work in New York in 1925 as part of the Puerto Rico–based Iglesia de Dios Pentecostal. Rev. Albelardo Berríos, who had been a pastor in Puerto Rico, was called to pastor a church in New York that was linked to the Iglesia de Dios Pentecostal. In 1954 Berríos led the church he was pastoring, Iglesia La Sinagoga, and other Puerto Rican congregations to separate from the denomination in Puerto Rico and to form CLANY. When Whitam wrote his report on Hispanic Protestants in New York in 1962, he reported that the denomination had 32 churches and 2,350 adult members.

The denomination is a Trinitarian Pentecostal denomination that includes a statement in its confession of faith to clarify that it is not a oneness (Jesus's name) denomination. Most of its growth has occurred among the Puerto Rican communities of the Northeast, though it reports congregations in 24 states and in several countries in Latin America, the Caribbean, and Europe. According to its current church directory, it has 217 congregations in the United States.[50]

### Churches of Christ

The Hispanic ministry of the Churches of Christ began in Abilene, Texas, in 1919, through the work of a language professor at Abilene Christian University. By 1930 there were about 250 members in various congregations in west Texas and the Rio Grande Valley. In 1958 there were 50 Latino churches of Christ with about 2,000 members. The number of churches grew from 1950 to the 1970s. The number of churches has not grown very much since that time.

In 1995 the Churches of Christ reported having 215 Latino congregations with about 10,000 members, mostly in Texas (143) and California (43).[51] The 2010 directory of Latino Churches of Christ lists 247 congregations, with churches spread throughout the United States, but fewer churches in Texas (65).[52]

The independent Christian Churches/Churches of Christ established a Spanish-language Bible institute, Colegio Bíblico, in Eagle Rock, Texas, in 1945. It has trained pastors and leaders for many independent Latino Protestant churches on both sides of the border since that time. A 2010 directory of Latino churches within this movement lists 143 congregations, mostly in Texas (32) and California (27).[53]

### Disciples of Christ

The Christian Church (Disciples of Christ) began ministry among the Mexicans of Texas in 1899 in San Antonio. By 1916 it organized the "State Mexican S.S. [Spanish-speaking] Convention" with seven congregations, five in Texas and two in Mexico. These congregations were never very strong, and some were started and closed more than once, depending on available missionaries and pastors.

The same year that ministry began in Texas, another group of Disciples began ministry in Puerto Rico, which had become a U.S. territory a year earlier (1898). Puerto Rican Disciples of Christ began a church in New York in 1939 ("La Hermosa") that eventually joined the denomination and became the sending church for establishing other Latino congregations in the region.

The Disciples established few churches during these early years. In 1960 the denomination reported having Latino churches with 1,851 members.[54] In 1969, when the Disciples established its Office of Programs and Services for Hispanic and Bilingual Congregations, it still reported having 18 congregations in the United States. The director of this new office was crucial for creating new interest in Latino ministry and organizing Latino leaders for ministry. As the number of churches grew and Latinos took more leadership, the Disciples structure also changed. The Latino congregations structured themselves as conventions, and the leaders developed a Hispanic Caucus.

The next important change occurred when the Disciples established the Central Pastoral Office of Hispanic Ministries in 1991. This office has developed several ministries and support resources for Latino ministry. Currently the Disciples of Christ has 200 Latino congregations that are organized in six Hispanic and bilingual conventions. These churches and conventions form the National Hispanic and Bilingual Fellowship.[55]

The links to Puerto Rico have been a blessing for the Disciples, but also a potential source of difficulty. Almost all of the key leaders among Latino Disciples have been Puerto Ricans trained in Puerto Rico. This has provided the denomination with solid leadership, which has been crucial in its growth. But because it has been easy to import leaders, few Latina Disciples leaders have been trained in the United States. According to leaders, since many of the Latino churches do not have a Puerto Rican presence, there will be a need to develop leaders who are more representative of the Disciples Latino churches.[56]

## Other Protestant Denominations and Movements

A growing number of evangelical and Pentecostal denominations have more than 100 congregations and are reporting new congregations. The only other mainline denomination with more than 100 congregations is the Evangelical Lutheran Church in America (ELCA). None of the Latin America–rooted denominations have reached this threshold, though it is likely that some will pass the 100 mark soon. Also, because most of the mainline groups are not growing very quickly, it is likely that some of the smaller denominations will soon have more Latino congregations than some of those that are included in this survey.

# Varieties of Latino Pentecostals

Because such a large percentage of Latino Protestants are Pentecostals, it is important to understand some of the varieties of Pentecostalism that exist in the Latino community. Of course one can find the various theological strains common in Pentecostalism: Wesleyan-Holiness, Reformed-Higher Life, and oneness Pentecostalism. The various charismatic strains and neo-Pentecostal teachings such as word of faith and the prosperity gospel are also found in the community.

But it is also very interesting to trace the origins of the various types of Pentecostalism among Latinos. The greater Los Angeles area serves as an excellent location to look at how Pentecostalism has developed among Latinos. Modern Pentecostalism began in Los Angeles, but now new people are bringing Pentecostalism back to Los Angeles in various new forms.

The most common forms of Latino Pentecostalism in Los Angeles are the churches tied to U.S. Pentecostal churches. All of the U.S. Pentecostal denominations have Latino churches in Los Angeles, including a traditionally African American denomination, such as the Church of God in Christ

(COGIC). Some of the Latino churches are part of Latino districts in their denominations, whereas others are part of the general district that includes mostly Euro-American congregations.

But there are also many churches from Latino Pentecostal denominations, such as the Apostolic Assembly, CLADIC, CLANY, or the Asamblea de Iglesias Cristianas. Each of these denominations was started by Latinos in the United States during the early years of Pentecostalism and has been led and financed completely by Latinos since its inception. These are the closest equivalents to the historic African American denominations found in the Latino community, and they have a small but growing presence among Latina Protestants.

There are also Latino churches linked to denominations that came out of the charismatic renewal movement, such as Vineyard and Calvary Chapel. Churches that follow such movements as word of faith or various forms of the prosperity gospel can also be found. Some of the Latino churches that teach these doctrines are part of movements where these teachings are practiced, though many are in denominations that oppose these teachings or are independent congregations.

In Los Angeles one can also find various forms of immigrant-based Pentecostalism. Some, like Elim—Ministerios de Restauración (El Salvador) and Elim (Guatemala), are direct imports from their countries of origin and have a large presence in Los Angeles because of the large Central American population. The Brazilian-based Iglesia Universal del Reino de Dios, commonly referred to by its popular theme, *pare de sufrir* ("stop suffering"), is also present in many Latina communities. Many other smaller movements also have churches in the Los Angeles area.

There are also movements such as Llamada Final, which was started by a Latin American immigrant pastor. Though this denomination, and others like it, began in the United States, it is a clear reflection of the transnational character of those Latino Pentecostals who live here but are strongly influenced by what is happening among Pentecostals in Latin America. Llamada Final is now developing a presence in Latin America. These types of movements have developed in Latin America, and to a lesser extent in the United States, around a strong apostolic personality who is able to prepare leaders to start new churches, but also to draw independent congregations into the leader's sphere of influence.

A variation on the transnational theme is when a church, such as Robert Schuller's Crystal Cathedral in Garden Grove, brought Dante Gebel to pastor its Spanish-language congregation. Gebel is a well-known Christian motivational speaker and author whose radio and television programs are heard and seen throughout the Spanish-speaking world. He was invited to pastor in Garden Grove because he already had a broad influence in Latin America and was seen as attractive to the Latino community in the region. (So far he has drawn many Latinos to the Spanish-language services at the cathedral.)

There are also many other Latin American pastors, conference speakers, and musicians who are regularly in the Los Angeles area. Some of the megachurch pastors who often preach or give conferences in Los Angeles include the Colombian pastors César Castellanos and Ricardo and María Patricia Rodríguez and the Guatemalan pastors Cash Luna and Harold Caballeros. Churches in Los Angeles also send their leaders to Latin America to participate in conferences led by these and other well-known pastors. Cross-fertilization of influences also occurs because many Latino pastors travel to Latin America to preach and give conferences on a regular basis.

The growth of Latino Pentecostalism in the Los Angeles area is also creating new types of relationships between churches in the area and within the various denominations. There are now at least 10 Latino Pentecostal churches in the region with more than 1,000 members, including megachurches such as Iglesia en el Camino/Church on the Way where the Spanish-language congregation is now larger than the English one that gave it birth and where many of those who attend the English-language congregation are Latinos. Because of the size of these churches, Latino Pentecostal pastors are having a growing influence in the region.

In addition, a number of churches are on the edges of the Latino Pentecostal community, such as Victory Outreach. Many of these churches do not openly identify themselves as Latina, though the vast majority of their members are Latinos and their services often have a Latino cultural flavor. Related to these churches are the growing numbers of non-Latino churches that have a growing Latina presence.[57]

## Latino Protestant Organizations: Evangelicals and Pentecostals

Throughout the years there have been several attempts at developing Latino Protestant organizations. Most of these have been regional or city-wide ministerial alliances. They have usually worked best when most of the people have been of the same national background and of similar theological perspectives or during planning for specific events. But it has been very difficult to develop a national organization given the wide range of differences in the community.

A number of things happened in the evangelical/Pentecostal world in the 1980s that created the environment for greater cooperation and the possibility of developing national Latino Protestant organizations, at least among churches from evangelical and Pentecostal traditions. That decade saw an increased interest among evangelicals in evangelizing ethnic-minority communities, particularly Latinos. A major conference, Houston '85 Evangelizing Ethnic America, encouraged evangelicals to open their eyes to the growing diversification of the country. The conference focused on all ethnic minorities, but it made it clear that Latinos were the fastest-growing group. Two books on Hispanic ministry from a Protestant perspective, *Los Hispanos en los Estados Unidos: Un Reto y una Oportunidad para la Iglesia* (1985)[58] and *Hispanic Ministry in North America* (1987),[59] helped evangelicals and Pentecostals gain a new sense of ministry in the community.

In this context of growing interest in Latino ministry, Rev. Daniel de León, pastor of Templo Calvario in Santa Ana, California, helped organize the Hispanic Association for Bilingual-Bicultural Ministries (HABBM) under de León's leadership, with Luis Madrigal as the first executive director (1985). The organization was short-lived, but it created the impetus for other efforts.

As the Latino Protestant community grew, a number of its leaders gained regional and national prominence, first within the evangelical and Pentecostal communities, but also in the political arena as politicians became interested in the Latino Protestant vote. Dr. Jesse Miranda, an Assemblies of God leader from the Southwest, became one of the first to gain a national platform. The others are both from the Northeast: Rev. Luis Cortés (American Baptist) and Rev. Sammy Rodríguez (Assemblies of God). Each leader has developed organizations that are having a national influence among Latino Protestants and in the nation at large.

### Alianza de Ministerios Evangélicos Nacionales (AMEN)

Dr. Jesse Miranda was key in bringing together Latino Protestant leaders from various theological traditions under the umbrella of Alianza de Ministerios Evangélicos Nacionales (AMEN) in 1992. Their goal was to unite Protestant denominations and community agencies that worked in the Latino community. Dr. Miranda hoped to cross the evangelical/Pentecostal–mainline divide by using the term *evangélico* purposely in Spanish and was able to get some mainline Protestant leaders to participate in the early meetings. During the first years of AMEN, the leadership worked alongside the National Association of Evangelicals (NAE) but did not join it because they hoped to integrate mainline Protestants into AMEN.

AMEN sponsored biannual convocations of Latino Protestant leaders and encouraged research into the Latino Protestant community. It was the Protestant cosponsor of the previously cited 2003 Pew study *Hispanic Churches in American Public Life.* Dr. Miranda also worked closely with the Bush administration on the faith-based initiative project. AMEN also worked alongside Esperanza USA to organize the first National Hispanic Prayer Breakfast.

In 2002 AMEN sponsored a major Latino Protestant convocation called Cumbre in Anaheim, California. During the closing activity of that conference, the leadership of AMEN symbolically passed the baton to a new generation of leaders. The AMEN board interacted with several Latino Protestant entities and decided in 2005 that the National Hispanic Christian Leadership Conference (NHCLC) most closely reflected AMEN's church-based vision, so they integrated themselves into the NHCLC.[60] Because the NHCLC is linked to the NAE, the earlier vision of an entity that could include mainline Latino Protestants was lost.

### Esperanza USA

Esperanza USA began in 1987 as a Philadelphia-based project to address the needs of the Latino community. As Luis Cortés gained prominence, Esperanza expanded its influence. In 2002, Esperanza became known nationally when it organized the first National Hispanic Prayer Breakfast and Conference in conjunction with AMEN and later became the lead organizer of this annual event. Every year Latino Protestant pastors and leaders from around the United States go to Washington, D.C., to pray for the nation, to lobby on behalf of Latino-oriented issues, and to receive training in political advocacy. National political leaders, including the president, always participate, making the event particularly attractive to many Latina leaders. The event also seeks to showcase Latinos and Latinas who are contributing to the community.

The prayer breakfast has provided a national platform for Esperanza and its leader, Luis Cortés. Esperanza has trained Latino pastors in community development, capacity building, and advocacy. It has helped develop locally based projects to address needs in the Latina community. Its other national initiative has been to organize Latino churches to work together on behalf of immigration reform.[61]

### National Hispanic Christian Leadership Conference (NHCLC)

Currently the National Hispanic Christian Leadership Conference (NHCLC) is the largest Hispanic Protestant organization in the United States. Rev. Sammy Rodríguez founded it in 2001 with the support of several prominent Latino Pentecostal leaders. It is historically linked to AMEN and sees itself as a daughter of the organization. It is the sister organization of the National Association of Evangelicals (NAE) and serves as the National Hispanic Association of Evangelicals. Some of the best-known Latino evangelical and Pentecostal leaders are on its national board. It represents all of the Hispanic churches within the denominations associated with the

NAE. Because most of the largest Latino Protestant denominations are part of the NAE, it represents the largest number of Latino Protestant churches of any organization in the United States. Also, many NAE member denominations and parachurch organizations have named the NHCLC as their representative for Hispanic-related issues.

The NHCLC and Rev. Rodríguez are currently the principal voice of Latino evangelicals and Pentecostals in the United States. National media refer to Sammy Rodríguez as the leader of the Hispanic evangelical movement and as one of the most influential religious leaders in the United States. The NHCLC is involved in networking among Latino evangelicals and is very prominent in public policy issues related to the Latina community.[62]

Though it is linked to the NAE, the NHCLC seeks to draw together "Hispanic born again Christians of all denominations in the United States." Using the 2003 and 2007 Pew studies as its source, the NHCLC states that "Hispanic born-again Christians make up 37% of the U.S. Hispanic population and 88% of all U.S. Hispanic Protestants, 43% of all U.S. Hispanic mainline Protestants, and 26% of all U.S. Hispanic Roman Catholics."[63] The NHCLC seeks to be the spokesperson for all Latinos who identify themselves as born-again Christians.

### The Coalición Nacional Latina de Ministros & Líderes Cristianos (CONLAMIC)

The Coalición Nacional Latina de Ministros & Líderes Cristianos (CONLAMIC) is led by Rev. Miguel Rivera. It is a coalition of Latino ministerial alliances, mostly from the Eastern Seaboard. CONLAMIC defines itself as a conservative social conscience. Though it is much smaller than the other organizations mentioned, it gained national prominence through its campaign inviting the undocumented to boycott the 2010 census unless Congress passed an immigration reform law.[64]

There is no similar grouping of mainline Latino Protestants, though they have the opportunity to caucus together through existing ecumenical organizations, such as the National Council of Churches. The NHCLC works from the assumption that since most Latina Protestants are evangelical or "evangelical like," that can be the basis for working together. Esperanza USA has provided some opportunities for broader participation since it focuses on community development and has worked with a number of mainline churches. But the AMEN goal of developing a broad-based Latino Protestant entity, using the term *evangélico* in its broader Latin American sense, has still not developed. Latina Protestants present many common characteristics, as is seen in the next chapter, but there are still very real differences that reflect the diversity of Protestantism in the United States and Latin America.

## CHAPTER FOUR

# Similarities and Differences with Other U.S. Protestants

Latina Protestants do not always easily fit into the common U.S. Protestant categories. Protestantism in Latin America and in the Spanish-speaking United States are both children of Protestant missionary work, led mostly by the United States. But as Protestantism grew in Latin America, it developed terms similar to, though slightly different from, those used in the United States to describe itself. More importantly, most of the Protestant growth in the region over the last half century has been among Pentecostal or neo-Pentecostal movements. There has been a proliferation of movements that have their roots in Latin America and are not linked to Protestant missionary efforts from the United States or Europe.

Latino Protestantism has developed as a combination of the mission work of U.S. Protestants in the United States and the growth of Protestantism in the Spanish-speaking world. Therefore, Latino Protestants reflect some of the influences of both. The common U.S. categories used to describe Protestantism in this country—mainline, evangelical, and Pentecostal—are a reflection of how U.S. Protestantism developed. But because of the influence from Latin America, the U.S. categories are often inadequate to describe Latino Protestantism because they do not necessarily take into account the overlaps and differences present in the Latino Protestant community.

If we want to understand the diversity of Protestantism in the Latina community, we need to understand both the history of U.S. Protestant mission efforts among Latinos (chapters 2 and 3) and a bit of the history of Protestantism in Latin America (chapter 2) and how these two have intersected in the Latino Protestant community in the United States. Both have shaped Latino Protestantism and have influenced how it sees itself.

## Faces of Latin American Protestantism

José Míguez Bonino[1] tells the story of Latin American Protestantism through the various waves of missionaries, immigrants, and Protestant movements that have come into the region. Each of the waves has been prominent during various periods of the 19th and 20th centuries. What he calls the liberal and ethnic faces of Protestantism were most prominent in the 19th century and the first part of the 20th. As the governments in Latin America attempted to define the future of those countries, there was an on-going battle between those who wanted to maintain the colonial model of church and state linked with those who had economic power (conservatives) and those who wanted to follow the French or American models toward a participatory democracy that would include freedom of religion and the separation of church and state (liberals). In practice, many of the "liberal" governments were dictatorships, but one of their goals was to break the power of the Catholic Church over the state and civil society.

With this in mind, various liberal governments invited Protestants to enter their countries. Missionaries were invited in to counteract the religious hegemony of the Catholic Church and to provide literacy, broader educational opportunities, and medical care. Some of the leaders of these governments were masons, but none were Protestants. They wanted the Protestants to offer a different model for their societies. This wave of missionaries is called "liberal" for several reasons. First of all, they came at the behest of liberal governments. Second, they came from "liberal" denominations in the United States, groups that had been influenced strongly by the social gospel movement. This meant, third, that their mission was strongly influenced by the liberal agenda of wanting to change society. They understood mission in terms of the social gospel and the sense of "mission" common in the United States among mainline denominations at the time—God had raised up the United States to be the "city on the hill" that would be an agent for the social transformation of the world.

During this period, several of the governments of South America created an immigration policy similar to that of the United States. People from Europe, including Protestants, were invited to migrate and work the land. The Protestant immigrants were like their U.S. counterparts. They brought their specific Protestant denominations, linked to their ethnic identity. The Protestants sometimes were not allowed to build churches, but were allowed to meet only in homes. Or if they were allowed to build churches, they could not look like churches or have signs identifying them as such. Most of these Protestant communities developed parallel religious practices and a separate ethno-religious identity. Míguez calls them the ethnic Protestant wave because they did not arrive in Latin America with a missionary intention, but as ethnic immigrant communities. It was well into the 20th century before many of them attempted to evangelize those within their country of adoption.

Missionaries, mostly from the United States, who rejected the liberal agenda brought the evangelical face of Protestantism to Latin America. Their goal was to evangelize individuals. From their perspective, change had to happen principally at the individual level. Many of them were dispensationalists and believed that Jesus was going to return soon (the second coming). People needed to repent and turn to God. Working to change a dying society was not on their agenda. Most of these groups came from evangelical denominations in the United States, from more conservative wings of the mainline denominations, or from independent fundamentalist churches. Since they were not part of the previous comity agreements between mainline Protestants, they spread their mission work through Latin America.

The fourth face of Latin American Protestantism is the Pentecostal face. As stated earlier, Pentecostalism arrived in Latin America by way of some Azusa Street converts. Years later, Pentecostal denominations, mostly from the United States, sent missionaries to the region. Pentecostalism began to grow and soon became the largest segment of Latin American Protestantism. The charismatic movement also opened the door for new Pentecostal movements (neo-Pentecostal) to develop and for charismatic influence to impact many of the other Protestant denominations. Today Pentecostals and Pentecostalized churches account for 60 to 85 percent of Protestants in any given country in Latin America.

So although the common U.S. Protestant categories have a parallel in Latin America, they look very different in the region. Most of the largest denominations and theological traditions from the United States and Europe have only a relatively small presence in the region. Pentecostal denominations and neo-Pentecostal groups that have their roots in the region are the ones that are growing and that increasingly define Protestantism in Latin America.

Jean Pierre Bastian has written many books on Protestantism in Latin America and Protestantism in Mexico in particular. He makes a clear distinction between "historic" Protestantism that developed from the work of Protestant missionaries and forms of Latin American popular Pentecostalism, which developed and grew in the midst of major political and social changes happening in Latin America, particularly after 1960. These new movements have several common characteristics: they have developed on the geographic and societal margins of Latin American countries; they have fragmented and proliferated as a large number of small religious movements (Bastian uses the Spanish term *sociedades*); and these new movements all have a Pentecostal bent. These new religious movements are confronting a society that keeps a significant percentage of its population marginalized and with little opportunity to have a voice in Latin America.

From Bastian's perspective, most of the new religious movements in Latin America have completely changed the face of Protestantism in Latin America. He argues that there is little in common between historic Reformation Protestantism, or the Protestantism that developed in Latin America before 1960, and these new movements, in doctrine or practice. He concludes that these new religious movements cannot be described as Protestant in any historical sense of the term. They may have their roots in Protestantism, but they are new popular religious movements that have developed in the midst of the rapid changes occurring in Latin America. They are forms of Pentecostalism, but they are, in fact, new religious movements that have much in common with popular Catholicism.[2]

Samuel Escobar and others challenge Bastian's basic premise since it seems to want to limit Protestantism to only a few "historical" groups that fit in a "liberal" definition of Protestantism.[3] But Bastian does challenge us to recognize that Protestantism in Latin America today looks different than it does in Europe or the English-speaking world. These movements have responded to the injustices of Latin American societies in much the same way that previous popular Catholic movements did, by preaching a messianic and millenarian message to those adversely affected by the situation. In that sense they look a lot like the African Initiated Churches that have taken root on the African continent in the midst of the disruptive changes occurring there, particularly after the end of the European colonial period.[4] A major difference is that many of these movements have roots within Latin American Protestantism and that most of the members of these new movements identify themselves with "those" other Protestants, even if they may not relate with them very much.

Because of this complex development, most Latin American Protestants define themselves differently from how Bastian, or historical Protestants from Europe or the United States, might define them. For example, most Latin American Protestants today do not call themselves Protestants. Most call themselves *evangélicos*. Some of these new movements do not use the term, but they would not deny being part of the *evangélico* movement on the continent. Its usage is much closer to the German than to its usage in the United

States, in that it includes most Protestants, though for very different reasons than in Germany. But the term also has the historical and popular connotation of referring to those who preach the gospel, something that is common to most Protestants in the region.

In popular parlance the difference between Protestants and Catholics is sometimes defined with the terms *cristianos* and *católicos,* a usage common to both Protestants and Catholics. Many Catholics do not see any problem with leaving the term *cristiano* to the Protestants.

As Pentecostalism developed in Latin America, another common, though derogatory, term that Catholics used to describe Protestants was *aleluyas* (those who shout hallelujah in church). This term is not as common anymore, but it reflects the history of Protestantism in the region.

All of these terms have been used, and continue to be used, by Latino Protestants when talking about themselves in Spanish. Because of the links to Latin American Protestantism, and a similar relationship to Catholicism within the Latino community in the United States, these terms are also part of the Latino Protestant lexicon.

## Protestant Identity in Latin America

Protestantism in Latin America has historically been seen as "other." Roman Catholicism was the only legally recognized religion during the colonial period. Protestantism was historically identified with the English enemy, such as the pirates and buccaneers who attacked Spanish ships and harbors. It was considered the faith of heretics and of those who wanted to destroy the unity of the Spanish Empire and of Latin American societies.

After independence, Protestantism took on a more complicated identity in Latin America. Some of the leaders of the Latin American independence movements looked to the United States as a model, and many Latin American liberal leaders thought that Protestantism could be helpful to the region. For others it was quickly identified with the imperial expansion of the United States, particularly after the conquest of the Southwest from Mexico. The clash between U.S. democratic ideals and the continual U.S. expansionism and interventions in the region left Latin American leaders with a much more complicated view of the United States. Even as one generation of leaders saw Protestantism as a sign of hope, another one suspected that the Protestant missionaries were part of the U.S. effort to control and take over Latin America.

Nonetheless, Protestantism continued to be been seen as a model and opportunity by many reformers in Latin America. For example, the great Mexican president and reformer Benito Juárez stated that Mexicans needed "una religión que les obligue a leer y no les obligue a gastar sus ahorros en cirios y para los santos" (a religion that requires them to read and not to spend their money on cirios and for the saints).[5] Juárez invited Protestant missionaries into Mexico and worked to reform the political and religious environment of the country. This has created an interesting situation in Mexico. Mexican Protestants have championed Juárez as a great reformer, but committed Catholics have not always known how to respond to him.

This situation became more complex during the East–West conflict of the latter part of the 20th century. The left and the right in Latin America developed very different narratives of the role of Protestants and particularly of the growing Pentecostal population. For many on the left, the United States was the problem in Latin America because it was supporting the oppressive right-wing military governments in the name of defending democracy and freedom. Protestant missionaries, and the Pentecostal message in particular, were seen as part of that problem. From this perspective, Protestant missionaries and converts were considered a fifth column that was helping the U.S. cause. And the Pentecostal message was an "opiate of the people" because it encouraged them to believe in God's future and not fight for transformation today.

The right tended to like evangelicals and Pentecostals because they were usually apolitical. Some of the military dictators, such as Augusto Pinochet in Chile, openly supported the Protestants, in Pinochet's case because the Catholic Church was questioning his actions. But the right often found that historic Protestantism sided with the Catholic Church on issues of justice and human rights.

After the end of the Cold War and the end of the military dictatorships, politicians on both the left and right have sought out the Protestants, particularly the Pentecostals, because of their growth. The Protestant/Pentecostal vote has been crucial in many Latin American elections. Some Protestant leaders have attempted to form their own political parties, with limited success, but most have worked within the existing system. In several recent elections the Protestant vote has been decisive. Candidates of both the left and right have seen the benefits of having Protestant leaders speak on their behalf.

## Overlapping Categories in the Common U.S. Parlance

Latina Protestants in the United States have been strongly influenced by the Latin American experience. But the Protestantism of the U.S.-dominant culture has been the strongest influence. Yet Latino Protestantism reflects much of the same complexity as that described by Bastian in relationship to Latin America. In his studies of Latino Protestantism, sociologist Larry Hunt concludes that the more Pentecostal/fundamentalist aspects of Latino faith are very similar to movements in popular Catholicism.[6] This would indicate that Latino Protestants, like their Latin American counterparts, not only are adopting a Protestant faith but also are reshaping it in light of their own experiences with God.

Because of the overlapping experiences of many Latino Protestant congregations, it is not always easy to clearly fit them into one of the categories common to U.S. Protestantism: mainline, evangelical, or Pentecostal. This can be particularly complex for many Latinos in mainline congregations. If a person doing a survey were to specifically ask them about their church's denominational links, most would likely be able to identify their denomination. But if asked whether they are mainline Protestants, many likely would not be able to answer the question. On the other hand, if they were first asked in Spanish whether they were *evangélicos,* they would likely say yes even though they might know that their denomination is part of a mainline tradition. This is particularly true of Latin American–linked Protestants who probably define *evangélico* as close in meaning to *Protestant.* If the first question asked were about Pentecostalism, some of them might also identify themselves as Pentecostals because many come from Pentecostal backgrounds, their church's worship style is Pentecostalized, and their congregation probably has relationships with Pentecostal churches. So depending on the language used and on the first question asked, the answers might be very different. Also, many Latino Protestants would likely identify themselves as *evangélico* and *Pentecostal* if the questions were asked in Spanish and if these were not treated as mutually exclusive terms.

The terms become more complicated because there are many Latino Catholics who identify with "evangelical-like" practices. Many identify themselves as being born again, and many Catholic charismatics have had "Pentecostal-like" experiences. There are also Latinos who maintain a Catholic cultural and religious identity, but who participate regularly in Protestant churches.

Both the 2003 and 2007 Pew studies asked Catholics questions about their identification with "evangelical like" experiences. The 2007 study found that 54 percent of Latina Catholics call themselves charismatic and that 28 percent have had a born-again experience.[7] Though there has not been a similar study of Catholics in Latin America, it is likely that a significant percentage of Latin American Catholics would also identify themselves as charismatic and/or born-again. There does not seem to be a tendency among these people to become Protestants. It seems more likely that these Catholics are stating that their faith is alive and vibrant for them, much like it is for Protestants who define themselves as charismatic or born-again. Nonetheless, this similarity provides potential bridges between Latino Protestants and Catholics.

## Categories Used by the Trinity Study and Latino Protestants

The common U.S. Protestant categories are not always adequate to describe the Latino Protestant community. But the categories used by the Trinity study (quoted in chapter 1) in relationship to non-Catholics were particularly problematic. The categories were clearly defined by those involved in the study and did not match theological categories or common parlance among Protestants or other non-Catholics. But they also did not follow any common sociological categories, so they grouped denominations and movements that have nothing in common historically, theologically, or ideologically. Because of this, several of the categories they use create significant problems when trying to describe Latina Protestantism. To start with, they use the common category "mainline," but they include the Orthodox within it. That likely would not skew the numbers very much since there are few Orthodox in the Latino community. But even the placement of the Orthodox in a Protestant category means that history and theology were ignored completely.

The next category, "Baptists," is not as problematic, though it does state that it includes African American denominations. There are few Latinos in traditionally African American churches, but many of those who are a part of these denominations participate in non-Baptist churches, such as Church of God in Christ or African Methodist Episcopal. If these Latinos were counted among the Baptists, then this raises another problem, since the first group would fit among Pentecostals and the latter among mainline churches.

"Christian Generic" is a name that makes little sense, though at least the denominations within this category more or less fit together. Most if not all of the churches the researchers placed under this rubric would self-identity as "evangelical." Why Trinity did not use that name for this category, again, is unclear.

Most of the churches in the "Pentecostal/charismatic" category would self-identify as such. But the category also includes churches such as the Church of the Nazarene and the Salvation Army. Both come from the Holiness tradition that has some links to other Holiness churches that are part of the Pentecostal tradition. But neither of the two denominations self-identifies as Pentecostal today, and neither is a member of any global Pentecostal or charismatic group.

The "Protestant Sects" classification is probably the most problematic of all. There seems to be no way to include Jehovah's Witnesses under any category of Protestant, unless the category also included the Mormons, which are placed in their own category. Neither of these groups identifies itself as Protestant, so what applies to the Mormons also applies to the Jehovah's Witnesses. This same argument can be made for Christian Science, another group that is also in the "Protestant Sect" category. Most other studies tend to put these groups together into a "marginal" or "sectarian" Christian category.

Even if one were to remove the Jehovah's Witnesses, it is still difficult to understand how the denominations put in this group fit together. If "sect" means "sectarian," in a sociological sense, then some of the groups might fit under this category. Nonetheless, how do Mennonites, Churches of Christ, Covenant, Messianic Jews, and Seventh-Day Adventists belong in a specific category together, even if one removes Jehovah's Witnesses and Christian Science? Since the published documents do not explain the logic used in creating these categories, it is difficult to know what the researchers hoped to learn about non-Catholic Christian Latinos by using these categories.[8] It is also practically impossible to compare this study to any other studies of Latino Protestants, since it groups denominations and movements in ways no other study does.

Dr. Efraín Agosto, academic dean of Hartford Seminary, a sister institution to Trinity College, also raises questions about the usage of the category "no religion" and the related options of "atheist," "agnostic," "secular," "humanist," or "having no religion." Since the latter term usually means "no organized religion," he wonders whether people who are not currently part of an organized religion, but who consider themselves spiritual, or are in the process of changing churches, would have found that the closest option to their current experience would be "having no religion." But this would have placed them in the "secular" category, which would likely not be descriptive of many Latinas.[9]

## Peculiarities of Latina Protestants

Though Latino Protestants reflect the broad spectrum of U.S. Protestantism, the percentages of each type of Protestant expression are very different from the percentages in the U.S. Protestant population at large. For the most part Latina Protestantism looks a lot more like Latin American Protestantism than it looks like Euro-American Protestantism in this country. The vast majority of Latina Protestants are part of existing Protestant denominations. Some look very much like their majority-culture counterparts. But most look different from the majority.

## Believers' Church Perspective

Most Latino Protestants are not only evangelicals or Pentecostals. They are more likely than the general Protestant population to be from churches or denominations that come from what is known as the "believers' church" tradition. All believers' churches, such as Pentecostals or Baptists, believe that baptism and church membership are for those who are able to publicly confess their faith in Jesus Christ; therefore, infants should not be baptized. Being a Christian is not something one can inherit from a Christian family, obtain because one lives in a Christian nation, or receive through infant baptism. Following Jesus Christ is a commitment that can be made only on a personal level; therefore, evangelization is always important even among those who grew up as Christians. Parents should raise their children in the faith, but those children have to make the decision to become believers and to accept "believer's baptism" before they are considered Christians and allowed to become members of the church.

For the vast majority of Latina Protestants, infant baptism harkens back to their personal Roman Catholic past in which they were identified as Christians because they were born into a Catholic family and were baptized, whether or not they had any personal faith commitment at all. Faith became real in their own lives when they made a personal commitment and were baptized. Even many Latino Protestants in churches that practice infant baptism, such as Presbyterians, Methodists, or Lutherans, relate to their own personal faith commitment as the point at which they became Christians.

Some Latino Protestants do not see their Catholic background as something to reject, but as something that is incomplete. One's Catholic parents might have been very sincere when they baptized their infant. But now that one is an adult, one needs to confess and affirm that one is a follower of Jesus Christ. What happened at infancy was about one's parents' confession. What a person does as an adult has to do with one's personal commitment. Baptism is always linked to the confession of faith of the one being baptized, not to parents or a believing community.

Historically, this has also meant that Latina Protestants have an uneasy relationship with the concept of Christendom and with the idea of a Christian country. Until recently, Latin American Protestants often could not participate in many parts of the political structure or of civic society because they were not Catholics. In practice, it also has often seemed like a waste of time to participate, since the powerful and the corrupt seem to have everything under their control. Latino Protestants have historically been a part of a doubly marginalized community, so they have often found little space for their political participation. Latino and Latin American Protestants of the believers' church tradition have not yet developed a theology to guide their newfound political voice.

### Pentecostal or Pentecostalized Faith

Protestantism in Latin America is largely Pentecostal or Pentecostalized, making up well over 70 percent of all Protestants. The percentages are not as high among U.S. Latinas, though Latino Protestants are much more likely to be part of Pentecostal/charismatic churches than the U.S. Protestant population at large. Latina evangelical and mainline churches are also like their Latin American counterparts in that they are more likely to have been influenced by Pentecostal or charismatic worship styles than their counterparts in non-Latino churches. In most Latino churches, even in many Catholic parishes, worship has a distinct Pentecostal or charismatic flavor to it.

This is much more than a religious experience. It reflects a worldview in which God and spiritual beings are very much a part of human existence. One goes to church expecting God's presence in worship and prayer. One recognizes that evil is real and that it creates havoc in the lives of people. Illness, chemical dependence, hopelessness, and injustice must all be confronted in the power of the Holy Spirit. If one depends on the social, political, medical, or economic structures, the poor have no hope, because the powerful and the evil always win in these arenas. But God provides the victory to those who seek his will in their lives.

The Holy Spirit is the great equalizer that gives the poor and uneducated spiritual gifts so that they can serve God and others. The ability to preach is not first something that is learned, but something that is given by God. Because of the firm belief that it is the Spirit of God who transforms lives, the poor and marginalized can also preach and anticipate that God will work through them. Because of the work of the Holy Spirit, poor Latinos can be agents, and not merely passive receptors, in God's mission in the world. They do not have to depend on the money or the education of others; they can be pastors, Bible teachers, and missionaries. This means that the poor, the undocumented, and the marginalized of society can establish their own churches, be involved in mission, and invite others to faith. Pentecostal faith has empowered Latinas from all social classes to believe that God wants to use them, if they are open to the Pentecostal power of the Holy Spirit.

### Evangélico Self-Identity

Most Latina Protestants, particularly those with strong Latin American Protestant roots and/or those who use Spanish as their dominant religious language, use *evangélico* as the self-designation that they share with other

Protestants, including those of different theological traditions. The vast majority of Latino Protestants, no matter what their theological tradition, are much more likely to call themselves *evangélicos* than *protestantes* when speaking in Spanish, even many of those who are English-dominant.

This usage has its roots in Latino Protestant history and tracks with how the terms are used in Latin America but often creates confusion in the U.S. setting, particularly in English-speaking scenarios. Some Latino Protestants use *evangelical* in English, assuming that it is synonymous with *evangélico*. Others use *evangelical* this way because all of the Protestants they know are *evangelical* and *evangélico*. Some go so far as to use the term *evangelical* to refer to all those who have had "evangelical-like" experiences.[10]

There are a few Latino Protestants who use *evangélico* in Spanish as synonymous to the common usage of *evangelical* in English. This usually means that the person, though potentially Spanish-dominant, was formed theologically in the English-speaking world. This is most common among Latinos from mainline churches who understand that they are not evangelicals. Since most of the *evangélicos* in the United States are evangelicals, therefore they conclude that they are not *evangélicos*.

### Belief in the Power of Prayer

Prayer and the belief in God's intervention in daily life is part of the Latino Protestant experience. People pray expecting God to intervene. Many churches have "testimony" times in their church services when people give public testimony of how God has answered their prayers or worked in their lives. The testimonies are an important part of how most Latino Protestants define their faith. Belief in the power of prayer is not only a doctrinal confession; it is a lived experience. Testimonies also serve to reinforce belief and to support those who are not seeing God's intervention at a particular moment. Individuals in the community know that God will work in their situation because God has worked in their own lives in the past and is working in the lives of those around them.

For some this belief almost feels transactional; God has to work because I have prayed or have prayed correctly. But for most Latino Protestants it is about believing that God is good, that God cares about humans, and that God intervenes on their behalf: because God is present in my life, I can bring my needs to God and anticipate that God hears and will work, sometimes through the actions of others and sometimes through miraculous intervention.

### Conversion-Oriented Faith Commitment

Most Latino Protestants have had a clearly defined conversion experience. They can tell others about when they "accepted Jesus," when they were baptized, and if they are Pentecostals, when they "received the Holy Spirit." Conversion and change are an important part of their experience, particularly those who were in destructive lifestyles. People give testimony, in word and action, of how their encounter with God transformed their lives, saved their marriages, or reconciled their families. What is often initially most attractive to nonbelievers is that they see that friends or relatives have in fact left destructive lifestyles and have become "new."

Converts still mostly come from a traditional Catholic background, one that was culturally Catholic but where they did not experience spiritual life. The preaching in most churches is more likely to call for a personal commitment and to invite people to a conversion experience, one in which the new life in the power of the Holy Spirit is emotionally and physically experienced. Pentecostal and charismatic churches also invite people to regular spiritual experiences, such as speaking in tongues or similar events.

Christian formation and development is also described in terms of conversion. Some Latino Protestants speak of several conversion experiences, those moments of encounter with God when they experienced a radical change in some aspect of belief or behavior.

## A People of the Book

The Bible has always been a key part of Protestantism. People's access to the book and the belief that individuals could understand its meaning, through the power of the Holy Spirit, were key parts of the Protestant Reformation. The stories about the Bible told by the 19th-century Latino Protestants (see chapter 2) and Protestants in Latin America were often described in terms of a new Reformation, a new access to the power of the Word of God. Latino Protestant history is filled with the testimonies of those who read the Bible or heard it preached and whose lives were transformed.

Early Protestant missionaries always gave away Bibles or made them available at a nominal cost. In some countries in Latin America, the first missionaries were actually Bible salesmen who wanted to be sure the Bible was available to all. Because the illiteracy rate was so high among Latinos and Latin Americans during the 19th and early 20th centuries, the Protestant message was often accompanied by literacy lessons. People needed to obtain a Bible, but they also needed access to it by learning to read it for themselves. Many a new Protestant believer learned how to read because of his or her desire to understand the Bible. This was also the motivation of the Bible translators in the indigenous regions of the continent; if people could read the Word, then their lives could be transformed through the power of the Holy Spirit.

The early stories were about the literal dangers faced and financial sacrifices made to obtain a copy of the Bible. Later stories told of the negative reactions of friends and relatives when one started reading the Bible on one's own.

Not too many years ago in Latin America and in the Latino United States, a sure sign of conversion to Protestantism was when people started using the *evangélico* deodorant, a Bible under one's arm on the way to church or a Bible study. To this day churches have pew Bibles or might project the biblical passage, but the implicit assumption is that those who have made a clear commitment to faith will bring their own Bibles to church. Personal devotional life is also linked to reading and studying the Bible regularly.

Latino Protestants consider the Bible vocative; God speaks directly to me when I read it, study it, or hear it preached. The power of the Bible is such that early Latino Protestant church services were organized around the preaching of the Word. This continues today, even in the newer Pentecostal movements that place a great deal of emphasis on the worship experience. Most Latina Protestants are used to long sermons in which Bible teachings and their implications for today are explained to the community. Home Bible studies are also a common part of the life of a Latino congregation.

Some Latina pastors may not have been able to formally study the Bible, and many lay leaders may have limited biblical knowledge, but the understanding is that God makes the Word alive through the power of the Holy Spirit. The Bible is also considered the final authority for faith and life. Theological and practical life quandaries are resolved by appealing to the book. There can be major disagreements about what specific passages mean or how to apply the Bible to specific situations, but the assumption is that this is the common starting point. (See more in the next section on Latino Protestant theology.)

### Faith and Ethnic Identity

The Pew study demonstrated the link that most Latinas, Catholic or Protestant, make between their faith and their ethnic identity. Latino Protestants are much more likely to practice forms of Christian faith that are informed by their cultural formation. For many this includes the use of Spanish, but it also includes worship services with a Latino flavor.

In spite of a common perception that Latinos become Protestants as part of their acculturation process in the United States, or because of some potential benefit within majority culture, both the Hunt study and the Pew (2007) study demonstrate that most Latino Protestants are not leaving their ethnic identity in the process of becoming Protestants. Most Latinos are becoming Protestants within their ethic identity and not as part of an assimilation process. They seem to be looking for ways to be Protestant and Latino.

But Latino Protestant churches have also played a proactive role in ethnic identity maintenance. Many U.S.-born Latinas learned to use formal Spanish by reading and studying the Bible in church and worshipping in

Spanish. Latino churches have also often served as safe spaces where young people could strengthen their ethnic identity even when majority culture was questioning that identity.

### Theologically and Socially Conservative

To say that Latinos in evangelical or Pentecostal churches tend to be theologically and socially conservative is to state the obvious. But Latino Protestants in mainline denominations also are usually theologically and socially more conservative than other members of their own denominations. This shows through at many levels. For example, U.S. mainline denominations usually find that their sister denominations in Latin America are theologically and socially more conservative than they are. This sometimes creates tensions where some Latin American denominations do not welcome missionaries from their sister U.S. denomination. But it can also affect relationships in the other direction when immigrants with a strong history within a denominational tradition find that the U.S. church does not believe or practice what an earlier generation of missionaries taught. For example, the National Presbyterian Church of Mexico was started by Presbyterian missionaries from the United States, and it is a sister denomination of the Presbyterian Church (USA). The teachings and practices of the National Presbyterian Church remain very similar to what the missionaries taught them. But the PCUSA has changed in many areas, so Presbyterian immigrants from Mexico may find that they cannot easily fit with Euro-American Presbyterians.

Because of the way personal and social morality are defined in this country, there is often an implicit assumption that certain types of issues go together. But Latino Protestants of all stripes tend to confound the Anglo leaders of their denominations. Evangelical and Pentecostal leaders struggle with the fact that their Latina counterparts support immigration reform and believe that the state should have a role in helping the poor. On the other hand, some mainline leaders struggle because many of their Latino counterparts place a strong focus on the importance of a personal conversion and the need for Christians to live in a way that is clearly different from the rest of the world. Latinas also tend to be pro-life and to oppose same-sex marriage.

Theologically, this means that Latino Protestants are more likely to believe that the Bible is true and should be their guide for faith and life than their Euro-American counterparts. Politically, this confounds politicians and church leaders because Latinas do not necessarily assume that immigrant rights and abortion rights belong on the same side of the ledger when deciding whom to vote for.

### Evangelism as Part of Being a Christian

Because a high percentage of Latino Protestants are converts or are from conversion-oriented and believers' church denominations, evangelism and witness tend to be more crucial for them than for the Protestant population at large. Inviting other people to faith and to a personal experience with God is considered a normal part of what it means to be a Christian and a crucial task of the church. This is closely linked to a commitment to serve the community in the name of Christ. But it is also the almost automatic response of those who have experienced the power of God in their lives and want others to also benefit from what they now have.

One of the reasons for the growth of Latina Protestantism, and of Protestantism in Latin America, has been the evangelism born from the commitment of the converted. New converts are most often a result of the preaching of those who do it because it is so important in their own lives. Latino Protestants are much more likely to view (and practice) evangelization as the task of all believers and not as a responsibility of mission experts.

Because most Latina Protestant churches are poorer than their majority-culture counterparts, they do not have the means to be involved in evangelism and mission in ways that often are assumed to be the normal ways of doing these things—at least in middle-class churches in the United States. Evangelism tends to happen in the normal walks of life as people share their experiences with their relatives, friends, and colleagues. Mission and service into the community are done within the financial realities of the people, often mission from the poor to the poor. Most Latina Protestant churches, particularly Pentecostal ones, do not assume that they need to have certain amounts of money or certain types of structures to be effective in mission. Since they assume that they are involved in God's mission, they assume that God will work, even if their efforts do not have a strong financial base.

### Importance of the Local Church Community

Latino Protestants go to church more regularly than their Euro-American counterparts or than Latino Catholics. This speaks to several types of commitments. Most Latino Protestants assume that the church is their place of primary allegiance; God comes first. They tend to understand their faith as linked to a concrete community of people walking together in their walk as Christians. Their congregation is often the place where they first encountered God, and it meets very important needs in their lives. Therefore, they are often willing to make major sacrifices to support their local church.

The local church is also the primary social network for many. In a world marked by movement and anomie, the church provides a place of belonging.

It fills the role of extended family for many Latinos. It is the place of regular meeting with fellow believers but also the place for social networking and mutual support. Believers encourage each other in the faith but also provide job leads, financial support when needed, lay counseling, emotional support in times of crisis, and prayer for each other. Because of the importance of the local church community, many Latinos will continue attending their same church even after they move farther away for work or housing opportunities.

Because Latinas have full local control of their churches, they have the freedom to express their faith in ways that connect with popular Latino culture. Many popular Latino Catholic devotional practices are done outside of a formal mass, so even very religious Latino Catholics usually do not go to church as often as very committed Latino Protestants. The popular piety and practices of Latino Pentecostals are a normal part of the liturgy of the common church service.

Though most Latino Protestants do not have the financial means to maintain church structures at the level of their majority-culture counterparts, they often make greater sacrifices than their counterparts to keep their church communities going. Many Latina pastors are bi-vocational; they have a job or business that provides the bulk of their financial needs, and they either volunteer their time or accept what the church can give them. Many smaller congregations have no paid staff; the pastor is a volunteer and serves whether or not the church can provide a salary or some financial support.

Because of their financial limitations, many Latino Protestant congregations meet in less-than-optimal facilities or situations. Congregations sometimes seem as migratory as many of the members. They meet in rented storefronts, they use other churches' buildings during their off hours, they meet in homes, or they rent auditoriums or halls. In most urban areas, owning a building means an extreme sacrifice for Latino Protestant churches. Yet many find a way to eventually purchase a permanent meeting place.

Worship in most churches is informal and participatory; everyone participates, and everyone is important to the liturgy. People come ready to talk about what God has done in their lives since the last community gathering. Because many of the churches are small, everyone is needed for the worship service to go forward.

Most Latino Protestant churches have Latino pastors, something that is not common among Roman Catholics. They provide spaces for otherwise marginalized people to find places to learn and practice leadership. People who have a sense of call can become pastors, even if they have not had access to formal theological education or cannot qualify because they do not have enough formal education, cannot study in English, or are undocumented. Because the churches depend on lay leadership, many working-class people have the opportunity to develop leadership skills even though they might never have an opportunity in other settings. In many churches the pastoral leadership is literally a person from among the people.[11]

Of course, this dynamic situation can also be a weakness for Latino churches. Many Latino congregations are short-lived, and many live on a financial edge. Some pastors make a virtue of their limited formation and do not work to improve themselves. Sometimes spiritual leading is used as a justification for lack of preparation. Since the churches are small, they can also create burnout among the leaders. Informality in worship can become repetitive and unattractive. All of these "assets" can become problematic when members of the church get a formal education and begin to expect their church to provide a better-prepared sermon or a better-organized worship service. The place that provided a space for people to develop can become too small for those same people when they do develop.

## Latino Protestant Theology

Latino Protestant and Catholic theologians have asked themselves what is unique about being Christian and Latino. Protestant theologians have often worked alongside their Catholic counterparts in addressing this question and have pointed to experiences that are common to most Latinos, whether they are Catholic or Protestant. But several of the Protestant theologians have also drawn on teachings and experiences that are more commonly Protestant to describe Latino Protestant theology and to suggest contributions that Latino Protestants con make to Protestant theology in general.

In their book *Introducing Latino/a Theologies,* Miguel de la Torre and Edwin Aponte argue that there are common cultural themes within the Latino community that create the environment for a community-based theology. Most Latinas, be they Catholics or Protestants, share similar cultural roots, similar cultural influences on their theology, and some common understandings of God and of how God works in the world.

Most Latinos either have experienced exile or have been treated like aliens or outsiders, even if they were born in the United States and have their historical roots here. Though this type of experience may feel more personal and direct for some than for others, just about all Latinas either have experienced this or are the descendants of those who lived through this type of experience. The Mexicans of the Southwest became foreigners in their own land after the U.S. takeover; Puerto Ricans are U.S. citizens but are treated like foreigners when on the mainland; and Latino immigrants are treated like foreigners, whether are documented or not.

The vast majority of Latinos have also lived in the same types of neighborhoods or communities. The barrios of the major cities and the poor farming communities have been the common lot or background of most. Only a very few have no links, personal or historical, to these places where the schools are deficient, social services limited, and crime higher than nearby locations. A large percentage of Latinos live in these types of places today.

Latinos are also a *mestizo* people. The vast majority are the children of many cultural, ethnic, and racial encounters. The European conquerors forcibly procreated among the indigenous. People of African descent were forcibly brought into the mix. Others have joined through migration. Today just about all Latinos are multiracial, even if they can claim one "race" as the one the principally defines them.

Most Latinas have also had similar influences on their lived theology. Popular religious practices reflect the *mestizo* background of the people. But there is also a clear sense of the poor listening to God and not allowing the powerful and the official religious elites to define them as mere spectators or receptors. Pentecostalism is a movement that has been proscribed and questioned. Yet many Latinos have found that Pentecostal faith bests addresses their search for ultimate meaning, provides them a way to worship God that connects with their lived experience, and allows them to be subjects of their service to God.

Spirituality is another common influence. There is a clear openness to the spiritual and a sense of God's presence in the world (see previous section). This leads to worship services that look like a fiesta. God's presence and mighty acts are celebrated in the family gathering that is a Latino Protestant worship service.

Religion is also lived out in a communal social location. Community is important in worship and religious practice. This is closely linked to the extended family, in the sense not only of blood relatives but of all of those who are connected to the family. Among Catholics one sees that popular religious practices are tied to family life. Among Protestants the church community often becomes the extended family. People call each other *hermano* or *hermana,* but they also provide the support one would expect from a strong extended family. Religion is not something experienced individually; it is something practiced in relationship with others.

These common experiences, influences, and social location create the space for reflection on who God is and what God is doing in the world. Latino/a theology cannot be separated from the lived experiences of real people. Latina/o theologians recognize that there is no such thing as

"objective" theology, an understanding of God separated from how concrete people experience God.[12]

It is in this setting that one needs to address the issue of Latino Protestant
theology. Is there something unique about being Latino and Protestant? If
there is, what does it have to offer other Protestants or other Christians?

Latino Protestants began reflecting on their unique experiences almost as
soon as the first Latinas were converted. There are a few extant documents
from the 19th-century Southwest in which Latinos reflect on their new faith
and its implications.[13] In these articles they spoke of their encounter with
God and of its importance in their lives. But most of them were apologetic,
defending Protestantism and their decisions to become Protestants and
calling on Catholics to also become Protestants. Their testimonies also addressed the difficulties of being a Latina Protestant or of being a Latino pastor in particular. The focus of most of these early documents was descriptive
and biographical much more than reflective or analytical.

The first signs of Latino theological reflection that was ethnically unique
happened in the midst of tensions with Euro-American Protestants. Several of the early Latino Protestant leaders found that they had to tell their
stories not only in contrast to Roman Catholicism but also in tension with
their Protestant brothers and sisters. Several of the early Latino Pentecostal
leaders spoke or wrote about some of the differences with majority-culture
Pentecostalism, but mostly, leaders such as Francisco Olazábal, Antonio
Nava, and Juan Lugo lived out their unique theology by separating from
Euro-American Protestantism and giving their people a space to grow and
develop as leaders.

It was in this environment that Pentecostal Latinas began to write their
own hymnology in which they expressed their faith and their understanding of God. These songs used the instruments and musical styles of the
people, something that Euro-American Protestant leaders were sure could
not be used to worship God. Whereas many Protestant missionaries were
sure that a guitar was too sensual and erotic for Christian worship, Latino
Pentecostals were using it because it was their instrument, one from their
culture and one that the poor could afford. Antonio Nava, one of the founders of the Apostolic Assembly, once stated, "*La guitarra...pa'al pobre...la
guitarra*" (The guitar...for the poor...the guitar).[14]

These songs were the first major step toward a Latino Protestant theology
because they were written in the idiom of the people and reflected the experience of Latinos with God. While mainline and evangelical Latinos were
singing mostly hymns translated from English, Latino Pentecostals were
beginning to write their own songs. Several of the major Latino Pentecostal
groups developed their own hymnals filled with songs written by people

from within their churches. Because of the migratory nature of the people, these songs also migrated north and south, mostly between Mexico and the Southwest and between Puerto Rico and the Eastern Seaboard, particularly New York.

These songs reflected on the lived encounter with God. For example, the songs of the people of the Southwest drew on their experience as migrant workers as they reflected on God and God's work in the world. But they also provided a means for the illiterate to "read" the Bible, by putting large portions of Scripture to popular music. Some of these songs even served to teach the history of the church by putting some of the key events into a *corrido*-style song.[15]

The 1960s created a new context for Latino theological reflection. The civil rights movement pushed many mainline denominations to acknowledge the minority voices among them. The growth of Latino Pentecostals and evangelicals was creating a critical mass that would not be easily ignored in those denominations. The birth of Latin American Liberation theology also created a space for Latinos to think about their own situation and to develop their own theology.

Justo González and Orlando Costas were the first Latino Protestants to write and publish formal Christian theology from a distinctively Latino perspective. They were influential both in Latin America and among U.S. Latinos, and both were influenced by their Latin American links and experiences and life in the Latino United States. Justo González has contributed to Christian theological reflection far beyond what he has written about Latino theology. He is a church historian and has written books on church history, the history of Christian doctrine, the history of Christian mission, and Christianity in Latin America. His books are used in many seminaries in the United States, and his work has been translated into many languages. He has been a leader in the Latino Christian community and has been crucial in the establishment of several Latino theological entities such as the Hispanic Theological Initiative, the Hispanic Summer Program, and the Asociación para la Educación Teológica Hispana (AETH, the Association for Hispanic Theological Education). Orlando Costas served as a pastor in Puerto Rico and the United States and as a seminary professor and academic dean in both Costa Rica and the United States. His influence was somewhat more limited because he met an untimely death in 1987.

González was born in Cuba and completed his first theological degree there. He came to the United States for further studies, and the Cuban Revolution kept him from returning to the island. He developed as a historian and a theologian within the experience of Latino Methodism. He has written several books and articles on Latino Protestant theology. Two books in particular frame his understanding of the unique contributions of Latino Protestant theology: *Mañana: Christian Theology from a Hispanic Perspective* and *Santa Biblia: The Bible through Hispanic Eyes*.[16] In each of these books, González begins with the lived experience of Latinos to develop his unique theological understanding.

The Latino Protestant experience provides a unique lens (a grammar) through which to read the Bible. In the first place, Latinos have a non-innocent reading of the Bible and of history. Many Protestants in the United States want to read U.S. history as if everything done was good or was at least done with a good intention. Latin Americans and Latinos have experienced the reality that all human structures, including the U.S. government and Protestant churches and missionaries, are fallen. This is an extremely important contribution to U.S. Protestantism, which has often fallen into the trap of believing in an American exceptionalism that does not recognize that even good governments are fallen and capable of hurting others. Reading the Bible through non-innocent eyes means facing the difficult parts of Scripture with the clarity that God works in broken human history. According to González,

> To those who think of their own history in terms of high ideals and purity, this may seem to detract from the power and inspiration of Scripture. This, however, is not the case with Hispanics. We know that we are born out of an act of violence of cosmic proportions in which our Spanish forefathers raped our Indian foremothers. We have no skeletons in our closet. Our skeletons are at the very heart of our history and our reality as a people. Therefore, we are comforted when we read the genealogy of Jesus and find not only a Gentile like ourselves but also incest and what amounts to David's rape of Bathsheba. The Gospel writers did not hide the skeletons in Jesus' closet but listed them, so that we may know that the Savior has really come to be one of us.[17]

The Bible is also a book that can be read by all, including those with limited education. Latina Protestants have demonstrated that the Bible in not the exclusive purview of those with a college or seminary education. Simple people can read the Word and also preach it.

Latinos also bring a series of unique experiences that make it possible for them to see things in Scripture that other might not see, because of a different set of experiences. To read the Bible *en español* is not only about language, though that is important, since the Bible we read is a translation, and no translation ever completely reflects the original message. But reading *en español* also has to do with how some of the common experiences of most Latina Protestants have shaped their reading of Scripture. González identifies five common experiences that affect how the Bible is read by Latinos: marginality, poverty, *mestizaje* (being of mixed race; mestizo), exile, and solidarity. Each of these allows Latinas to grasp teachings from the Bible that might not be obvious to those who have not had similar experiences. By reading from this perspective, Latinos find in the Bible insight and strength for dealing with the injustices that are often justified biblically, but also a clear sense that God walks with the poor and the marginalized.

Orlando Costas was born in Puerto Rico but raised on the U.S. mainland. He became a believer in the United States but returned to the island, where he married and served as a pastor. Later he pastored Latino congregations in the United States. From there he went to Costa Rica to teach at the Latin American Biblical Seminary in 1970. He arrived there as that seminary was beginning to go through tensions related to the growing influence of Liberation theology. During his time in Costa Rica, he was influenced by Liberation theology, the Latin American Theological Fraternity, and the Church Growth movement. His area of expertise was evangelism, and he began to develop a perspective of evangelism and mission that took into account all of these influences. After service in Latin America, he decided to return to the United States to serve the Latino community, once again.

After he returned to the United States, Costas published *Christ outside the Gate: Mission beyond Christendom*.[18] In this book Costas brought his Latin American experience to bear on his developing missiology, but also on his understanding of ministry in the Latino community. His last major publication was *Liberating News: A Theology of Contextual Evangelization*,[19] which was published after he died in 1987. These books lay out his theology of mission and evangelism that had already been expressed in previous publications in Spanish. But he also presented key components of a Latino Protestant understanding of mission and theology.

The principal concept that comes through in his writings is that mission has to be contextual. The gospel is good news to those who are in need. But only those who recognize their own need can effectively share it. Only the beggar can tell another beggar where to find bread because only a person that recognizes his or her own need for bread will understand the value of sharing that message.[20] This speaks to both the missionary strategy and the missionary. Christ is outside the gate of power and privilege; therefore, those who want to share the gospel in ways that will truly be good news have to be willing to leave the comforts and privilege of Christendom so that the gospel can transform both the missionary and the one accepting the message. This is much more that connecting the gospel to the context of the hearer; it means communicating "the good news from the 'base' or 'margin' where we find the absentees of history, the most vulnerable and needy people of society. This perspective implies returning the evangelistic ministry to the grass roots of the church and establishing a preferential option of the marginalized of society."[21]

Costas recognized that as a "Hispanic missiologist," he needed to help Protestantism in the United States understand the perspective of the absentees of U.S. missionary history: Latinos, African Americans, Asians, and Native Americans. His role was to do missiology from the periphery of the U.S. metropolis.[22] One of the key contributions of Latino Protestantism, particularly Pentecostalism, is that it has opted to work on the margins. Latino Pentecostalism is good news to the poor because it is working from among the poor, outside the gates of power. The call of Latino missiology to the U.S. church is that it can be faithful to the Christian gospel only if it is willing to let go of the "comfort and security of our ecclesiastical compounds… in order that we might serve the world and witness to the new creation."[23] It is outside the gate that it will find its way. The final paragraph of *Christ outside the Gate* frames the invitation of Latino theology most clearly:

> Therefore let us not be co-opted by the structures of Christendom but, rather, let us become apostolic agents in the mobilization of a servant church toward its crucified Lord, outside the gate of a comfortable and secure ecclesiastical compound. Let us not sell our missional birthright for the mess of pottage of a cheap social activism but, rather, let us be prophets of hope in a world of disillusionment and false dreams, pressing forward to the city of God—the world of true justice and real peace, of unfeigned love ad authentic freedom.[24]

Eldin Villafañe builds on the thinking of González and Costas but works specifically from the perspective of Latino Pentecostalism. What are the unique issues and contributions of the largest segment of Latino Protestantism? He has developed his thought in such books as *The Liberating Spirit: Toward a Hispanic American Pentecostal Social Ethic,*[25] *Seek the Peace of the City: Reflections on Urban Ministry,*[26] and *Fe, Espiritualidad y Justicia: Teología Posmoderna de un Boricua en la Diáspora.*[27] Villafañe was born in Puerto Rico and formed in the Puerto Rican Pentecostalism of New York. He brings together the marginality of Latino Pentecostalism and the exile theme, common to most Latino immigrants, and calls Latino Pentecostals to be a community of the Spirit for the world so that they will avoid the negative elements of upward social mobility, that is, becoming a "church" in the sociological sense, a part of Christendom.[28] Villafañe also develops that thought for the church's mission in his appeal to the exile motif and to the Old Testament prophet Jeremiah's letter to the Israelites in Babylonian exile. All Christians need to take seriously an understanding of exile as a motif for the Christian life. They need to seek the peace of the city in which they live, even as they recognize that their goal and vision is the city of God, not the incomplete visions of any earthly city.[29]

Justo González has not only taught and published; he has also encouraged a new generation of Latina theologians to reflect on what it means to be Latino and Protestant, but to do it in collaborative ways, *en conjunto*. In the last 20 years, a number of younger Latino and Latina theologians have taken the basic ideas developed by González and by Catholic theologians and looked at specific theological issues. Many of the new generation of Latino/a theologians have worked *en conjunto* (working together), reflecting on *lo cotidiano*[30] (daily lived life) of the Latina experience. From their perspective these are another two key contributions that Latinos give the larger Christian community. Theology is the reflection of how a concrete community of believers experiences God and how that community articulates its experience. In addition, the theological task is the task of the people who experience God in their day-to-day situations. In other words, all theology is contextual and communal.

Many of the newer works of Latino theological reflection have been collections, often put together as part of joint conferences. Three representative collections from a distinctively Protestant perspective are *Teología en Conjunto: A Collaborative Hispanic Protestant Theology*,[31] *Protestantes/Protestants: Hispanic Christianity with Mainline Traditions*,[32] and *Vivir y Servir en el Exilio: Lecturas Teológicas de la Experiencia Latina en los Estados Unidos*.[33] Each of these collections seeks to take seriously the concept of working *en conjunto* while learning about Latino theology through *lo cotidiano*. The first was born out of a conference of Latino/a theologians who came together in 1995 to address historical Christian doctrines from a distinctively Latino perspective. The second looked at the Latino Protestant experience as the basis for understanding Latino theology. The third collection developed in the theological reflections of the Los Angeles chapter of the Latin American Theological Fraternity, by men and women who serve within the immigrant communities of greater Los Angeles. The specific focus of each collection is how Latinas experience God within the complexities of our *cotianidad*.

A "third" generation of Latina theologians is now developing that is broadening the discussion, presenting a wider variety of issues and concerns. Since Latino Protestants reflect the diversity of the Latino community and the diversity of Protestantism in the United States, so their theological reflection also reflects that diversity. A sample of that broadening can be found in *New Horizons in Hispanic/Latino(a) Theology*.[34] The editor of the collection, Benjamín Valentín, states that because Latino theologies aspire "to transformative social relevance," they need to take steps to further develop the key contributions of Latina theology up to now. Latino theologians need to (1) go from recognizing the importance of culture to incorporating it in the theological conversation, (2) expand from the concerns of identity and culture to issues of justice, and (3) expand the concept of *en conjunto* to include conversations with other minorities who can enrich the conversation from their own experiences.[35]

Because this is an expanding field, it is impossible to name all of the voices or perspectives that are developing. The new voices come from across the theological perspective represented in the Latino Protestant community. Some are revisionists, questioning some of the ways that the earlier generations developed theological themes. Others are discovering the importance of a Latina perspective within their own theological and denominational families. But all are asking what is unique about being Christian and Latina and how that contribution can enrich our understanding of God and what God is doing in the world.

## Issues for the Future of Latino Protestant Theological Reflection

Latino theological reflection has raised important issues for theological reflection in the U.S. context. It has identified a number of crucial areas that need to be taken into account as part of the theological task. But standing outside the gate will mean continuing to move toward the margins even as Latino theology is being accepted in the theological and academic center. Because of the unique nature of the Latino experience, this process will continually have much to contribute to the theological task.

One of the key motifs of Latino theology has been exile. But currently the most clearly defined struggle among Latinos is that of the undocumented. Most Latino Protestants have identified themselves with the struggles of the undocumented and are working for immigration reform. But are Latino Protestants ready to incorporate "undocumented" into the theological lexicon, with all the marginalization that this implies? The experience of the undocumented offers a powerful way to read the migrant narratives of the Old Testament patriarchs and matriarchs, but also is related to the "sojourners" and "diaspora" language of the New Testament.

But for many Latino Protestants the undocumented also raise difficult questions about the role of the state and how Christians understand law and order, ethics, and national identities. The transnational movement of peoples, documented or undocumented, raises questions for Latino theology. Is the concept of being undocumented a theological metaphor that all Latino

Protestant theologians are ready to embrace? The undocumented are doing theology as they migrate.[36] Incorporating being undocumented into the core of Latino theological reflection will place Latino theology firmly at the margins, outside the gate, but will raise many serious questions, particularly for Latino evangelicals and Pentecostals.

Valentín raises the question of who should be a part of *en conjunto* conversation. Even as Latino theologians need to reflect with those outside the community, there are also important voices within the community that are having an influence but are not always recognized. For example, Latino theology has been influenced by Latin American theology, but mostly by example. Most of the books and articles published by Latina theologians have been written with the U.S. scholarly community in mind and published in English. They have served as an explanation of who we are to the Euro-American Christian community.

But two areas of conversation have yet to be developed. On the one hand, there is a need for a more conscious conversation with the south. Latino Protestantism is influenced by its southern background, but also by the movement of religious ideas in the globalized and transnational reality of those Latinos who live on both sides of the Rio Grande River or who continue to be connected to the Caribbean. Latina Protestants are doing popular theology in conjunction with their Latin American counterparts as they move north and south. How is that conversation included in the *en conjunto*?

The other conversation partners who are not clearly included are the Spanish-dominant in the Latina community and those who will never read scholarly material. Latino theologians are committed to doing theology *en conjunto* and *en lo cotidiano*. But they also need to be more intentional in reflecting with those in the church and community and in producing materials that both reflect them and also allow them to be agents of their own theological reflection.

Because Latina identity is fluid and polycentric, there is also the need to reflect on the lived and changing identity of those who have been in the United States for several generations. Is "exile" still a term that helps them understand how they experience God in the world, or are there new terms that need to be brought into the conversation? Since culture is not static, it is clear that Latina theology will need to expand the lexicon of terms that helps the community reflect on its common encounter with God.

Some Latin American scholars and a few Latina scholars have seen popular Pentecostalism as a subversive Protestantism that points to radical change in life and society. The temptation is to assume that these movements are "merely" a reflection of the struggles of those who have been excluded and are trying to find a way in to the structures of power. But are they something more profound—a different way of thinking about social order, one in which the biblical eschatological vision of God's reign, where there is social, political, and economic justice for all, is central? Might this type of popular Pentecostalism offer an answer for a postmodern reality that is looking for spiritual answers but that recognizes that they will not be found in the structures of Christendom? Orlando Costas invited Christians to find their mission outside of the structures of comfort, and Eldin Villafañe has warned Latinos about the dangers of wanting to "fit." That seems to be the place where Latinos Protestants are today, wanting to know how to fit in U.S. society, or whether that is the right way to frame the issue. How do Latino Protestants most effectively contribute, as an ethno-religious minority group, to the United States? What does it mean to seek the "peace of the city" in this country that represents both hope and exile to many Latinos?

## CHAPTER FIVE

# *Protestantes* and Protestants in the Latino Community

The 2007 Pew study reviewed in the first chapter hinted at the fact that although most Latinos attend churches that have clear ethnic characteristics, a significant minority do not. Only 5 percent stated that they attend churches with none of the ethnic distinctions Pew defined, but others went to churches where only one or two of the characteristics were present. Though the study did not define how many people fit in this category, it made it clear that many Latinas who have been in the United States for several generations do not attend "Latino" churches.

Another thing that did not seem clear from the way Pew reported the results was whether those who answered participated in Latino-oriented activities or only went to churches where they were available. For example, did some of those interviewed go to a church that offered a worship service in Spanish, even though they might go to a service in English at the same church?

There are many reasons that some Latinos choose to attend "non-Latino" churches. In this chapter we want to understand some of those reasons and describe the types of churches that tend to be most attractive to these Latinas. To do that we need to set a very brief historical framework of the relationship between Protestantism and ethnicity in the development of denominations in the United States and how Latino Protestants have fit into this history. We also want to look at the relationship between ethnic identity maintenance and religious practices within the Latina community.

## A Very Brief History of Ethnically Oriented Protestant Christianity in the United States

Most European-background churches in the United States, whether Protestant or Catholic, started by having a clear "national" focus. European immigrants brought their religious practices with them, including pastors or priests, and usually settled near each other. This meant that these churches had a clear ethnic and/or linguistic link. There were Swedish Baptists, Ukrainian Catholics, German Lutherans, Scottish Presbyterians, and so on. Many of these Protestant groups eventually organized into denominations, but with a clear ethnic core. Some of the Catholic groups formed national parishes in which the liturgy, religious festivals, and language reflected the background of those who funded the parish.

The American experience affected all of these churches, though in different ways, often linked to their ecclesiology and their specific ethnic experience in the United States. On the one hand, Catholic immigrants were often suspected of not truly being American. So the U.S. Catholic leadership often pushed to have the churches be "American" and eventually discouraged the forming of new "national" (i.e., ethnic) parishes. So when the U.S. Catholic Church took over the Mexican Catholic churches of the Southwest, they did not strengthen the existing local clergy, nor did they actively recruit new priests from the local population. They did not even bring many priests from Mexico or other Spanish-speaking countries. They mostly removed the existing priests and replaced them with people from the eastern United States or with European immigrants. The people of northern New Mexico had maintained their own churches for centuries and had produced their own local priests. But the new U.S. leadership did not allow them to continue leading their churches.

Though there are some Catholic parishes with a clear ethnic identity, the U.S. church does not encourage the "national parish" model. This means that when a Latino Catholic immigrant comes to the United States, that person may find that his or her local parish does not have masses in Spanish or that the liturgy and popular devotion do not match what he or she is used to. The immigrant's choices are to go to another parish, to try to get the local parish to begin masses in Spanish, or to focus on the religious practices he or she is used to. He or she is not free to attempt to start a new parish, even if the immigrant had the means to do so.

The Protestant experience in the United States went in a very different direction. Some denominational traditions eventually joined together across ethnic and even linguistic lines to form one denomination, once ethnic identity or language was no longer deemed fundamental to religious practice.

Other ethnically or linguistically based denominations took longer to open themselves up to people of different ethnic backgrounds. Sometimes they stated their openness, but the principal ethnic flavor tended to remain in those churches for several generations. To this day some denominations still have a very clear ethnic majority group, even if they no longer identify themselves with a specific ethnic group and even if they have opened their churches up to people from other ethnic backgrounds.

The American experience also brought new denominations into the picture. On the one hand, the American Civil War caused several denominations to split into northern and southern denominations. Some of these denominations did not reunite until well into the 20th century. Even today one can clearly trace the impact of these splits within and across denominational lines. These splits would directly impact the first Latino Protestant converts, since the southern Baptists, Methodists, and Presbyterians would mostly evangelize in Texas during the 19th century, and the northern Methodists, Presbyterians, and Baptists (and Congregationalists, to a lesser extent) would mostly evangelize in the rest of the Southwest.[1] Latina Protestant converts became a part of the northern or southern branches of denominations based on where they lived.

Racism was behind the creation of the historically African American denominations. The white majority would not worship with African American slaves or even with free blacks. African Americans accepted the Christian faith, but they were forced to develop parallel churches and denominations. The pattern was set for segregating out those who were not considered equal.

Another important impact of the American religious experience was the development of new Protestant movements. Revivals, doctrinal disputes, charismatic leaders, and class differences all contributed to the formation of new denominations and new churches within denominations. Western migration created a need for many new churches, and many of these new movements gave pastors and leaders a great deal of freedom to establish new churches. Though most of these movements would not impact Latinos directly until the 20th century, they would provide a model for Latino Protestants, making it relatively easy for them to also start their own churches or denominations.

Protestant ecclesiology continues to encourage the establishment of new churches, even in areas where there are many existing congregations. Protestants typically do not go to a parish church, but rather go to one of their liking, even if they drive past many other churches of the same theological tradition. In the past, denominational links played an important role in deciding on a church. But today most Protestants attend churches based on other types of attraction. Among ethnic minority communities such as Latinos, language, ethnic identity, and social networks usually play an important role in a person's decision of what church to attend. Historical Protestant denominations assumed that they would decide when a new Latino church would start and where it would be established. But the current Protestant practice is to start a new congregation where language and ethnic identity can be affirmed as core values, if that attracts new people.

Early Pentecostalism attempted to cross the ethnic and racial divides of that time and was successful for a short period of time. But in the end the Pentecostal denominations that developed out of the Azusa Street revival accepted racial divisions in one of two ways: (1) Most of the Trinitarian denominations started "Mexican" or "Hispanic" districts; Latinos remained within the denominations, but they developed their own churches and structures with the denominations. (2) The oneness Pentecostals ended up with separate denominations by racial group, though they committed themselves to working with each other. These models continue among Pentecostals, though Latinas are breaking the molds by establishing churches in the "other" district or "other" denomination or by attending Euro-American congregations.

Latino Protestants became a part of a unique Protestant experiment in the United States. People established new churches and denominations as they moved west and as they experienced God in new ways. Ethnic and linguistic minorities were free to establish their own congregations and denominations, if they had brought their faith with them from Europe. But the situation was also one where the Euro-American leadership of existing denominations assumed that non-whites would worship separately from whites. New missionary work started from the assumption that non-white converts needed their own churches. Latino converts in existing denominations soon found that they would have more freedom for self-determination if they developed separate or parallel institutions. The Latino churches that had the most autonomy were also the ones that grew the most. They had the most freedom to effectively evangelize in the Latino community and to develop their own leaders. They also had the most freedom to establish new churches.

## Latino Converts and Latino Church Development

When the Protestant missionaries first began evangelizing the Mexicans of the Southwest, they always began new churches with these converts. In many areas this made obvious sense, since there had been no Protestant church in many communities before the arrival of the missionaries. But even in cities and towns where the new immigrants from the Eastern Seaboard were settling, the missionaries encouraged the establishment of two churches, one for the Mexicans and one for the new Americans from the East. (They also began different congregations for European immigrants who spoke other languages and among Native Americans.) By the end of the 19th century, there were Anglo and Mexican churches of the same denomination, sometimes started by the same missionary, in most of the larger population centers of Texas and New Mexico.

The missionaries assumed that there were clear linguistic and ethnic differences that made it necessary to have different churches for each distinct minority community, which was usually true. But the early Protestant missionaries also had a clear sense that whites and non-whites should be kept separate for reasons that had much more to do with class or racist assumptions than with the specific ministry needs of those they were evangelizing.[2]

But since Americanization was part of the missionaries' goal, they were faced with a complicated set of questions. Should Latinos develop parallel churches and structures, or should they be encouraged to assimilate into the English-language congregations? Because of the major class and racial differences between the communities, the issue did not come up very often. But as some young Latino Protestants learned English and went to school, they sometimes preferred going to the English-language church. For some it had to do with acculturation; for others it was tied to intermarriage. But underlying these reasons was the implicit, and often stated, assumption that the English-language congregations were better, that they were better reflections of what it meant to be a good Protestant church. These congregations had more resources, better-educated clergy, and better church buildings. The Mexican churches were usually only pale imitations, translated copies of the "right" way to do church.

Throughout the 19th and well into the 20th century, most denominational leaders, apart from the Pentecostals, assumed that Latinos could not develop churches like those led by people from majority culture. They needed help and resources, but even with long-term assistance, it would be very difficult for them to succeed. The model of a successful church as defined by mainline denominations was impossible for most Latino congregations to ever reach. It assumed class and socioeconomic characteristics that most churches could never surmount. No matter how hard they tried, the Latino churches would always be less than their majority-culture counterparts.

This was different from the beginning in Pentecostalism. Most of the converts, no matter what racial background, were poor. There were no established churches and structures to serve as models of what new churches "should" look like. There was also an implicit assumption that people could establish their own congregations and that each congregation could become immediately responsible for it own leadership and finances. The early Latino evangelists usually preached without outside support and established new congregations among the new converts. The long-term success or failure of these congregations depended on the congregations themselves from the very beginning. But Latino Pentecostal leaders also learned the freedom of taking on this responsibility; they were not dependent on Anglo money, so they did not have to submit to Anglo leadership and control.

During the early years, language was a clear barrier between Latino and Anglo Protestants, and it continued to be with each new wave of immigrants. But as U.S.-born generations learned English, this was no longer a barrier in and of itself. Racial and class barriers still existed, but they were not as clearly marked for Latinos as they were for African Americans. Latinos could pass if they wanted to, and some chose to do so. But leaving the barrio or the rural Latino community also represented the opportunity for success in the United States. The cost of success for most young Latinos was leaving behind a strong ethnic identity. Young Latino Protestants often found that once they went to school and developed a profession, they no longer fit in their former churches. The class difference also meant that they often felt somewhat more comfortable in the English-language congregations, though they were not always easily welcomed.

This created a number of difficulties for the missionaries and for the converts. As stated in chapter 2, at the end of the 19th century, longtime northern Methodist missionary Emily Harwood was lamenting that some of the young people were leaving the Spanish-language churches to join the English-language congregations.[3] But many of the missionaries and mission agencies assumed that Latinas would completely disappear as a distinct ethnic group, overwhelmed by the new settlers coming west.[4] So it was not clear where they assumed these "absorbed" new Protestant converts would go to church.[5]

Southern denominational missionaries in Texas saw Latinos as "Mexicans" and treated them as foreigners. Therefore, they assumed the converts would have their own churches, though there were also cases of Latinos becoming part of majority-culture congregations. That perspective would not be seriously challenged among southern denominations until the middle of the 20th century, as they began to deal with the implications of segregation.

If becoming a Protestant was supposed to open the door into majority culture, it was not successful. Most Anglos did not want "Mexicans" in their churches, unless they were of the same socioeconomic class. But most mainline and evangelical leaders also clearly communicated, implicitly and often explicitly, to their Latino counterparts that the Latino churches were not equal partners in ministry and that they could never reach the threshold of equality unless they were willing to become as Anglo as possible.

This played out differently in each denomination. Presbyterians and Methodists pushed for Latino churches to have equality, but often at the cost of closing some Latino churches. Most evangelical and Pentecostal denominations continued to develop many new Latino congregations, allowing each church to develop within its own socioeconomic and ethnic reality. This meant that the Latino churches were always poorer. Most evangelicals tried to "help" them economically and often created patterns of economic dependency that lasted decades. Pentecostals allowed the churches to develop completely on their own. Churches were not financially dependent, even if they were small, because they had simple buildings and lay or bi-vocational pastors.

But the implicit assumption about most Latino Protestant churches was that they were located on the other side of the tracks and were for people that lived there. If one was able to leave the barrio, there was no Latino Protestant church for a Latino middle class or for those aspiring to become middle class. Until the second half of the 20th century, almost the only church option for "successful" Latino Protestants was a majority-culture church.

## The Complexities of Latino Identity and Church Participation among Latino Protestants

All the issues related to ethnic identity maintenance, acculturation, and assimilation impact how Latino Protestants make choices about the church they are part of. The assumptions of the larger society about how minorities participate in U.S. society have had an impact on how Protestants have developed their mission strategy, but also on how Latinas have responded to the Protestant message. Generations of Latino Protestants have continued grappling with the relationship between their religious and ethnic identities and have come to different conclusions about how they fit together.

The early Protestant missionaries were "successful" in that Latino Protestant converts have adapted to life in the United States, as have Latino Catholics. But the implicit assumption was that the converts would shed their culture and adopt Euro-American culture. Some did, but many found ways to maintain parts of their culture and their ethnic identity even as they converted to Protestantism and adapted to Euro-American culture.

Latinos have acculturated; every new generation has learned how to fit with U.S. society and has adopted a U.S. identity. But most Latinas have not assumed that "fitting" necessarily has to include the loss of one's culture or that it reduces the importance of one's ethnic identity. If becoming Protestant was supposed to cause Latinos to lose their ethnic identity, then it has failed. Both the Pew (2007) and Hunt (1998) studies quoted earlier clearly demonstrate that most Latino Protestants see the importance of their culture and ethnic identity in relationship to their faith.

The same can be said of the assumption that conversion to Protestantism eventually leads to secularization. There might be some truth among a few Latinas who joined historic Protestant denominations, but it does not seem to be true of those who are part of "subversive" Protestant movements, such as the Pentecostals. Popular Protestant denominations seem to fit quite well within the religious worldview of most Latinas.[6]

Even many of the Latino Protestant churches that were started with an assimilationist assumption have ended up supporting ethnic and cultural maintenance. Latino churches have often been one of the few places where a new generation learns formal Spanish. Through much of the 20th century, schools were teaching English, often punishing children for speaking Spanish, and working for children to make a language shift. But Latino Protestant churches have usually been one of those places where the use of Spanish has been encouraged and defended. The churches also have historically been a safe haven for young Latinas to test and affirm their Latina identity.

But the issues have never been clear-cut. Latino churches have always had to address the issue of cultural adaptation and identity. Those in leadership have resolved the issue in their own lives. Some are immigrants who still hearken back to their countries of origin. Others are a part of Latino churches because that is where they were formed as Christians or because they have chosen to clearly identify with the Latina community.

The issue usually becomes complicated with the second generations, either literally the children of immigrants or merely children who are struggling with their own issues of identity. On top of all the other issues related to adolescence in our globalized world, Latina young people also have to deal with the social pressure to leave their Latinoness behind. Latino Protestant churches have struggled with this issue and have come to different conclusions. Some have assumed that the church should be a place for ethnic identity maintenance. Churches that have taken this perspective are intentional about making sure that programs are in Spanish and that children and young people learn about Latino culture. Others go in the opposite direction, assuming that their children will fully assimilate, and so they do not directly offer programs for their children and youth, but link those programs to an existing majority-culture sister congregation. A third option is that of adjusting programs depending on the tendencies of the adolescents themselves.

At the same time, these young people also make their own decisions. They struggle with their own identity, and the church sometimes becomes a testing ground for that struggle. This means that Latino youth ministry has to deal with all the issues of adolescence and ethnic identity issues within a minority community.[7] The clearest point of contention is usually language. Youth who have recently immigrated will probably enjoy Spanish, but most of those born or raised in the United States will tend to feel more comfortable with English.

But the underlying issue is the ethnic identity of minority peoples in the United States. No matter what perspective Latino churches take, they become players in the issue. There is no neutral position; either they reflect that ethnic identity maintenance of minority peoples is important in the United States, or they reflect that it is not important. The ambivalence reflected in the larger society plays out in Latino Protestant churches as they struggle to understand how best to frame the gospel message for their polycentric children.

Figure 1.1, which was used to describe the various ways Latinas identify with Latino culture and ethnic identity in relationship to Euro-American culture, is very useful in thinking about cultural expectations related to church participation. This allows us to identify who is most likely to be drawn toward or away from Latino churches and what are the ethnic and cultural issues that will likely draw them in one direction or another (see Figure 5.1).[8]

People who are "nuclear" Latinas are not likely to be attracted to a non-Latino church because it is outside of their normal experience. They are not likely to be invited to such a church or to feel very comfortable in one if they are invited. It also means that Latino churches are likely to have more nuclear Latinos than the Latino population at large. This also means that Latino churches are likely to reflect Latino culture in all their activities and that Spanish is likely to be the principal or only language of worship and interaction.

At the other end of the drawing, those who have structurally assimilated into Euro-American culture ("new ethnics") are not likely to be drawn to a Latino church because it is outside of their frame of reference. They are of Hispanic descent, but their ethnic background does not shape their culture or identity today. Such Latinas will likely be in the same church as their Euro-American neighbors.

It is the Latinos who have a polycentric identity who do not easily fit in churches that seem monocultural. The bicultural, marginal, fleeing, and

# Latino Ethnic Identity and Church Participation

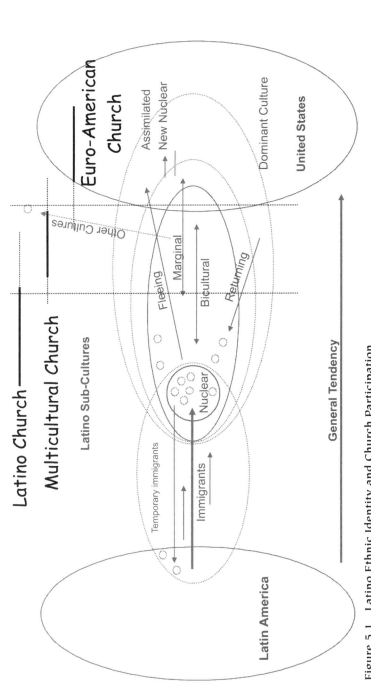

Figure 5.1   Latino Ethnic Identity and Church Participation

returning are people who have a fluid ethnic and cultural identity, or who compartmentalize their lives, expressing certain cultural traits in one environment and claiming a strong ethnic identity in another. These types of people are most likely to move between Latino and non-Latino churches or look for a church that addresses the complexities of their own cultural experience.

The drawing attempts to demonstrate that ethnic identity is an evolving process in the life of most Latinas. People start from where their parents raised them but then are influenced by the forces in U.S. society that work toward structural assimilation. If the person is involved in structures that encourage identity maintenance, such as a Latino church, a strong extended family, or continual links to Latin America, then there are forces that keep the person closer to a Latino identity. Some Latinas also occasionally strengthen their ethnic links through marriage. For Latino youth this process is going on in the midst of generational changes that encourage a questioning of parental values and culture.

Today the types of churches that Latinos participate in are usually described as Spanish-language churches, English-language Latino churches, intentionally multicultural churches, and traditionally English-language churches. These categories reflect a continuum that tends to parallel the drawing on Latino ethnic identity maintenance. But these are not always mutually exclusive categories. For example, many churches have services in both Spanish and English. There are also many predominantly Latino churches that do not self-identify as Latina. But it is within this continuum that Latino Protestants look for a church community in which to express their faith.

## Why Do People in the United States Shift Churches?

It is far beyond the scope this book to analyze why people in the United States change churches or denominational affiliations. But it is important to recognize that Latinas are impacted by the same influences and make similar types of decisions.[9] People who already go to church are sometimes attracted to the new church that is currently the "talk of the town." People move and become disconnected from the church of an early stage in life. Their life situations may change, and they feel that a new church might better meet their new needs, such as a ministry for children or youth. Mainline churches that were once at the center of religious participation in the United States are now struggling to redefine themselves as they interact with a new generation that questions the best way to be a faithful church and to be an effective church in mission. These questions are linked to the desire for renewal, the sense that culture and society have changed, or the fact that structures and styles that were developed by one generation no longer seem to speak to a new generation.

Though the decision by a Latina to go to a non-Latino church is usually analyzed in light of assimilation or the loss of ethnic identity, it is important to recognize that all of these other issues also come into play. Ethnic-identity shift and acculturation issues may play a role, but they will not necessarily be the principal reason Latinos leave a specifically Latino congregation to become a part of a congregation that is not primarily Latina. Those other types of reasons would likely be similar if they decided to go from one Latino congregation to another one or if they joined a Euro-American congregation.

## Why Latinas Go to "Non-Latino" Churches

We want to review some of the reasons Latinos decide to attend non-Latino churches, particularly when their decision is linked to cultural or ethnic issues. There have been no detailed studies of this specific process, so this section is based on observation and the comments made in popular Latina Protestant culture.

### Euro-American Church as First Option

Attraction to a Protestant church and ethnic identity shift are not always linked. Many Latinos with a strong ethnic identity go to churches that are "non-Latino" because that is where they were first invited to church. Friends or relatives invited them, and they had an encounter with God there and have become a part of the church community. They might have had some formal religious identification in the past, probably Catholic, but they were not an active part of any congregation. They never made a conscious choice between a Latino and a Euro-American church. Their choice was between a culturally framed religious identity that was not linked to regular church attendance anywhere and the church they now attend. Some of these people take their ethnic identities into the lives of the congregation and enrich them.

### Shift from a Latino Protestant Church toward a Euro-American Protestant Church

Latino Protestants have been leaving Latino Protestant churches and becoming part of Euro-American churches since the 19th century. That movement can usually be attributed to social mobility and/or acculturation.

In the past it was also linked to geographic reality, since Latino Protestants who moved into areas with a small Latino population might not find a Latino Protestant church in that new location.

Usually the first time that Latino Protestants face the question of church participation is when they become young adults. Educational, vocational, and relational issues all create a new reality, and these young adults have to choose a new church because they are far from the church of their youth. Latino young adults also tend to disconnect from church during this transitional period. But it is during this period that most Latinos consider the possibility of leaving the Latino Protestant church of their childhood. As they continue to define their own identity, the role of the church in that process also comes into play.

For Latina Protestants who became members as adults or who have been part of Latina churches all of their lives, this process is often evolutionary and does not always have a clear transition point. The factors that influence their decision may be more complex than ethnic identity issues.

The most common reason stated for leaving a Latino church is language. Latinos have always had an ambivalent attitude toward Spanish. For many it is seen as a marker of cultural pride and ethnic identity, whereas for other it seems the language of the uneducated or something linked to an immigrant past. Even those who proudly use it often actually speak Spanglish because they have never had the opportunity to formally study Spanish. Yet even though recent studies indicate that Latinos tend to lose Spanish in about two-and-one-half generations, the use of Spanish continues to grow, and Spanish-language media continues to expand in the United States.[10]

Limited Spanish usage is a reality for many Latinos, but language preferences also reflect the fluid identity issues mentioned in the previous section. Many Latinos choose English-language congregations because they are looking for a place where they can better understand and participate. But for others the issue of language is a marker of the complexity of ethnic identity issues and the desire to find a different way to bring their polycentric identity into church. The Pew (2007) study also demonstrated that some people choose to go to a church that uses Spanish even though they are English-dominant.

For a young Latina who is being strongly encouraged to structurally assimilate, the Latino church often feels like the cultural past. It is attractive when there is a desire to reaffirm a Latino ethnic identity but feels odd when one is fleeing from that identity or when one one's identity feels broader than the Latino focus of the congregations. It is not that non-Latino churches are culturally neutral, since they reflect the culture of the majority. But some churches consciously celebrate many identities, which seems to fit many polycentric Latinos. Latino churches clearly have a cultural identity that is minority and alternative. Many times the majority of church members are immigrants or people who maintain strong ties to Latin America. This type of congregation reflects a culture and values that seem to run counter to those that a young Latina is now adopting.

Another common reason given for leaving a Latino church is that it does not provide a specific type of program or the quality of ministry that is expected. One of the complexities faced by the majority of Latino churches is that they can never provide the level or quality of ministry of their majority-culture counterparts. Most Latino churches are smaller or have a smaller financial base because their members are usually poorer than their majority-culture counterparts. So when a Latina member is looking at the "quality of services," the Latino church almost always loses out.

There are times when younger college-educated Latinas almost feel pushed out of the church they grew up in. Many working-class Latino pastors often feel threatened by church members who are better educated than they are. They have the ability to pastor working-class people like themselves, but their limited education and theological formation make it difficult for them to deal with the issues that more educated members bring to church. Sometimes these younger members propose changes that reflect what they have seen in other churches. Or they question teachings and practices that are often more linked to issues of class or culture than to Christian faith. They may want to bring more order to worship or church organization. Any or all of these things can feel very threatening to someone who does not have their level of education. Though the pastor may use "spiritual" language to describe the issue, the end result is that these people usually end up leaving the church.

A variation on this theme arises when a Latino church calls a pastor who is a recent immigrant and who does not understand the values and practices of those who have been born or raised in the United States. Since these people express their faith and commitment in ways that are very different than in Latin America, the pastor often perceives these people as not being truly committed to the faith.

Small churches are a place where everyone has a part and where all the members are needed. Most Latino Protestant churches fit this mold. This is a great way to create community, but it can often create burnout in those most willing to serve. Some Latinos leave their small Latino church because they are looking for a large church where they can be anonymous; they want to have a good worship experience without being expected to serve.

The Greeley and Hunt studies demonstrated that upward social mobility is also a factor in the religious changes of some Latinos. They were looking at the movement from Catholicism to Protestantism, but it can also be linked to the decision to attend a non-Latino church. In many large cities it is linked to the relationship between financial success and living in suburbia. A sign of economic success is the ability to purchase a home. But in most urban areas this means moving into a new area. Many Latino Protestants continue to be connected to their churches because of social and familial links. But in many large cities the distances are large, and people do not always find a Latino church in parts of suburbia, though that is changing rapidly. Because they moved for economic benefits, they often weaken their social networks, making it easier to think about going to church outside of the Latino community.

Most Latino churches are multicultural; they have people from many national, racial, and cultural backgrounds, though all are identified as Latino. But in some areas specific Latino churches have a specific national background or regional tendency. Latinas who are not from that background may find it difficult to participate because of cultural differences and may find it easier to be in a non-Latino church where they know they are different than to be in a church where they feel they should fit but do not.

People make their decisions about church participation in the movement and polycentric reality that is Latino identity. Some of those who choose to leave treat Latino churches as reflections of the past, places frozen in time that continue to reflect what was and what might be remembered with nostalgia, but not a live and developing institution. There is sometimes also the temptation to compare the worst of what is in a Latino church with the ideal of what a Euro-American church wants to be. The fact that Latino churches are dealing with the same tensions between tradition and innovation as their majority-culture counterparts often does not come into play: the Latino church is part of "my" past, and the majority-culture church is part of "my" future, even if the specific Latino church is more innovative than a traditional Euro-American congregation.

## Do Latinos Shift from Non-Latino to Latino Churches?

Latina Protestants also move between Latino Protestant churches for many of the same reasons majority-culture Protestants move around. But there are also Latinos who go from non-Latino churches to Latino churches. Some may have first become Protestant believers in a non-Latino church and are now moving to a congregation where they sense a better cultural fit. There are also Latinos who left a Latino church and who decide to return. The reasons may have little to do with culture or ethnicity, but to the extent that these are factors, it is also important to describe this movement.

The Latino identity drawing can be helpful with this issue. "Returning" Latinas are those people who are rediscovering their ethnic identity. Going to a Latino church becomes one of the ways to explore, discover, and redefine one's identity. Religion has always been a key factor in Latino identity. Therefore, going to a Latino church becomes one of those potential spaces where a "returning" Latino can reexamine his or her identity.

A variation on the returning theme is the Latina Protestant who "took a break" from his or her Latino church and then decides to return. Because these types of people are usually leaders, they often return to take on leadership roles again. When they return, they are often more enthused for ministry in the community. Their time in another church gave them new experiences and generated new ideas that they want to bring back to their previous setting.

Manuel Ortiz, in his book *Hispanic Challenge*, also called on young Latinos to purposely move back into the barrios of their youth and to be agents of transformation.[11] Committed Christian young adults often are willing to live in depressed communities and support local institutions, such as Latino churches, as a way to give back to their communities.

Another pattern that is becoming more familiar is that of Latinos who left a Latino church and found a church that they liked, but now would like to see what the new church is providing become available to the Spanish-speaking community. The process goes something like this: I like my new church, I like my Latino identity, and I want to serve my community. Is there a way that the richness of what I am experiencing can be made available in Spanish?

Most of the large urban areas have at least one Latino megachurch where the pastor was already a celebrity in the Latino Protestant world before becoming a pastor. These types of churches are attractive to many people and usually grow very quickly. They usually have access to more resources than the average Latino church, so Latinos who left a Latino church often find that these new "celebrity" churches provide programs that most Latino churches cannot provide (as do many Latinas who are still attending Latino churches). These Latino megachurches are also becoming attractive to small numbers of non-Latinos.

A phenomenon becoming more common in many urban areas is for churches to make major transitions in their ministry focus because the neighborhood around them is changing. Older established churches need to work alongside younger Latino congregations as the former fade and allow the latter to take over, or as the former redefine their mission in this new reality. Inevitably, the former congregation has some Latino members who now must decide whether to fade away as part of the former congregation or join with the younger congregation that now reflects the composition of the neighborhood.

Latino Protestants are not unlike their Euro-American counterparts in that they also choose to move from one church to another, even though they will often stay within the same theological tradition. A significant change is that the existence of so many and varied Latino Protestant churches in most urban areas gives those Latino Protestants one more set of options as they church-shop.

## What Non-Latino Churches Do Latinos Attend? Historical Links

The 2007 Pew study clearly identified one group of Latinos that is most likely to attend non-Latino churches: those who have been in the United States for several generations (even though the study demonstrated that a large percentage continue to go to churches with a strong Latino identity). The implicit assumption behind the study is that these people are more likely to be "new ethnics" or "marginal Latinos," people completely, or almost completely, assimilated into Euro-American culture. Mainline churches were more likely to have this type of member than the evangelical or Pentecostal churches.[12]

Since mainline denominations such as Methodist, Presbyterian, American Baptist, and Disciples of Christ have had Latino churches and converts for more than 100 years, it is not surprising to find third-generation-plus Latinos in these churches. Some of the Latinas who attend these churches have been Protestants for several generations and are descendants of those early Latino converts. These Latino Protestants may wear their historical links proudly, though they feel more comfortable worshiping in English. But many of them maintain links with both English- and Spanish-language congregations.[13]

Traditionally it has also been assumed that since many mainline churches have a class status attached to them, upwardly mobile Latinos may be attracted to these churches, since they potentially represent who they are becoming or want to become. As stated earlier, Hunt has challenged this assumption,[14] though there might be a small number of Latinas who are drawn to mainline churches in part because of status issues.

Most evangelical and Pentecostal denominations have a shorter history of ministry in the Latino community, so there are not as many potential third-generation-plus Latino Protestants in their midst. But there are also Latinas in some evangelical or Pentecostal churches who either grew up in Latino churches of the same denomination or are descendants of people who did.

Because of language and/or upward mobility, they feel more comfortable in a Euro-American version of the church they or their parents grew up in.

But many Latinos are also attracted to the same types of churches that have become popular in the United States. Some of these churches may have a significant minority of Latina members in their midst. These churches may not be reaching out to the Latino community, but may attract them in the same way they attract other members. (In the next section we will describe non-Latino churches that are intentionally trying to bring Latinas into their congregations.)

One of the issues related to Latinos in Euro-American churches has to do with their impact or contribution. An assimilationist perspective would assume that Latinos in a Euro-American church either have already made the cultural and ethnic identity changes that make it possible for them to fit or are in that process, and that is why they are attending such a church. But that is clearly not always the case. Some of those Latinas recognize that they are "different" and simply accept that as a given and conform to the majority because they are "guests." But their presence raises the larger societal question that is constantly in the background: Should these Latinos seek to impact the congregation or conform to it? Are ethnic identity and cultural differences important contributions to church life, or should they be conformed to the dominant culture of a church community? Since the United States is changing, how do minority communities participate?

## Churches for Those "In Between"

Being a polycentric person means living "in between" many times. Many churches have recognized the growing diversity in their midst and have responded by developing new congregations or a more intentionally multicultural focus, starting from the assumption of cultural pluralism and not assimilation. This usually starts within Latino churches. In most urban area, Latino Protestant congregations are often very multicultural and multiethnic, reflecting the vast diversity of peoples who fit under the Latino "umbrella," whether or not there was an intentionality guiding that result. But there are also many Latina Protestant churches that are intentionally developing a multicultural ministry.

Historically, Latino churches have responded to polycentric, bilingual Latinos, often their children, in one of three ways. Some have defined themselves clearly as Spanish-language and Latino-culture congregations. They use programs for children and young people to try to develop a strong linguistic and cultural identity in them. At the other extreme, one finds some congregations that decide to change with their children. Some other

Latino churches have "disappeared" as distinctively Latino congregations, not because the Latino community is dying, but because they have chosen to focus on their children exclusively.

Most Latino churches are bilingual, in one form or another. Some larger churches have parallel programs, one in Spanish and another in English. Others use English for activities with children and young people and Spanish with adults. Another common response is to have bilingual activities, whether they include full translation of everything or feature the more common model of "sprinkling in" some English into a Spanish-language service, assuming that all the English speakers understand Spanish to some extent and merely need occasional "pointers" to help them fully understand. There may be an internal debate as to whether the role of the English-language activities is to serve as a bridge so that young Latinos can go back and forth or to serve as a transition toward English-language dominance and the loss of Spanish. But the result is a recognition that Latino churches usually have to be bilingual to minister to all the people in their congregation.

Some Latino churches are also working with English-dominant pastors to develop congregations that have a clear Latino ethnic identity and cultural flavor but that minister completely in English. Some of these congregations look like their Spanish-language counterparts, but others clearly want to focus on their differences. In his book on intentionally multicultural Latino Protestant churches, Daniel Rodríguez describes this audience this way:

> The challenges confronting many native-born Latinos [is that they are] faced with the choice of attending either a Spanish-only or Spanish-dominant (e.g., bilingual) church or a church of the dominant group. . . . most English-dominant Latinos usually prefer something in the middle, a church in the hyphen *con el sabor latino*.[15]

Some of the churches reaching out to this audience are niche churches, focusing on a fairly specific segment of the Latino community. There are churches that cater to younger Latinas who grew up in Latino Protestant churches but are somehow recovering from the experience. These types of congregations usually react against some of the legalisms common in some Latino Pentecostal or evangelical churches. The core members can all point to a similar type of childhood church experience, which they may recall with nostalgia, but which they do not want to be a part of. Their marketing is similar to that of many congregations that cater to members of a younger generation who grew up in the church and are committed to Christian faith, but who do not feel that the church they grew up in has anything to offer them. For example, a church in south Florida put up a banner to advertise their meeting place that said, "Calvary Fellowship: Not Your *Abuela's* Church."[16]

Other predominantly Latino congregations go in an opposite direction in relationship to culture and ethnic identity. They may be in a predominantly Latino neighborhood, and the vast majority of their leaders and members may be Latina. But the message they want to communicate is that their church is just like any Euro-American church. Their worship services and programs intentionally do not look different from that of their Euro-American sister congregations. Most, if not all, of their members may be of Hispanic descent, but cultural distinctiveness and ethnic identity play a very limited role, if any, in how the church expresses its faith.

A growing number of intentionally multicultural congregations also are developing models of ministry that draw minority young people of various ethnic backgrounds who often share a similar experience of being polycentric. These churches attempt to affirm both the distinctiveness of the various ethnic backgrounds represented and the commonality of the intercultural and interethnic experience of many urban people. Young people from majority-culture backgrounds are also drawn to these types of churches as they discover the cultural diversity around them and choose to be a part of it.

Some of these congregations are connected by values other than a common ethnic or cultural background, such as socioeconomic and educational similarities. But others are intentionally attempting to minister across all of these lines, particularly if the church is located in a mixed neighborhood. These churches usually try to intentionally reflect their diversity in all aspects of church life, be it leadership, worship, or outreach programs. Their music and their potlucks celebrate the distinctive gifts of the various cultures represented in the congregation, and they attempt to develop models of cultural interaction that allow people of various backgrounds to feel comfortable together.

Another version of this model appears when congregations of various ethnic or linguistic backgrounds work together, even as they maintain their distinctive congregational life. They may be organized as one church with several distinct congregations or as several churches using one building. In this multicongregational model, Protestant churches, usually of the same denomination or theological tradition, work together and occasionally have joint worship services in which they celebrate their unity. But they continue their distinctive activities. A variation of this practice is the church that offers worship services or Bible studies in various languages or focused toward specific communities as part of its overall church ministry.[17]

These types of churches are addressing the increasingly multicultural and multiethnic reality of most urban areas. Though the United States has not become the postracial society dreamt by many, an increasing intercultural reality is being experienced by many. Because Latinos are the single largest minority group, their growing presence will play an important role in this intercultural reality. As the Latina community continues to diversify and express its polycentric identity in many different ways, churches like these will continue playing an important role among Latino Protestants who are not a part of Latino Protestant churches.

## Latino *Evangélicos* and Latina Protestants in the Future

Latina Protestants and Latino *evangélicos* reflect not only the increasing diversity in the community but also the continuum of experiences and the role of religion in ethnic identity. The encounter between these two groups within churches and Protestant denominations is often as complex as the community itself. The temptation is to simplify the situation by assuming that one segment is representative of the whole or is the most important segment of the community. Some effectively only recognize those Latinos who are part of Latino churches, whereas others assume that Latinos will structurally assimilate, so they see Latino churches principally as temporary structures that serve as placeholders or as support structures for people as they assimilate. Will Latino pastors and leaders look at each other in the same way across this divide?

Latina Protestants are changing the face of U.S. Protestantism both as distinct churches and as part of churches where they are only a segment of the congregation. Both will face the challenge of recognizing each other in the "other" Latino and of working together, particularly when they are a part of the same denomination. The diversity will also challenge the assumptions of Euro-American Protestants about how best to relate to ethnic minorities.

## CHAPTER SIX

# Faces of Latino Protestantism

In chapter 1 we addressed some of the key differences between various Latino communities and how some of these difference impact religious preferences. In this chapter we want to deal with the complexity of being both Latino and Protestant. Because Latinos are an ethnic minority, but Protestantism is the religious expression of the majority in this country, this creates a complex situation in which it is difficult to maintain an identity that is both Latino and Protestant in the United States. But generations of Latino Protestants have lived out their faith and developed various expressions of it in this environment. Protestant missionaries evangelized Latinos with a certain set of assumptions about how conversion would affect them. Studies of Latino religion often ignored the Protestants or assumed that their conversions could be fully explained as a response to the pressures of cultural adaptation or the desire to succeed in the United States. In this mix Latino Protestants have developed identities as complex as the environment in which they live. The many faces reflect their common religious and ethnic experiences, but also the influence of the larger environment in which they are living out their faith.

## Protestant and Latino: Missionaries' Assumptions

The Protestant missionaries, missionary teachers, and mission leaders of the 19th and early 20th centuries were convinced that they had a God-given responsibility to evangelize the Mexicans of the Southwest, the Puerto Ricans, and the Spanish-speaking immigrants on the Eastern Seaboard. But they closely linked Protestant conversion to Americanization. From their perspective, American society, in its ideal form, reflected the effects of

Protestant faith, which was a good reflection of the gospel. To become a Protestant and to adopt an American lifestyle was to become a good Christian. If Latino Catholics were to become good Protestants, in this perspective, they would not only have God's blessing; they would also be able to become good citizens of the United States.

The missionaries assumed that there was little in Latino culture that could be "rescued." Their religion was a dead faith, and their culture was part of a dying past that would soon disappear, swept away by the new superior culture being brought into the Southwest by the westward migration or into Puerto Rico through the new influences of the U.S. takeover. If the new U.S. citizens of the Southwest, and later Puerto Rico, and the Spanish-speaking Catholic immigrants were to have any future in their new country, they needed to adopt the culture of the future.

Becoming a Protestant was a key component of the hope for the future in the United States. If Latinos would leave behind their superstitious faith and practices and adopt a biblically based faith and U.S. Protestant religious practices, this would go a long way toward making it possible for them to succeed in the new reality. It was not clear whether Latinos would be swept into or swept away by the Americans moving west across the continent. They needed the hope of the gospel, but also had to deal with the new reality of the U.S. takeover. Some of the missionaries assumed that Latinos would be able to quickly fit into the new reality, and others assumed that Latino Protestants might need "extra help" in this transitional process. But none of them assumed that Latino culture could survive in the United States or that Latinos had anything to offer Protestant faith. Other than using Spanish in their churches, there was little that the missionaries assumed Latinos would bring into their new faith. Many Protestant missionaries assumed that Latino churches in the United States would be only a temporary phenomenon until Latinos began to acculturate and fit into existing churches.[1]

Some of the early Protestant converts followed the path of structural assimilation. They left their communities and families to live among Euro-Americans, and a few intermarried. But this path was open to very few, and most Latinas either did not have the option or rejected it. Even among most of the first converts, there was a sense of wanting to express their faith in their own cultural idiom. Many were very open to the biblical message, but when they became converted and started to preach the message to their own people, they framed it in ways that fit into their culture, religious perspective, worldview, and language.

These conflicting assumptions and actions created tensions in relationships to Latino Protestant churches. Protestant denominational leaders assumed that successful Latino churches would look like their Euro-American counterparts. They would develop similar structures, adopt a similar worship style, prepare their pastors in the same way, and eventually be full participants in denominational structures, either alongside Euro-Americans or by developing and maintaining their own parallel structures. But the Latino churches never seemed to make the grade. They were always a step away from becoming full participants in Protestant denominations. As late as 1970, Grebler, Moore, and Guzman described the tension faced by the Protestant denominations in the following terms:

> Protestant denominations [Presbyterian, Methodist, and Baptists] are simultaneously institutions of the dominant society and also religious bodies. The Mexican is a nonmember, but he must be seen as a potential member. However, access to membership for the Mexican American is made difficult because he is not simply a *non*believer, but has an *erroneous* (that is, Roman Catholic) attachment. To destroy this attachment, the evangelist must also struggle with the "potential Christian's" special Mexican characteristics. The Mexican people have been to a degree pariahs. In order to cope with them or overcome the distaste caused by "Mexicanness," the evangelist must either be Mexican himself or have a special liking for or "vocation" for these people (which is often defined as rather peculiar). This extension of the church to the "pagan Mexican" is thus *not* an extension of the church as an institution, but only of those within it who (rather absurdly, perhaps, to the mundane Southwestern Protestant) are committed to its religious mandate to extend membership. Simple conversion does not succeed in making Mexican Americans into Anglo Protestants—it just makes them "Christian" rather than pagan.[2]

Pentecostalism turned all of these assumptions upside down. Since Pentecostalism was a revival movement, it did not have a clearly defined model of what Pentecostal churches should look like. Most of the early Pentecostal leaders were poor people who did not make the class assumptions of other Protestants about church structures. Under Pentecostalism Latinos became agents of their own churches and their own mission efforts. Latino Pentecostal churches used their own musical instruments and musical styles in worship. They established churches that reflected the economic level of their members because the members had to support them with no expectation of outside subsidies. The Latino converts were the missionaries, and they also became the pastors of their own congregations. Some of the pastors had some formal theological education, but many did not. But what was most valued was not the educational level, but "giftedness"—the demonstrated ability to preach and lead. The abilities of the people and their cultural idiom were appreciated and used to spread the Pentecostal message. Poor, Spanish-speaking Latinos with little formal education could be agents of their encounter with God, calling others to conversion and establishing churches and worshiping God in their own language and in their own cultural style.

Latina Pentecostals demonstrated that they did not need the resources of Euro-American Protestants to develop their own churches, only the power of the Holy Spirit. Not only did they not need these resources; they could also question the value of some of them. Latino Pentecostals could meet in tents or simple buildings where God's presence was "real." Latino Pentecostal pastors could preach with the power of God without seminary education and might even do it better because they were not encumbered by their education. Even the Latino Pentecostals soon discovered that Euro-Americans might be willing to help, but that they would want some level of control. Latinos would be free to worship God in their own way only if they did it on their own.

Latino Pentecostals also became culture creators and "contextual theologians." They evangelized in ways that affirmed their own people and started their own churches. They developed their own liturgy and wrote their own hymns of the faith, hymns that reflected their own culture, experience, and worldview. They taught in their Bible institutes and eventually led those institutions that had been started in conjunction with Euro-Americans. In the midst of all of this, they began to practice an identity that was both Latino and Pentecostal.

While Latino Pentecostals were beginning to grow during the first half of the 20th century, Latino Protestants in mainline and evangelical denominations often found it more difficult to develop their own voice within their denominations. The expectation was that they would "learn" the voice of the majority and make it their own. But even in the midst of learning this new voice, some worked to at least add a distinctive accent. As Latino and Latin American Pentecostalism began to have a broader influence, other Latino Protestants also started finding ways to express their faith in their own cultural idiom.

Latino mainline Protestants began to find their own voice in the midst of the civil rights struggles of the 1960s. They formed caucuses and similar organizations to work for change within denominational structures. Latina theologians began to reflect on who they were as Christians and Latinas and on their unique contribution to the larger church. It would take longer for Latino evangelicals to address these types of questions, but by the latter part of the 20th century, they were also asking questions about what it meant to be both Latino and evangelical.

### Sociological Studies of Latino Protestants

Until fairly recently there were few studies of Latino Protestants. Studies of the various Latina communities might address religious or ethno-religious issues. If they did, they would focus on the role of Catholicism in the community and on ethnic identity maintenance. Protestants were seldom mentioned, if at all, giving the impression that they did not exist or that they played no important role in the community.

If and when Latino Protestants were mentioned, it was as an afterthought after discussion of Catholicism. Manuel Gamio, the Mexican sociologist and anthropologist who studied Mexican migrants in the United States during the 1920s, was the first sociologist to mention the Mexican Protestants of the Southwest. Gamio wrote two books about Mexican migrants in the United States. During his extensive interviews he met a few Latina Protestants. He concluded that the Protestant message preached among Mexicans was often linked to Americanization ("foreignization") and that immigrants were open to the Protestant message because they were no longer under the social control of their communities, but that these conversions were often "doubtful" or "merely conventional."[3] The link between conversion and Americanization and the assumption that these conversions were not significant became common themes if and when later sociologists mentioned Latino Protestants in their studies.

The Chicano movement created a renewed interest in understanding the history and experience of the Mexican Americans of the Southwest in the 1960s and beyond. Scholars studied many aspects of the community and published numerous books and journal articles. Some of these studies looked at the religious aspects of the community after the U.S. takeover, particularly at the popular devotional practices of the people. Most of the authors completely ignored Latino Protestants and accepted the idea that Mexican and Mexican American ethnic identity was closely linked to Catholicism. If they were mentioned at all, it was usually as an afterthought, recognizing that a "few of them" had become Protestants.[4]

This perspective is clearly reflected in the seminal work *The Mexican-American People* quoted in chapter 2. The authors dedicate one chapter to Protestants, in their section on the role of churches. But they begin on the assumption that "Mexican-American Protestants are not worth much special attention" because of the relatively small number of Latino members reported by Protestant denominations.[5]

Even many of the more recent sociological studies look at Protestants only in relationship to the Catholic majority. Because the Latino Protestant community continues to grow, a new series of studies attempted to understand why Latinos were defecting from the Catholic Church. Both the previously quoted Greeley and Hunt studies analyze Latino Protestants from this perspective. Hunt also refers to a series of studies that look at Latinas and their religious practices in specific regions of the country. Interestingly, all of the studies look at the practices of Latino Catholics and reference Latino Protestants only in relationship to Catholics. None of the studies are about Latino Protestants, nor do they figure prominently in the conclusions of the authors.[6]

A common issue among all of these scholars is the relationship between Latinos becoming Protestants and their cultural adaptation in the United States. That was one of the goals of the early missionaries and one of the assumptions of several of the studies: if Latinos became Protestants, they would find it easier to adapt and succeed and would more effectively assimilate into Euro-American culture, leaving behind their distinct cultural and ethnic identity. Hunt demonstrated that there is no necessary link between becoming a Protestant and socioeconomic success or between Protestantism and the loss of ethnic identity.[7] Hunt and the Trinity study both imply that there may be a relationship between assimilation and secularization, but Whitam's assumption that Latinos might become Protestants on their way to adaptation and then secularization has not been demonstrated.[8] Again, both Hunt and the Trinity study recognize that U.S.-born Latinos may be drawn toward secularization but are more likely to be drawn to Pentecostalism or evangelicalism.[9]

### Scholarly Studies of Latino Protestants

A growing corpus of scholarly works focuses on Latino Protestants or Protestant mission work among Latinos. (The works dealing with Latino/Hispanic theology were addressed in chapter 4.) Most of those studies have looked at Latino Protestantism in the Southwest, which is not surprising, since there is a longer history there, it has the larger Latino population, and the largest number of Latino Protestant churches is in the region. Specifically, the Presbyterian work among Latinos in northern New Mexico and southern Colorado is the one that has been studied the most.

The Presbyterian ministry in New Mexico presents a number of important issues related to Latinos and Protestantism. Northern Presbyterians were the denomination that worked the hardest and invested the most in the "American mandate"[10] of 19th- and early 20th-century liberal Protestantism. They were strongly committed to evangelizing and Americanizing the people of New Mexico. The missionaries connected themselves with the communities and worked hard to understand local culture and faith. They were the missionaries who connected most successfully with dissatisfied *Penitentes*,[11] and as a result, several *Penitente* leaders became Presbyterian lay pastors. One of the Presbyterian missionaries wrote a detailed account of *Penitente* beliefs and practices.[12] When the missionaries arrived in the region, there were few public schools, so the Presbyterians funded school buildings and teachers in many of the small communities well into the 20th century, even after there were public schools in the communities. They established the first formal theological school to prepare Latino pastors. They established hospitals and clinics in several isolated communities. Yet in spite of this large investment, there were few Presbyterian converts. Many Latinas from the region became Protestants, but few joined Presbyterian churches, and many of those who joined eventually left for other denominations.

The Presbyterians have kept the most complete record of their work, something that facilitates scholarship research. Menaul Historical Library in Albuquerque and the Presbyterian Historical Archives in Philadelphia contain the most complete account of Protestant mission work among Latinos of any denomination. There are scholarly works profiling the missionary endeavor, missionary attitudes toward the *Penitentes,* the Presbyterian school system, and the Presbyterian College of the Southwest.[13]

Others have studied northern New Mexico and southern Colorado more broadly, since the Northern Methodists, the Northern Baptists, and the Congregationalists also worked in the region during the same period. Each group made similar assumptions about the role of Protestant missionaries among Latinos, but they approached the task in slightly different ways, so these comparative studies provide the opportunity to understand how these different denominations approached the task.[14] The southern denominations working in Texas approached their task with a slightly different focus, which has been the subject of another detailed study.[15] There also has been a study of all of the Protestant work among Latinos in the Southwest during the 19th century.[16]

Several histories have been written of specific denominations and/or regions. Some of these have been collections of stories or descriptive and chronological works. But other denominational studies have also addressed some of the more complex issues such as missionary motivations and majority–minority relations. Pablo García Verduzco, a Methodist pastor who worked in both Texas and northern Mexico, has the distinction of being the first Latino to publish a history of Latino Protestants; he wrote a history of the Southern Methodist work in northern Mexico and among the "Mexicans" of the Southwest in 1933.[17] There are scholarly histories of Latino Presbyterians[18] and of the Disciples of Christ in Texas.[19] There are also more popular histories of the Methodists,[20] the Baptists in Texas,[21] the Mennonite Church,[22] several of the Apostolic Assembly,[23] and the Seventh-Day Adventists.[24]

In the 1970s Latino Protestants, particularly those in the mainline churches that had a longer history within Protestantism, started asking a new set of questions, many times related to the issues of the civil rights movement. Chicano studies scholars also began to link the military conquest of the Southwest with the religious "conquest" of the Protestant missionaries. From this perspective the role of Protestantism was to "deculturate" Chicanos so that they would try to fit within dominant society. According to radical Chicanos, the only solution was for Chicano Protestants to break away from Protestantism and re-embrace their Catholic roots.[25]

The vast majority of Latino Protestants rejected this perspective, though they did recognize that the early missionaries had closely linked evangelization and Americanization. For example, in *Iglesia Presbiteriana,* a history of Presbyterian work among Latinos, the authors address the issue head on, but they demonstrate how linking Americanization to evangelization made it so difficult for evangelization to succeed.[26]

Most of the studies of Latino Protestantism have been published in the last 20 years. The early 1990s saw the beginning of several Latino theological organizations mentioned in chapter 3. These spurred the vision for research into various aspects of Latino Protestantism. The Hispanic Theological Initiative (HTI) helped a number of younger scholars complete their doctoral studies and publish their research on Latino Protestantism.[27] The Lily Endowment provided the funds to develop an extensive bibliography of extant materials on Latina Protestantism that was published in 1998.[28]

The U.S. chapter of the Comisión de Estudios de Historia de la Iglesia en América Latina y el Caribe (CEHILA) had published a book on the history and development Latina Catholicism in 1983[29] but had never published its companion volume on Latino Protestantism. The first steps in that direction were taken by the short-lived Academy for the Study of Latino Church History (APHILA by its Spanish name)[30] and by the Asociación Hispana para la Educación Teológica (AHET).[31] Renewed interest in Latino Protestant history resulted in the CEHILA Protestant volume in 2004.[32]

Newer scholarly works have focused on specific denominations, regions, or segments of the community. *Avance,* the study of Latino Adventists, mentioned in chapter 3, is the broadest of any of the studies to date. Apart from the works already mentioned, there have also been studies of Latino Pentecostalism,[33] Victory Outreach,[34] and the Pentecostal preacher and social activist Reies López Tijerina.[35] There have also been a number of books on various aspects of the Latino community and their implications for Protestant ministry. (See the bibliography for a sampling of those types of publications.)

## Religion and Latino Identity in the United States

These scholarly works and the ones mentioned in chapter 4 all recognize the complexities of being both Latino and Protestant. Latino Protestantism was born in the clash between Protestant and Catholic powers in the Southwest and has developed in the ongoing relationship between a predominantly Protestant United States and a predominantly Catholic Latino community and Latin America. Most outside scholars have addressed conversion to Protestantism as a way to cope in the midst of this encounter. But most Latino Protestants did not experience their conversions in this way. For them, God became real in their lives through the preaching of the Protestant message. They became Protestants because of their encounter with God, not as a way to adapt to U.S. reality.

Throughout the book we have pointed to some of the issues Latino Protestants face as they deal with both their Protestant Christian confession and their ethnic identity. These are the issues and themes that are common to all of the scholarly works on Latino Protestantism.

### Protestantism and Americanization

The Protestant evangelization of Latinos does not happen in a vacuum. All of the historical studies point out that Protestant evangelization happened in the midst of the westward expansion in which concepts such as Manifest Destiny, the Monroe Doctrine, the White Man's Burden, and the U.S. sense of a mission in the world guided how Americans viewed their role in the world. This affected not only how Protestant missionaries did their work, but also how the United States interacted in the Americas and beyond.

Studies look at how these themes motivated the missionaries, how they affected their attitudes toward Latinos, and how this shaped the relationship between Euro-American and Latino Protestants. The studies all conclude that this background created a unique type of relationship and that the consequences of that relationship continue into the present. To this day there is an uneven relationship between majority and minority, even in denominations where Latinos are a significant percentage of the membership.

### Latinas' Encounter with God

Most Latino Protestants have had conversion experiences. These conversions have created profound changes in their lives and the lives of those who interact with them. Conversion has also made Latino Protestants agents in their encounter with God and in their commitments to being a part of God's mission in the world. Several studies focus on the impact of Protestant conversion, how it changes destructive relationships, and how it creates agency among the poor and marginalized.

Another aspect of scholarly study is the conversion narrative itself. The ability to tell one's story and to have a community that hears it and affirms it empowers those who gain that voice. That voice not only transforms the immediate situation, but also provides a growing voice for people to become agents of change in other areas of their lives.

### Acculturation and Latino Protestantism

Most outside studies of Latino Protestantism address this issue from the perspective of the role of Protestantism in acculturation and assimilation. The key question for those scholars is whether Latinas become Protestants as part of the process of adaptation. Most Latino Protestant scholars are looking not at the relationship of conversion and assimilation, but at the continuing impact of dominant society on Latino youth who are part of Latino Protestant churches. Growing up in a church and family that nurtures a Latino identity, while living in a society that strongly encourages young people to assimilate—this is the concern of Latino Protestant scholarship on the issue.

How does this experience impact Latino Protestant youth? How do Latino and Euro-American churches need to adapt to effectively serve those who find themselves in between? In other words, Latino Protestant churches are seen not as agents of assimilation, but often as entities that are defending Latino identity, many times in tension with their own young people.

### Subversive Pentecostalisms

This theme is most common in Latin American studies of newer Pentecostal movements. But it is also a theme that can be seen in studies of Latino Pentecostalism. Popular Pentecostalism challenges the official religious order, not by directly confronting the religious powers, but by offering a counter-narrative that is more compelling and that allows people to be active participants in God's work in the world.

This theme raises the question of acculturation in a different way. Are subversive Pentecostalisms an invitation to a new way of thinking about the church and its role in the world or "merely" a counter-narrative that is discarded if the excluded find a way into the structures of power? Can the tendency to become a church in the sociological sense be avoided?

### Catholicism and Latino Identity

The idea that Catholicism is a crucial component in maintaining a strong Latino identity continues to be an object of study and debate. Latina Protestants have demonstrated that one can be Latina and Protestant. But Catholicism has been a key component in the development of the Spanish language and in Latin American and Latino culture. This raises the question of the links between Catholicism and Latino culture and the Spanish language.

The questions raised link worldview, language, and identity. How linked are Spanish and Catholicism? Are they so linked that anyone who speaks Spanish is reflecting a Catholic worldview, even if they are Protestants?[36] A related question is whether one continues any real links to *latinidad* if one neither is a Catholic nor speaks Spanish. What would be the core of a Latino Protestant identity without Spanish or a traditional (Catholic) worldview?

### Latinos and the Encounter with World Religions

A new area of study is the Latino encounter with other religions, particularly Islam. There is a small but growing Latino Muslim community in the United States.[37] But there is also a growing missionary encounter between Muslim and Latino immigrants. Even as both attempt to deal with cultural adaptation and the realities of being minorities in the United States, both are compelled by a missionary mandate and by the memory of an encounter that began 1,300 years ago on the Iberian Peninsula.[38]

## Latino Protestants in Their Own Voice

Latino Protestants have been writing about themselves since the 19th century. The most common form of oral communication, the testimony, was also the most common form of published writing. Latinos told about their conversions, their ministry, and the cost of being a Protestant. Occasionally, sermons by Latino pastors were also published. These types of communications were printed in denominational periodicals, conference reports, and gospel tracts.

By the 1930s Latino Pentecostals were also communicating by song. They sang about their lives and their experiences with God. But they also used this method to teach doctrine and church history. But the focus of these songs was usually also a testimony. Narratives became the principal way to talk about God and about God's role in their lives. Because of the importance of narrative in Latino Protestant self-identity and theologizing, it is an important way to learn about the Latina Protestant experience.

Latino Protestants represent all of the diversities of the Latino community and all the variations of Protestantism in the United States. As seen in the previous chapters, Latino Protestants are much more likely to be Pentecostals or charismatics than the U.S. Protestant population in general. One of the ways to understand Latino Protestant diversities is to describe specific people. The following stories are all part of this author's experience in the Latino Protestant community.[39] Names and other clearly identifiable information have been changed, though an effort was made to maintain as much information as possible to clearly frame each vignette within one of the specific varieties of Latino Protestantism.

### From the Gangs to the Pulpit: Another Pentecostal Success Story

Johnny Cruz was born in Los Angeles. He grew up in the gang culture and ended up in jail. Many of his friends died either in gang violence or from drug overdoses. He was converted through Victory Outreach and their ministry to Mexican Americans involved in drugs and gangs. Currently he is the pastor of a Victory Outreach church. The congregation does not identify itself as Latino, though the vast majority of its members are of Latino descent. He loves to minister in Spanish, though he speaks Spanglish.

Johnny knows that Victory Outreach is usually much more successful than any government gang- or drug-intervention program. A very high percentage of those who are converted through Victory Outreach are able to leave that lifestyle behind permanently. At times he gets frustrated with the local government because they spend a lot of money on gang- and drug-intervention programs that have a much lower success rate. But he wonders whether their church should try to obtain government money. Will the money make it possible for them to expand the program, or will it make them less dependent on the Holy Spirit?

### How Do Single Latinas Pastor in the Latino Context?

Flor Martínez had a clear sense that God had called her to be a pastor. Flor is a Mexican American who was born in Texas, but whose family migrated to California after having been migrant farm workers for a period of their lives. She was raised in a Latino Assemblies of God church, and that was where she felt the call to ministry. She went to college and then earned a seminary degree. After that, an existing Assemblies church invited her to begin a ministry among migrant workers. Though Flor feels more comfortable speaking English, she has worked very hard to improve her Spanish so that she can serve her church community more effectively.

Because of her success in ministry, she has become a model for other single Assemblies of God Latinas who have a call to ministry in the Latino community. It seems like Latino churches can accept the leadership of younger single Latinas like Flor, even though most of the few women who serve as pastors of Latino Assemblies of God churches are married and middle-age. Seminary education seems to provide a credential that makes it possible for a Latino church to accept her leadership.

## A Protestant Church of Hispanic Descent

One of the original goals of the Protestant missionaries was to Americanize the Mexican population. That certainly was the implicit goal of the church that sent a bus through David Perez's neighborhood to take children to church. The church leadership described their work as helping these young "Mexicans" escape the poverty and be able to dream of a better future by becoming Protestant Christians. David's parents wanted the best for him, and they allowed him to go to Sunday school. He became a believer in that church, and his parents saw many positive changes in his life. The church helped him get a scholarship to go a Bible college. Little by little, he felt compelled to leave his parents' old ways and use his pastor as a mentor and model of the future. By the time he finished Bible college, he no longer identified himself as a Latino or Hispanic. If someone insisted that he define his ethnic heritage, he would say that he is an American of Hispanic descent.

David became a pastor and is now leading a charismatic church in a predominantly Latino neighborhood. Services are all in English, even though there are many Spanish-dominant people in the area. The church is part of one of the charismatic movements that developed in the Los Angeles area, and it makes sure its congregation looks like the larger majority-culture congregations of the movement. Just about everyone in the church is Latino, and the movement of which they are a part has several Latino congregations. But they do not want to identify with anything Latino. The church does not relate to Latino churches and has decided not to allow a sister Latino church to use its facilities. The church members perceive themselves as people who have successfully integrated into U.S. society, and they want to be sure that everyone around them knows it. They are a growing congregation that seems to have tapped into the sentiment of many Latinas in their neighborhood.

### Liberal, Protestant, Latina

Marisol González's life will challenge anyone's stereotypes about Latina Protestants. She is an Episcopal priest of Puerto Rican descent who was born and raised in New York City. Marisol leads a small parish of mostly Mexican immigrants, but she understands that her principal focus of ministry should be the broader Latino community. She is very involved in community issues and is at the forefront of abortion rights and issues related to the gay community.

But Marisol is very proud of the fact that she became a Protestant believer through the influence of a large charismatic church. She wants to be a bridge between her charismatic Latino roots and the mainline denomination of which she is now a part. Marisol is proudly a liberal Latina Episcopal priest.

## A Mexican American with a Vision for the World

Joe Nava has his roots in the Apostolic Assembly of the Faith in Christ Jesus. His ancestors were among the founders of the movement in 1925. He has served in various senior roles within the denomination. He currently pastors one of the largest Apostolic churches in the country. The church has Sunday worship services in both English and Spanish. The denomination has a history of work in Mexico, and its links to its sister denomination in Mexico go back to the origins of the movement in California. Yet even though the denomination's roots are among Mexicans and Mexican Americans, and most of the members of his church are Mexican or Mexican American, he is not convinced that the denomination should continue to put a strong mission emphasis on Mexico.

He hopes that the Apostolic Assembly will focus less on Mexicans and make more time to reach out beyond the Latino community. He is particularly interested in seeing the Apostolic Assembly become more mission-oriented around the world. He knows that many of the people in Apostolic churches have ecclesial, historical, and familial links across the U.S.–Mexican border, but he would like to see the denomination broaden its mission focus. Nonetheless, his denomination is so closely tied to Mexico and to the ongoing migration north and south that he knows that this work will likely continue to absorb most of the denomination's energy.

## How to Rapidly Grow a Latino Protestant Church

José Guerra has been a well-known international conference speaker in the Latin American and Latino *evangélico* community for many years. A well-known English-language congregation has invited him to become their pastor of Spanish-language ministries. The assumption of the church is that because he is well known in the Spanish-speaking world, he will attract many people to the congregation. So far the plan seems to be working. The church is now expanding its reach through Spanish-language radio and television.

Of course, many of the pastors of the Latino churches in the area are not too happy. A person they had previously admired as a public personality has now become their competition and is drawing people from their congregations. Nonetheless, the church is having an impact and is encouraging other Euro-American churches to seriously consider doing something similar.

## Does He Speak with a Tejano or Texan Accent?

The lines between "Hispanics" (previously "Mexicans") and "Anglos" in the Baptist world of Texas have historically been well drawn. All the churches are part of the same convention and of the same associations. But historically each group of churches has ministered in their own world. That is changing as English-dominant Latinos such as Héctor García have made their mark in both Latino and Anglo denominational structures. Héctor has earned his stripes in both Latino and Euro-American Baptist circles. He has been a successful pastor and church planter in the Latino community, but he also has an advanced theological degree and has served the denomination for many years, in both Latino and Anglo Baptist organizations. He is a third-generation Baptist and is very committed to his denomination.

Yet Héctor sometimes seems to find himself caught in the middle. How should he define himself in the Baptist world? Is he one of those "Mexicans" that Baptists wanted to evangelize more than 100 years ago because they would eventually take over the denomination? Is he just one more assimilated Latino? Or is he part of something new that is happening among Baptists in Texas?

### Shouldn't Latino Youth Ministry Be in English?

The Especialidades Juveniles conference in the United States breaks all of the stereotypical molds related to Latino youth. It is part of a larger Protestant ministry that does youth conferences in English. It holds major conferences in Latin America but has found that many Latino Protestant youth are very connected to Latin American Protestant youth culture. It began a national conference for Latino youth, in Spanish, and is now expanding the project to facilitate the linkage between Latin American and Latino youth. The lines between Latinos and Latin Americans are often blurred since many of the youth workers live transnational lives.

Most of the Latino youth pastors and leaders who are part of Especialidades are proudly and completely bilingual. They teach seminars in Latin America and do youth conferences in English. They inhabit the bilingual world of the young people they work with and feel comfortable working in English or in Spanish, with Latinos, with Latin Americans, or with majority-culture young people in the United States. Especialidades has recently taken steps to expand its Spanish-language work in the United States and to further link Latino and Latin American youth through international youth conferences in Spanish in the United States.

### What If You Really Want to Serve the Latino Church?

Adán Martínez reflects many of the tensions faced by U.S.-born Latinos raised in Latino Protestant churches who want to serve the Latino community but who have been formed for ministry by majority culture. Adán grew up in a Latino evangelical church. At an early age he made a commitment to follow Jesus, and he became the youth pastor when he was only slightly older than the young people he was leading.

When he finished high school, Adán went to a Christian college of his own denomination. There he was exposed to the expectations and opportunities of the majority-culture churches of his denomination. Because of his sense of call to ministry, his professors encouraged him to go to seminary. Now that he is at seminary, he finds that (1) pastors from majority-culture churches are very interested in his future and are offering him ministry opportunities, and (2) the Latino leaders of his youth are not so sure about him because he has not earned his stripes by serving as pastor in a church before going to seminary. Both the majority-culture and Latino leaders are glad he went to seminary. The problem is one of process. Adán is in trouble with the Latino leaders because he went to seminary at the encouragement of Anglo leaders, before he had proven himself as a leader in a Latino church. The Anglos expect their leaders to go to seminary first, so they are very happy with him. It seems like Adán's mistake is that he did the right thing by going to seminary but did it in the wrong way by not following the common model among Latino pastors in his denomination. It is yet to be seen whether the Latino leaders of his denomination will be able to make room for him to develop as a leader, or whether he will choose to minister with only the blessing of the Anglos.

### Puerto Rico Is Not Part of the Future

Francisco and Elizabeth Peña are like many young educated Puerto Ricans. They both grew up in churches of one of the largest Pentecostal denominations on the island. They made a personal commitment to faith and sensed that God called them to ministry. They both completed their university studies in Puerto Rico and decided to come to the mainland to study at a seminary.

But they made the decision with a fairly clear sense that they would not return to the island. They want to serve God and their community, but they do not see a role for themselves in Puerto Rico. From their perspective there are already too many churches, too many leaders, and too few opportunities for them to serve and have an impact on the island.

While they are completing seminary, they have become very involved in serving a Latino church in their area. As they get closer to completing their studies, they are looking at various urban areas with large Latina populations so that they can establish themselves and serve the Latino community. They enjoy going to Puerto Rico during vacations and always come back energized. But Puerto Rico is not part of their future.

### Proudly Latino in His Mestizo World

If you run into Joe Williams, you are not likely to immediately think "Latino." His name and his look do not fit any common stereotype of who is Latino. But Joe has deep Latino Protestant roots. He is directly related to one of the first ordained Latino Protestant pastors from the 19th-century Southwest. Joe is part of a long line of Latino pastors in his denomination. Because he is also the family historian, he inherited his great-great-grandfather's theological library.

Joe is proud of his Latino Protestant heritage and of his family's contribution to Latino Protestantism in his denomination. But he sometimes wonders whether his children will carry on the legacy. With a last name like Williams, they do not always identify with things Latina. They are committed Protestants, but he is not sure that they will be Latino Protestants.

### Dreaming with an Incomplete Dream Act

The "Dream Act" children in California are those whose parents brought them as undocumented aliens when they were little, but who went to school here. Because of California law, Julia Motessi was able to study in a public university paying in-state tuition. She is an active member of her large Latino congregation and is actively involved in the community development programs of her church. She worked very hard with many other Dream Act children to try to pass the national Dream Act that died in the Senate at the end of 2010. She is part of a program that works with undocumented minors who were caught by immigration agents crossing the border without parents or adult guardians. Julia is fully integrated into U.S. society and has most of the legal documents that would identify her as a legal resident in the United States.

Julia is considering entering seminary to become a pastor. Because she fits so well, she can easily pass. The likelihood that immigration authorities would ever catch her is next to nil. But this leaves her with an ethical and moral dilemma. Should she publicly let people know of her status so that the majority culture can see her value and contribution, risking her future in the United States? Julia continues dreaming, caught in a reality she did not create, but which will influence her future.

### Latin American Pentecostals in a Liberal Mainline Denomination?

Eliseo Méndez was a Pentecostal pastor in his country of origin for several years. His father was a pastor, and he worked alongside his father before becoming a pastor himself. He came to the United States to study at a seminary on a student visa. While he is studying, he has begun to pastor a small Latina congregation. He later learned that the church is part of a liberal mainline denomination, but that Latin American Pentecostal immigrants, like him, pastor most of the Latino churches of that denomination in his area.

The denomination seems to be desperately looking for Latino pastors and so has been willing to accept people who are not from the denomination's theological tradition, as long as they have a seminary degree. At times Eliseo feels uncomfortable because the denomination is too liberal from his perspective, particularly on issues such as same-sex marriage. But so far he has stayed because he has been free to lead the church without much outside influence and has found that even the older members of the congregation, who have strong denominational links, disagree with the denomination's position. The small Latino congregation is starting to grow, though some Latino Protestants from other denominations leave when they find out the church's denominational affiliation. Denominational leaders have promised to help him apply for a religious worker visa when he completes his studies, something they have already done for other pastors. Eliseo is still trying to make sense of this situation. He confesses that he came to the United States to study with the intention of finding employment and staying. But he never thought he would potentially become an ordained pastor in a denomination with which he disagrees so much.

## A Foreigner in His Own Land and Also in His Denomination?

All those Latinos whose roots are in the Southwest know that the Census Bureau does not acknowledge their existence. The 2010 census gave Latinos many boxes they could mark to clearly distinguish their "race" and national background. But nowhere was there a box that gave them the option of stating their national background as "Southwest when it was part of Spain (or Mexico)" or anything like this. So Joe Maes marked the "Other" box, once again.

Joe seems to have spent his life marking "Other" when describing himself. He is a fifth-generation Latino Protestant, so he grew up being "other" in his predominantly Latino Catholic community. His denomination has spent a great deal of money evangelizing his people but has never quite figured out how Latinos fit in the denomination; again he is an "other." But he also seems to be an "other" in his ministry commitments. He has worked in Latin America for his denomination, but most Latin Americans do not understand the history of Latinos whose history is in the Southwest. Their tendency is to see him as an Anglo, though most people can see that Joe is not that. So even in Latin America he is "other."

## The Undocumented Serving the Undocumented

Elisa Gómez came to the United States more than 20 years ago, fleeing the political violence in her country. She requested political asylum because she and members of her family had been specifically threatened, but her application was rejected. Because of the threats on her life, Elisa decided to stay in the United States and lost her legal status. While in the United States, she became a Protestant believer and later studied in a Latino Bible institute to become a pastor. Her congregation knows of her status, and many of the church members are in a similar situation. The denomination of which she is a part is attempting to get her a religious worker visa, since she has been a pastor for several years, but it is not clear whether that is possible. But the denomination also faces an ethical dilemma: should they ordain Elisa, knowing that she has no legal status in the United States, even though she is effectively serving a congregation and meets all of the requirements for ordination?

### Sacrificing Friends and Family to Follow Jesus

José Cantú is a border person who happened to be born in Mexico, even though several of his siblings were born in the United States, when the family was doing migrant farm work in the States. He was raised as a nominal Catholic but never practiced that faith. José became an undocumented worker, on a whim, many years ago and then married a Latina who had been raised in a Latino Protestant church. Within a few years of marriage, both had a strong conversion experience and soon went to a Spanish-language Bible institute to prepare for ministry. His siblings ostracized José for becoming a Protestant, though over the years most of them have since also become Protestants.

José and his wife were taught that one had to be willing to sacrifice everything, including friends and family, for ministry. They moved far from their extended family to plant churches among Latino migrant workers and served in migrant farm-working communities all of their active lives. But they continued to evangelize their extended families and eventually became the unofficial family chaplains, even of the members of the family who remained Catholic. Now that they are officially retired, they continue providing pastoral support to a small congregation meeting in the facilities of a large majority-culture congregation.

They have never had a doubt about God's call on their lives or about the importance of sacrificing all for ministry. Yet they recognize that their children are not so sure about this decision. Would they have had stronger ties to family if they had grown up nearer to their extended family? Would their grandchildren feel closer to them if they had not made this sacrifice?

### Marrying Back into Latino Ministry

Joe Pérez was well on his way to becoming an English-dominant Mexican American and might have become a nominal Protestant, but he married a South American immigrant who was part of a well-known Pentecostal family in her country of origin. They have now been married for many years, and they have been pastors of several Spanish-language congregations. Joe and his wife are co-pastors of a church linked to one of the newer charismatic movements in the United States. But because of his wife's links, their church is strongly influenced by what is happening in Latin America, and their church interacts regularly with churches from the south.

Because the movement of which they are a part now has churches in Latin America, their social networks cross denominational and international borders in a web of relationships that cannot be easily untangled. They are also linked to Latino churches of other denominations through family ties. If you start describing the links of their church members, their web of ministry ties is truly a spider's web, beautiful to look at, but impossible to easily track.

### Migrants as Missionaries

José Garza was a Cuban exile who was widowed after raising a family and retiring. He became a Pentecostal Christian and met a widow from Nogales, Sonora, on the U.S.–Mexican border, at his new church. He has always had a heart for serving others and was looking for a place to dedicate the last active years of his life when he and his wife visited Nogales. They saw the need in a new neighborhood made up mostly of people who went north hoping to get into the United States but who have ended up on the Mexican border. Because it was a new neighborhood, there was a lot of need and many opportunities for service. Occasional food bags became a regular feeding program for children so that they could have a nutritional meal before going to school. Tutoring became an after-school program, and all of the work become a church planting project.

José's church in the United States supports their work in Nogales. Some of the church members are undocumented, so they cannot visit Nogales without danger of not being able to return. But they can sell tamales to raise funds for the project. Those who have legal documents travel regularly to Nogales to help however they can, always taking supplies for the various projects. Jose's U.S. church is part of a Pentecostal denomination that has a sister denomination in Mexico. But because of the politics between both denominations, he cannot legally identify the Mexican church with the denomination in Mexico.

The pastor of José's U.S. church is a Central American immigrant who is now the overseer of the young congregation and ministry in Nogales. He is ordained in his Pentecostal denomination, and their church gives the expected amounts for denominational support and mission projects. But the denominational projects are seen as that: something from out there.

The congregation in Nogales is their project and part of their ministry commitment, similar to what they do in their neighborhood.

Nogales also became the point of encounter with others interested in working in the same neighborhood. Maribel, a daughter of *tejano* migrant workers who later became a public school teacher, heard God's call to leave teaching and to develop a mentoring program for the children of the migrants in Nogales. She and her husband have a number of friends in the States who provide financial support for their efforts. Maribel and José are coordinating efforts with each other and with the local schools to best serve the children.

### What If You Outgrow Your Latino Church?

Rut Pérez is a Latin American immigrant, but she came at an early age and grew up in the United States. She is proudly Latina. Rut grew up in a Latino evangelical church where she made a confession of faith and was baptized. She got married in that church and participated in its leadership. Several years ago she had tensions with the pastor of her church, who was a recent immigrant, and she and her husband decided to join a large English-language charismatic church. There are many Spanish-speaking Latinos in her church, and they relate well to each other. Rut loves all things Latino but always compares Latino churches negatively to her church, even though she knows very few Latino churches.

Because a close relative is the pastor of a Latino church, she occasionally visits and is even willing to help out, as necessary. But she is convinced that the Latino church is part of her past, an institution for those who do not fit in a church like hers.

### Immigration and Customs Enforcement (ICE) as a Missionary Sending Agency?

Rafael Gutiérrez worked many years in Los Angeles, where he learned the construction trade. There he had a strong conversion experience and became a Pentecostal lay pastor. He and a fellow lay pastor, Francisco, would often travel to Mexico to support the mission work of their church.

After a few years Rafael wandered away from his Christian commitment and got himself in legal problems. Because of those problems he lost his legal status in the United States and got deported. His wife, who is a legal resident, was originally from Tijuana, so he ended up there. His first response was to return to the United States as an undocumented worker, but while in Tijuana he reconciled his life with God and began to work in one of the many poor neighborhoods of the city.

Gradually he and his wife started a church, which included a preschool and a feeding program for children before they went to school. Because he had building experience, he built the church's sanctuary and rooms for the preschool and feeding program.

One of the things that stood out for Rafael was the extremely substandard housing many of the people lived in. He worked with one of the church's families, who owned a small property, and learned that he could build a small U.S.-style, wood-frame house for about $2,000, as long as all the labor was donated. This was still a great deal of money, but he got some friends in the United States to help him raise the funds, and they built one home.

He was able to reconnect with his old ministry colleague, Francisco, who connected him to his working-class Latino Pentecostal church in Los Angeles. The church had several members with roots in Tijuana, some with legal documents and others without them. But because of these links, they decided to begin working with Rafael. This became a joint venture of poor people working together, a poor people's Habitat for Humanity, if you will. The families in Tijuana had to obtain legal title to a property and had to be willing to work as volunteers on several building projects. The U.S. congregation would raise the $2,000 through yard sales and the selling of tamales and *pupusas*. Since many of the church people were involved in the construction trade, those who had legal documents would volunteer on weekends, working alongside Rafael, the homeowners, and other local church members.

One of the regular supporters of this project is João Mendoça, who arrived in the United States as an undocumented alien from Brazil in 1986, when the United States passed the Immigration Reform and Control Act. A friend encouraged him to go to a rural Latino community where a farmer was willing to sell him a letter stating that he had been a farmworker during the last few months so that he could qualify for amnesty. He ended up becoming a resident and then a U.S. citizen. But the links to working-class Latinos tied him closely to the Latino community. Later, João became a Protestant believer and naturally joined a Latino Pentecostal congregation. He learned the building trade and was looking for a way to use his skills to serve others as part of his Christian service.

When João heard about the building project in Tijuana, through the Central American pastor of his church, he decided to become a regular part. He now goes to Tijuana a couple of weekends a month, whenever a building project is going.

Rafael now says that God worked through ICE, sending him to Tijuana where he reconciled himself with God and found an important place to serve. This project just finished building its 12th home, and they assume that they will be able to continue pastoring the church and providing services, such as affordable housing, for a long time. As long as there are migrant workers in Los Angeles and migrants in Tijuana trying to make it to Los Angeles, they have a place to serve.

This transnational network of migrants consists completely of working-class people who never would be able to raise enough money for traditional Protestant missionary efforts. But they are sure that God called them to be a part of God's work in the world. Their only concern is that the international border is an inconvenience for their ministry. It does not define their relationships or the places where they serve, but it does make it difficult for some people to serve directly; and it sure takes a long time to get back across the border when they are returning to the United States!

## What These People Have in Common

All of the people whose stories have been told have a Protestant understanding of Christian faith. Their faith is clearly an important part of who they are as people, and they are committed to their faith. There is a clear Christian core, though there is significant movement out from that core. In that sense they reflect the diversity of Protestantism, but with a strong Pentecostal tinge. Commitment to God and to God's mission in the world is a common theme among them all; they serve because God changed their lives.

They are also all Latinos, or Hispanics, at least as far as the Census Bureau is concerned. Most wear the term proudly, though they have taken it many different directions. For some it is an important part of who they are today, and for others it is part of their heritage. Some more recent immigrants are not even sure why they are called by those terms. Others, particularly those who have been in the United States for several generations, seem to be fleeing from a Latino or Hispanic identity.

For most of them, their Protestant faith, their culture, and their Latino ethnic identity are all part of who they are. Most Latina Protestants tie Latino and Protestant into a sometimes uneasy knot. Others have separated their Latino and Protestant identities but have kept both, and some seem to have chosen one over the other.

These are the varied faces of Latina Protestantism.

## CHAPTER SEVEN

# *Mañana* as a Way of Being

The word *mañana* has a wide meaning and many connotations. Though it literally means "tomorrow," in common parlance it usually just means "not today." It can refer to any undetermined time in the future. For some, *mañana* carries the negative connotation of putting things off indefinitely, creating a sense that Latin Americans never get around to doing things. In his book *Mañana: Christian Theology from a Hispanic Perspective,* Protestant Latino theologian Justo González also recognizes that *mañana* has sometimes become the "discouraged response" of those who have worked to bring change, only to see that their efforts never seem to become reality. From this perspective *mañana* becomes utopia (the non-place) or only the hope for life after death.

But *mañana* is also the "radical questioning" of today, a belief that God is yet at work in the world creating something new. To be a Latino Christian—and a Latina Protestant in particular—is fundamentally to believe that the God who continues to interact with humanity will continue to do so in the future. *Mañana* is also a word of judgment since it points to the fact that things could be better in the United States and in the world. It is a willingness to question and to challenge the "innocent" reading of U.S. history, calling the country to address its corporate sins, so that it can continue to grow toward a greater *mañana*.

This is Latino Protestantism at its best. As a people of *mañana*, Latino Protestants can confess that

> the world will not always be as it is. It will not even be an outgrowth of what is. God who created the world in the first place is about to do a new thing—a thing as great and as surprising as that first act of

creation. God is already doing this new thing, and we can join it by the power of the Spirit! Mañana is here! True, mañana is not yet today, but today can be lived out of the glory and the promise of mañana, thanks to the power of the Spirit.[1]

It is from a *mañana* perspective that we venture to guess about what the future might be like as Latino Protestants grow and have an increasingly important role in the United States.

Latinos have been a part of the United States for more than 160 years. They have contributed to the United States through their labor and their sacrifice. They have adapted to the dominant culture in many ways but have not disappeared into the melting pot. Because of the varied experiences and responses of the Latina community, the United States is today the second-largest Spanish-speaking country in the world. But at the same time, the number of Latinas who have fully assimilated into dominant culture, do not speak Spanish, and are marrying outside of the Latino community continues to increase. The flow of legal immigrants from Latin America continues at a steady pace, and everything seems to indicate that the United States will need more laborers from Latin America, especially once the bulk of the baby boomer generation retires. And until the country develops a comprehensive immigration reform law that takes into account the needs of future flow, which, sadly, seems unlikely, the labor demands will probably also contribute to an increase in undocumented migration from Latin America.

The unique history, geography, and economic relationship between the United States and Latin America make it probable that migration south to north will continue to be an important part of the Latina story for the foreseeable future. Latinos look like previous immigrant groups from Europe in many respects. But the unique aspects of Latino reality make it probable that Latinos will always be one step away from becoming exactly like those previous immigrant experiences.

As the Latina population continues to grow, everything seems to indicate that it will continue to diversify. There are many different visions of what the future might look like, of how Latinos will participate in U.S. society in the future. The religious dimension is one very important variable in the community that will likely continue to diversify, but one that will also have an important impact on how Latinas impact the United States. As Latina Protestants continue to diversify, a number of issues, both internal and external, are likely to influence how Latino Protestantism develops and how Latinos participate in Protestant churches and in society.

# Looking into the Future of the Latina Protestantism— Harbingers of the Future

The future of Latino Protestantism is closely linked to the future of Latinas in the United States. Latinos will be affected by dominant society's attitudes toward how minorities participate in broader society and by the future flow of immigrants, U.S. foreign policy in Latin America, and a number of related issues. Each of the following issues portends a different scenario for the future of Latinos in the United States, even though, even as dominant society seeks to define us, we will also define ourselves and impact this country. The directions these issues take the United States will also have a direct impact on Latina Protestantism.

## Immigration and the Latino Community

At the time of this book's writing, the most controversial national issue affecting how Latinos "fit" in the United States is immigration reform. The combination of a weakened economy with the overall changing demographics of the country has created an "anti-Latino" environment in some parts of the country that could expand. Immigration is not a new issue in the Latina community, since, as we saw in chapter 2, migration from Latin America has historically increased or decreased depending on labor needs in the United States and on the changing political and economic situations in various Latin American countries, particularly those that have sent significant numbers of migrants in the past. U.S. laws related to immigration and attitudes toward the undocumented have also varied, depending on the national mood. But the fairly constant legal and undocumented migration from Latin America has created complex issues related to national identity, how to deal with a broken immigration system, relations between the United States and Latin America, transnationality, and the place of minority communities in this country.

Because of the way the terms *Hispanic* and *Latino* are used, they include people born in the United States, Puerto Ricans if they move to the mainland, and both legal residents and the undocumented alien who just crossed the border while you were reading this section. Because the terms are used so broadly, they create confusion both within the community and with larger society. For those who fear the cultural and ethnic changes happening in the United States, Latinos are the clearest manifestation of the "threat." It does not matter whether they were born here, whether they are here legally, or whether they are migrant workers—Latinos are perceived as a threat by some because they are growing and because many choose to maintain their own culture and language, even as they participate in and contribute to U.S. society. In practical terms this means that for many people in the United States, practically all Latinos are assumed to be undocumented, particularly if they are speaking Spanish.

But undocumented migration also creates dilemmas within the community. A small percentage of Latinas agree with those who want tougher action against the undocumented. But most find themselves trying to figure out how to respond in light of such negative attitudes in some segments of the United States. A key question for many Latinos at the end of 2010 and early 2011 had to do with how to respond to the law in Arizona (S1070) that authorized law enforcement to ask for legal documentation if a person "looked" undocumented. How does one confront a policy that for many Latinos seems like "legalized" racism, but that enjoys the support of the majority of people in the United States, even though many of those same people recognize that it might result in racial profiling? Many Latinas have undocumented relatives, friends, or fellow employees. How does one walk with them? How does one deal with a broken immigration system, and its changing and inconsistent application, that sometimes accepts and sometimes rejects the undocumented and sometimes rejects those who have a legal right to be here? What does the individual Latino do when he is treated as undocumented, even though his ancestors have been here for generations? How do Latinos help the country address the complexities of the links between U.S. political and economic policy in Latin America and migration? What about future flow and the increased labor needs the country is likely to face in the next few years?

The issue of immigration reform has created a strengthened commitment to political participation among many Latina Protestants. Before this topic came to the forefront, the Latino Protestant vote, particularly of evangelicals and Pentecostals, was being courted by social conservatives because of issues such as abortion and same-sex marriage. But Latina Protestants demonstrated that their concerns cross the traditional political lines. If the issue of comprehensive immigration reform remains unresolved, they will likely decide to become more involved in the political and civic process, both to serve the undocumented and to work alongside non-Latinos to create a different political environment.

Latino Protestants have already brought the issue to the forefront in their denominations. Several denominations have taken strong pro-immigrant stances because of the influence of Latina Protestant leaders. Even conservative denominations such as the Assemblies of God and the Southern Baptists have taken strong stances in favor of immigration reform. The National Hispanic Christian Leadership Conference (NHCLC) worked closely with the National Association of Evangelicals (NAE) to get them to work on behalf of immigration reform. This issue continues to affect all Protestant denominations at several levels. For example, during the writing of this book, the Mennonite Church USA has been debating whether it can afford to cancel a national convention it had scheduled for 2013 in Arizona. Latino Mennonites have made it clear that they will not attend if the conference is held in that state.

Migration patterns also create ministry opportunities and responsibilities for Latina Protestant churches. The existing legal flow means that churches need to be constantly aware of new immigrants and how to best serve them. But the existing undocumented community presents a different set of challenges. Most of the 11–12 million undocumented have become part of the national social fabric, yet have no way to influence decisions made about them. Many of them are part of Latino Protestant churches. What does pastoral care and support mean in relationship to these people and their U.S.-born and raised children? What role should Latino Protestant churches and pastors take in advocating for them in a system that benefits from their labor but does not want to deal with their presence?

Because the United States is so closely linked to Latin America, it is likely that issues related to migration from that region will continue to be part of the national debate into the foreseeable future. Latino Protestants—even those who historically have not wanted a voice in the public arena—will be impacted and will likely have to respond. Will they choose to seek acceptance among those who are anti-immigrant, or will they take the risk of standing with those who have no voice?

### Puerto Rico's Future

The long-term status of Puerto Rico continues to be an unresolved issue. The 2010 census pointed out two important issues related to the island. First of all, more people of Puerto Rican descent now live on the mainland than on the island. Second, Puerto Rico was one of only two states or entities to lose population between 2000 and 2010.[2] This seems to be due not to a dropping birth rate, but to the fact that more Puerto Ricans are leaving the island than are being born there. Since Puerto Ricans are U.S. citizens, they are free to move to the mainland and seek new employment opportunities, if they so desire.

Since Puerto Ricans are the second-largest Latino group, the short-term situation on the island and its long-term political status both affect the Latino population directly. If Puerto Rico were ever to become a state or go in the opposite direction and become independent, this would create many other issues that would affect the Latino community. But currently the situation is that one of the constant migratory sources of the growth of the Latina population is legal and completely unregulated. Many of those moving are more educated than the Latino population at large, so Puerto Rico is likely exporting an educated labor force.

This is having a direct impact on several Latino Protestant denominations, particularly those with a historical connection to the island. Several of the mainline denominations have a growing number of new Latino churches because of the new patterns of Puerto Rican migration. These denominations are drawing on Puerto Rican pastors and leaders because these leaders usually have a seminary education from a U.S.-accredited seminary on the island (the Evangelical Seminary of Puerto Rico), and many have ministry experience. Denominations such as the Disciples of Christ and the Presbyterian Church (USA) are "overrepresented" in the percentage of Puerto Ricans who are in leadership positions among Latinos. Several of the Pentecostal denominations, particularly those with Puerto Rican ties, are also growing and are drawing new pastors and church members from the island.

Since Puerto Rico has a high percentage of Protestants, this type of situation is likely to continue. Denominations that require seminary education for their pastors can easily obtain a graduate from the island without a major investment. Given the current economic situation on the island, continued migration to the mainland is likely. This makes it likely that Puerto Rico will continue to provide educated leaders for Latino Protestant churches and denominational positions into the foreseeable future. Puerto Rico will also continue to be a key component in the transnational cross-fertilization of Latina and Latin American Protestantism.

### The Role of Spanish in the United States

Spanish has now surpassed English as the second-most-spoken first language in the world, behind Mandarin, and the United States is one of the largest Spanish-speaking countries in the world. Even though a significant percentage of Latinos do not speak Spanish, the number of Spanish speakers in this country continues to grow. Because, overall, U.S. Latinos are economically better off than their counterparts in Latin American countries, the Spanish-speaking population represents an important market for global Spanish-language media.

Univisión, the principal Spanish-language network in the United States, often competes with English-language networks for market share in strong Latino markets. Spanish-language disc jockeys are usually competing with each other for the number one position in several radio markets, with English-language jockeys behind them. The number of broadcast, cable, and satellite offerings in Spanish continues to grow. Recently the newspaper

*El Mundo* from Spain established a U.S.-based Internet news service because of the growing Spanish-speaking readership in the country. Mexican multimedia giant Televisa, the largest provider of Spanish-language media in the world, recently signed a multiyear contract to invest in Univisión, which means that Televisa is betting that the Spanish-language market in the United States will continue to grow.[3]

There has been some backlash against this growth, particularly in the form of English-only initiatives and the curtailing of bilingual education in some states. Latinos also have not demonstrated a strong commitment to the language after two to three generations. But the role of Spanish in the public arena continues to increase. It currently seems likely that the number of Spanish speakers in this country will continue to grow, though the total will be only a percentage of the Latina community. What could change that equation would be a very strong anti-Spanish attitude throughout the country that might result in legal actions against the use of Spanish in the media or strong enough social pressure such that fewer Latinos would be open to continuing to use the language. But the traditionally libertarian attitude toward business makes it likely that Spanish-language media will continue to be free to expand, serving as one of the principal supporters of continued Spanish language usage in the United States.

The number of Spanish-language Protestant churches continues to grow, even as many Latino churches are expanding their programs, offering activities in both Spanish and English. Spanish-language Protestant media is alive and well in this country, though it is being impacted by the same market forces affecting the larger market, particularly in the area of print media. But Spanish-language Christian radio is particularly popular among Latina Protestants in most major Latino markets.

If Spanish continues to have a strong role in the United States, Latino Protestant churches likely will continue to have an increasingly important role in the mission and focus of their denominations. On the other hand, if social pressures and/or the end of significant migration from Latin America were to cause the role of Spanish to diminish, then Latino Protestant churches might need to rethink how they define their mission. Given the probability of a long-term role for Spanish, but also of an increasing number of English-dominant Latinos with a strong Latino identity, it is likely that Latino Protestant churches will need to work at models that take into account both languages for the foreseeable future.

### Latin American Economy and Politics

The complex relationship between the United States and Latin America has always tended to get more attention from Latin America than from the

United States. From the time of the Monroe Doctrine, the United States has defined a special role for itself in the region. But it often seems to forget about its "backyard," unless something happens to get the country's attention.

The most compelling issue at the time of this writing is the drug war in Mexico. The Mexican government has been trying to destroy the drug cartels, and the cartels have responded with a major wave of violence. This violence has created a lot of insecurity in various parts of Mexico, but it has also created a great deal of fear in several of the border areas of the United States. One interesting unintended consequence has been that some of the rich in northern Mexico have moved some of their assets into places such as Houston. Since they have no trouble getting a U.S. visa, some have bought a second home in the States and are spending most of their time in the States, waiting for things to calm down. Many of these rich people from northern Mexico have always been transnational people, but at this moment their movement north is linked to the wave of violence.

Some of the potential game-changers in Latin America would be the fall of the Castro brothers in Cuba or increased unrest in places such as Venezuela. Another earthquake or natural disaster, such as the one in Haiti, would also put pressure on the United States. Any changes such as these would affect the U.S. role in the region and would likely create a new migratory flow to the United States. Of course, the growing political and economic stability of much of South America could create a very different scenario, if it became a real competitor for jobs and migrant workers.

The United States is closely linked to Latin America, and a large percentage of Latinos have personal links to the region. Any abrupt social, economic, or political changes could have an impact on U.S. attitudes toward the region and toward Latinas. Latinos, and Latino Protestants in particular, need to be alert to how they can be bridges that can serve the rest of the country in understanding this complex relationship and in awareness of the need to take all of these issues into account when formulating policies related to Latin America in general and to immigration reform and border security in specific.

### Politics of the Border

Though this section could be addressed under the previous one, it is a unique situation because the border region of the Southwest has been a "borderlands" region for hundreds of years. This has been a place of encounter between ethnic groups since before the Europeans arrived and has continued to be since the time of European colonization. It has been a region where it is impossible to draw clearly defined boundaries between the region's various groups. The United States took over the Southwest and drew a clear political boundary in the area. But the border regions on both sides continue to be linked to each and to influence each, maintaining a borderlands reality. Many of the peoples of the Southwest have had relatives on both sides of the border since before there was a border there. The historical territory of some of the native peoples of the Southwest crosses the border between Arizona and Sonora. The area also has several border sister cities that depend on each other for their economic livelihood.

But the borderlands area has also often been a point of contention between the United States and Mexico. It was conquered from Mexico in a war that most people in the United States do not remember, but many in Mexico will never forget. Today the principal issues are undocumented migrants and illegal drugs. Those on the U.S. side of the border want to reinforce it to control the flow of people and drugs. But many on the Mexican side wonder why they have to pay the price of the drug cartel wars, since they are fighting to control access to the U.S. market, which the United States has not been able to control.

The recent (2010) passing of SB1070 in Arizona is an example of the connection and the tension. Those in Arizona are convinced that they need to take this type of action because the federal government does not control the undocumented from crossing the border, most of whom cross in Arizona. For Mexicans this is a sign of racial profiling, and many people with legal documents have decided not to cross into Arizona to shop. Another example is the border crossing between San Diego and Tijuana. It is the most used border crossing in the world. In spite of the recent violence, people cross the border every day, in both directions, to work, shop, and play.

The Mexican side of the border has been an area of ministry and service for U.S. Protestant churches for many years. There are many crossboundary ministries that have offices in U.S. border towns, but that work on the Mexican side. One of the rites of passage for many Euro-American Protestant youth is to do short-term missions, often in a Mexican border community and in conjunction with a Latino Protestant church that provides translators. This has decreased due to the recent violence, though it is likely to increase again once the violence subsides. More recently, many Latino Protestant churches that have members with ties to the border area have increasingly become involved in this type of ministry. These links tend to strengthen the borderlands reality since people who live on the U.S. side continue to travel regularly back across the border.

A more controversial border ministry being supported by some Protestant churches is providing water and emergency services to the undocumented who get stranded in the Arizona desert. Many people have died trying to cross the desert, and many churches and agencies see providing service as an act of compassion. But many in Arizona see this action as aiding and abetting criminals. Will Latina churches be ready to help the undocumented this way, particularly in a state that has created so much insecurity for many Latinos and where so many Euro-Americans are opposed to such ministry?

## Transnationalism

Globalization has created people who have more than one passport and more than one national allegiance. Many of these people have learned to live and navigate in more than one national environment. There are many rich people from Latin America who have homes and investments in the United States and who move back and forth regularly. There are also many U.S. citizens who have chosen to retire in Latin America because of the cheaper cost of living. But there are also many poorer people who regularly move back and forth between the United States and Latin America, both legally and without legal documentation.

These transnational people are having an impact on Latino Protestant churches. Their movement serves to cross-fertilize churches, but also as a conduit to mission. Churches are learning from each other and are moving pastors and leaders in both directions. Latino churches are also using the networks these people follow as they become involved in ministry across national boundaries. For many of these people, the national borders are inconveniences that complicate ministry but not lines that significantly differentiate a local church's work in Los Angeles from work in Tijuana or in San Salvador. These congregations follow their natural networks, many of which cross that inconvenient line called the U.S. border.

Even as the United States attempts to more clearly define and "protect" its border, more Latina Protestants are treating it merely as a bother that they need to take into account, but that does not define who they are or how they think about their relationships or their mission as Christians. Increased globalization is likely to increase this missional border crossing, even as it also increases the attempts, on the U.S. side, to define the border more clearly.

## Latino Youth Subcultures

All of the census projections assume that the largest area of future growth in the Latino community will be among U.S.-born Latinos. Immigration will likely continue to be an important source of Latino growth into the foreseeable future. Even though many people in the United States assume that most Latinos are immigrants, the reality is that most Latinas are born in the United States. Because of the size of the community, there is likely never going to be a time when most Latinos are immigrants. The U.S.-born are and will continue to be the majority and a growing percentage of the Latino population.

Latina young people are going to be the single largest area of demographic growth in various parts of the United States. In some places, such as California, Latino children are already the largest group starting school.

Clearly Latina youth represent all of the diversity presented in the drawing on Latino ethnic identity maintenance. Instituto Fe y Vida, which is involved in pastoral work among Latino youth, has identified four broad categories of young people in the life of the church. *Mainstream movers* are those who are pushing toward structural assimilation. They seem to be saying that they assume that their future lies in becoming part of majority culture. *Identity seekers* are Latina youth who are struggling to understand who they are as Latinos in the United States. *Immigrant workers* are Latinos who have migrated to the states as young adults and have a clear sense of identity with their country of origin, but who are likely to live their adult lives in the States. *Gang members* are those who have gotten lost in the midst of identity formation and seek out their community and identity in gangs. Each of these presents different challenges and responsibilities for the church.[4] Latino youth are experimenting with all of the identity options, and the church needs to be a part of the support base where they can grow to become Christians who understand how their ethnic and religious identities fit together.

Latino youth are also culture creators. In the midst of their experimentation, they are drawing from many sources and developing subcultures that will impact how they define themselves in the future. They are fleeing, returning, forming, and reforming the culture they received from their parents, mixed with the cultural influences of others. Many are choosing to marry outside of the Latino community, though the vast majority marry other Latinas. They clearly will shape the future of the Latina community. Latino churches need to both walk with them as they develop and respond to them as they ask new questions about who they are and how they fit in their world. Many of those same young people will be the pastors of some of these Latina churches and will shape the future of Latino Protestantism.

### The Changing Face of Protestantism in Latin America

Because of the historic and ongoing links between Latino and Latin American Protestantism, both are affected by what happens to the other. Many denominations continue to maintain structural links in their Spanish-language ministry that cross the Río Grande River in both directions. The practice of bringing pastors and leaders from Latin America has its counterpart in U.S. Latinos who are working in Latin America. Spanish-language Protestant media moves in both directions, often produced in the United States, but used principally in Latin America. When linked to the circular migratory patterns of transnational people, this means that changes in Latin America will affect Latino Protestants.

One of the unanswered questions is the role that the churches will have in civic society over the long term. It is not always clear whether they will be agents of transformation and renewal or whether they will eventually be absorbed into the existing social patterns. Latin American *evangélicos* have already demonstrated that they are not the clients of one political faction or another, but that they can push for change. Might Latin American Protestantism offer a different way forward for Latino Protestants than the traditional tensions between church and state in the United States or the traditional left/right categories used by the dominant political parties?

It is also clear that several churches and movements from Latin America are going to continue to send missionaries to the United States. Will these people be seen as a blessing to the church here, or will they be perceived as proselytizers? What can Euro-American Protestantism learn from the growing and dynamic church of the south?

### The Changing Migratory Patterns

Because migration is a global phenomenon, Latino Protestants also will be affected by increased migration from other parts of the world. Latinas are not only interacting with Euro-Americans; they are often interacting as much with minority peoples from other parts of the world. A sudden increase in migration from other parts of the world would also challenge Latina Protestant churches to develop a more multicultural sense of ministry in the world around them.

All of the issues mentioned in this section are pieces of the puzzle. No one issue will determine the future, but all will have an impact. Latino Protestantism will need to keep track of these issues as it seeks to be faithful to its understanding of its role.

## Latina Protestants and Protestant Churches—Issues in the Immediate Future

Latino Protestants will continue to face many of the same issues as the Latina community in the United States, including, how do Latinos fit in the denominational structures? The various Protestant groups have developed different models of participation, some of which seem to work better than others, but all of which present opportunities and challenges. And this question is being asked as the concept of denominationalism is going through major shifts.

Currently most denominations with a Latino ministry have some type of Hispanic ministry office. The Latino churches usually have some type of parallel structure for ministry and fellowship. Some have completely separate districts, and others have councils or caucuses that bring the Latino leadership together. A few groups, such as the Assemblies of God and the Church of the Nazarene, have more than one type of structure for Latino churches. It is likely that these two denominations will be the first to have to think about these relationships in new ways.

Part of the difficulty has to do with how Protestant denominations view Latinos. Some seem to view them as some type of salvation for churches that are dying. Many denominations are reporting that their only current area of growth is among Latino churches. Other segments of most denominations seem to be losing members. But Latinas also represent new ideas and ways of doing mission and thinking about the church. How much will Latinas be allowed to influence the direction and ministry of existing denominations?

Most of the denominations have Latino "experts," people whose role is to understand ministry in the community and guide the denomination toward new ministry possibilities. The question will be whether denominations are ready to have Latinos in denomination-wide positions and allow them to influence planning for the future. Up to now Latinos who have made it into higher positions have usually reached the positions as a form of affirmative action or because they were Anglicized enough that the majority felt comfortable with them. As the Latino presence becomes more prominent in several denominations, the majority will need to rethink how it is that Latinas fit.

That Latinos clearly do not have a common perspective on how to fit will make the task that much more complicated. Denominations will constantly have to respond in different ways to the various segments of the Latina community.

These issues get more complicated as the traditional Protestant model of denominationalism continues to erode. Growing numbers of independent churches will be making decisions about how to relate to Latinas, without the advantages and limitations of being a part of larger structures. Given the various ways Latinas want to be a part, the growing diversity of the community likely will be seen in the various models that churches and denominations will develop to work with and in the Latina community.

Another complexity is that it is very likely that Latin America—and other parts of the majority world—will continue to send Protestant missionaries to the United States. From the perspective of these churches, Christians in the United States have lost their way in the midst of an increasingly non-Christian or even anti-Christian culture. Whether or not U.S. Protestants agree with this perspective, they will need to decide how they are going to respond to these new missionaries. Will they be seen as a threat or a bother, or will they be accepted as sisters and brothers in Jesus Christ who can work alongside the churches in the United States?

## Contributing to U.S. Protestantism Today

Because of their unique history and location, Latino Protestants have the opportunity to contribute to religious life in the United States today and dream about how they might contribute in the future. U.S. Protestantism is going through profound changes, and Latina Protestants can help address many important issues, contributing to the continued spiritual vibrancy of the churches in this country. Most of the issues addressed have been mentioned in different places throughout the book. They are brought together here to focus on some of the specific ways Latina Protestants can be catalysts for the future.

### Working Together in Transitional Neighborhoods

As Latino Protestants take on a more active role in mission, they will not be the objects of mission in transitional communities, but significant actors in continuing to give Christian witness in these areas. As Latinas move into many of those neighborhoods, there is an excellent opportunity for Protestants of various ethnic backgrounds to develop ministries that serve both the older community that is leaving and the new community that is moving into the area.

Bilingual pastors can serve as pastoral support for the generation that is passing, providing the opportunity to celebrate what has been accomplished and to point to a new future of ministry. If denominations and churches are proactive in this process, dying congregations in urban areas can become thriving with a new vision. This gives a clear message to the generation that served that their contribution and commitment to their local community continue. It also provides an excellent way to be wise stewards of the buildings and investments in ministry of a previous generation.

### Rereading U.S. History

As the U.S. population continues to diversify, the country has to find new ways to tell its national narrative. The answer is neither a naïve Euro-centric "Christian" retelling of the story as it was told to a previous generation nor a tearing down of the legacy of this country with a secularized version that tries to deny the role of Christian faith in the formation and development of the United States or to blame Christian faith for all of the ills of the country. Latino Protestants, particularly Latino theologians, can offer a way forward using Justo González's non-innocent reading of U.S. history and of God's working in the world.

Minority peoples and new immigrants will fit in the "official" U.S. narrative to the extent that the story can be broadened to include those who have been traditionally excluded. But that will often mean having to directly address the parts of the U.S. story that are not exceptional, such as the destruction of native peoples, slavery, imperial conquest, and the use of migrant laborers from Latin America, Asia, and other parts of the world without giving them full legal status and rights. Many of the people who took these actions were Euro-American Christians who assumed they were doing God's will. To confess that these actions were wrong, and that the country still needs to address some of the legacy of those actions, merely means to accept the reality that the United States is a country of imperfect people. The best ideals of the United States will be fulfilled when its citizens are able to tell the national narrative in a non-innocent yet hopeful way. Until these parts of the story are fully incorporated into the national narrative, most minority peoples will never fully be a part.

## Connecting U.S. Protestantism to the Majority World

Protestants in the United States are connected to Protestants around the world through many formal relationships, most of which were started by the United States. But most of those relationships are unidirectional, ways for the church in the United States to "serve" others. Most U.S. Protestants do not have a truly global sense of the church. Latina Protestants—and other Protestant immigrants from the south—can serve as a bridge to the vitality of Christian faith in the global south.

As Euro-American-based Christianity continues to wane, Latinos and others linked to the global church can share from their own experience and provide the opportunity for a new revival of the churches in the United States. Latino Protestants can walk with their sisters and brothers into the new globalized reality where the church is not a Euro-American entity, but one that is truly global, one where the average Christian is more likely to be a poor Brazilian or Philippine woman than a European male.

## Learning to do Mission from Below

Protestant understandings of mission in the United States have usually been linked to a Christendom model of mission and to a concept of church linked to the nation-state. Mission has been the work of the powerful to those without power, from the center to the periphery. National borders have also traditionally defined mission. Work that crosses national borders is mission, and that which does not cross borders is ministry or "home mission."

Latina Pentecostals are turning these concepts upside down (as are many other majority world Christians). The poor are doing mission from the periphery, often to other peripheries, but also toward the center of traditional Christendom in the United States and Europe. It is the powerless who are involved in mission to the powerful, a model that looks like the church of the first century. Mission is a labor of love from the poor, not dependent on the amounts of money available for mission.

Migrants are also crossing national boundaries without distinguishing what is done within national borders and what crosses borders. Because their familial and social networks freely cross national boundaries, the ways they do mission also follow the same patterns. Transnationalism marks how they provide for their families, how many live their lives, and how they do mission.

Mission from below will be a difficult concept for many U.S. Protestants, who have always assumed that missions, money, and power go together. But as Latinas live out a missional way of life, they will model a different way of thinking about mission. Also, as the United States becomes more religiously diverse, missionaries from the majority world will provide a different way of thinking about how God is working in the world.

### New Models of Interethnic Relations

Because of how Latinos became a people, they can make no claim to any kind of racial purity. *Mestizaje* is the Latina story. In the midst of that *mestizaje,* Latinos have learned to adapt to new cultural realities, even when those realities have been imposed from outside. The new intercultural realities of being part of Latino churches in the United States are creating new *mestizajes* in the Latino diversity.

But Latinos are also developing new models of intercultural church life with other minority peoples and with Euro-Americans. They are finding ways of making room for people to worship together even as they express themselves in their own cultural/ethnic idiom. Because they are now the largest ethnic minority, Latinas will likely be one of the key components of new expressions of intercultural church life. Because of their lived experiences they will likely be able to provide models of how to go forward in this area.

### An Embodied Spirituality

Latino Protestants, and particularly Latina immigrant Pentecostals, embody a spirituality that is often missing in much of Euro-American Protestantism. They worship God in a lively manner that connects them with the divine at a deep emotional level. Their experience takes forward a commitment toward God, the church, and mission that is often missing in more established churches.

Latinas, and other majority world Protestants, will likely be at the forefront of a revival of Christian commitment among Protestants in the first world. They may even be a part of a new Protestant Reformation, one that takes into account the call of the Reformation while also connecting that call to a strong encounter with God's Spirit.

## A Diversified Future—Latino Protestants in All Segments of Life

As Latina Protestants seek to define the future, the temptation will be to assume that "my" experience is the definitive experience. Those who have taken the path of structural assimilation can easily assume that all Latinos will eventually look like them and seek to have ministry decisions shaped accordingly. Those who have fought hard to maintain Latino Protestant structures may be tempted to assume that all Latinos should care about what they have accomplished and seek to continue to support them.

Yet if current and historical trends are any indication, the Latina community will continue to diversify. A significant percentage of Latinas will marry outside of the ethnic community, though this will not always mean that the person will be structurally assimilating; some will bring their spouses into the Latino community. Nonetheless, it is clear that full structural assimilation will be the future of some segments of many Latinas. The drawing used in chapters 1 and 5 will continue to reflect the various segments of the community and the movement related to ethnic identity maintenance. Because of the likelihood of increasing labor needs as baby boomers retire, it is extremely probable that there will also continue to be new temporary and permanent migrants from Latin America. All of this movement will enrich and further diversify the people who are grouped under the Latina umbrella.

The relationship between Latino Protestants and Euro-American Protestants has a tortured history, and it is likely that there will still be a lot of pain before a good new model of working together completely emerges. Latinos have gone through many negative experiences, and many could be unsure about the value of working toward a joint future. *Mañana* might always feel like it is another step away. Yet believing in *mañana* is to believe that God continues to work.

# Conclusion

This book started as a family history, if you will. It continued as a look through the extended family picture album. But since we are the reflection of our Protestant forebears, we are as diverse as the larger Protestant community. The family includes many who hardly recognize each other, be it because of different historical backgrounds, different denominational experiences, or significant theological differences. Because of the fractured nature of Protestantism, people from some of the denominations mentioned in this book will question why others were included. Because of my own background, I personally had to push back against the voices in my head that kept questioning why I included the Seventh-Day Adventists or oneness Pentecostals.

Latinoness was created in the painful encounter of European imperial conquest into the Americas. One can almost literally say, "My Spanish great-grandfather raped my indigenous great-grandmother, and here I am." Something similar can be said of Latino Protestantism. U.S. Protestant missionaries began preaching in the Southwest and in Puerto Rico as a result of U.S. imperial expansion. Both of these painful experiences are part of the story of Latina Protestantism. Yet the experience of encounter with God trumps the painful memory for most Latino Protestants.

Latino Protestants are a very clear indication of the need for a non-innocent reading of the history of the church and of the history of the United States. In the midst of these painful encounters, men and women have experienced God's presence in their lives and have found faith and hope for *mañana*.

To be Latina and Protestant is to be at a number of crossroads and points of encounter: between Euro-American North America and Latin America, between Euro-American Protestantism and Latin American Catholicism, between the first world and the majority world, between a dying Christendom and the vital new Christian expressions of the global south, between changing notions of the nation-state and the new transnational reality of migrant peoples, and between old racialized understandings of life together in the United States and the new intercultural relationships that are developing. Yet the moniker "Latino Protestant" is so diverse that there are often at least a few Latina Protestants on both sides of all these encounters.

Latino Protestants often seem no more united than the diversity reflected in the terms *Latino* and *Protestant*. Yet there is a common thread of history and a common understanding of a personal encounter with God. It is that divine encounter that continues to provide meaning to many who live at these crossroads.

# Notes

## Introduction

1. Later, one of her sons, Deantín Guerra Jr., would also enter Protestant ministry as the director of a Christian nonprofit on the Texas–Tamaulipas border that provides affordable housing for the poor on the Mexican side of the border.

2. See Juan González, *Harvest of Empire: A History of Latinos in America* (New York: Penguin, 2001).

3. In *Who Are We? The Challenges to America's National Identity* (New York: Simon & Schuster, 2005), Huntington argued for an Anglo conformity model of participation in U.S. society. He considered Latinos a threat to that model not because they are not learning English, but because many of them are bilingual. Huntington is probably correct in stating that Latinos are a threat to the Anglo conformity model.

## Chapter 1

1. *Changing Faiths: Latinos and the Transformation of American Religion* (2007) can be found on the Pew Hispanic Center website at http://pewhispanic.org/reports/report.php?ReportID=75 (hereafter cited as Pew 2007).

2. Gastón Espinosa, Virgilio Elizondo, and Jesse Miranda, "Hispanic Churches in American Public Life: Summary of Findings" [from HCAPL project funded by Pew Charitable Trusts]. Institute for Latino Studies, University of Notre Dame. *Interim Reports* 2 (March 2003), http://latinostudies.nd.edu/pubs/pubs/HispChurchesEnglishWEB.pdf.

3. The Trinity College study, *U.S. Latino Religious Identification, 1990–2008: Growth, Diversity & Transformation,* is available on the website of the American Religious Identification Survey 2008 at http://www.americanreligionsurvey-aris.org/latinos2008.pdf (hereafter cited as Trinity study).

4. Pew 2007, p. 10.

5. Trinity study, p. 1.

6. Ibid., p. 23.

7. The study did not attempt to separate evangelicals and Pentecostals.

8. Pew 2007, p. 11.

9. Ibid.

10. The Pew study does occasionally use "3rd+" though this usage is inconsistent. For example, it is used on a chart on p. 52, though not on other charts or graphs.

11. Like most other studies of the Latino population, it does not provide a category for Latinos who trace their history to the Southwest before the U.S. takeover in 1848. Potentially, at least some of the people who fit in this category identified themselves as "Other."

12. Pew 2007, p. 11.

13. Ibid.

14. Trinity study, p. 15.

15. Oral report presented in Washington, D.C., when the report *Hispanic Churches in American Public Life* was presented to the public (author's private notes).

16. "Overview of Race and Hispanic Origin: 2010." 2010 U.S. Census Briefs, Issued March 2011 (www.census.gov/prod/cen2010/briefs/c2010br-02.pdf).

17. Pew 2007, p. 31.

18. U.S. Census Bureau, "Hispanic Heritage Month 2010: Sept. 15–Oct. 15," Facts for Features, CB10-FF.17, July 15, 2010.

19. See "Protestantism by Country," *Wikipedia,* http://en.wikipedia.org/wiki/Protestantism_by_country (last modified February 11, 2011).

20. Mexico declared independence from Spain in 1810, and by 1846 most of the Southwest was under U.S. control. The war with Mexico ended in 1848 with the Treaty of Guadalupe-Hidalgo, which ceded the Southwest to the United States and provided U.S. citizenship to the Mexicans who stayed in the United States.

21. Pew 2007, pp. 12, 41.

22. Trinity study, p. 17.

23. Pew 2007, p. 42.

24. Ibid., pp. 42, 43.

25. Ibid., p. 44.

26. Ibid., p. 47.

27. Ibid., p. 49.

28. Ibid., p. 50.

29. Ibid., p. 52.

30. Ibid., p. 50.

31. Ibid., p. 51.

32. Ibid., p. 47.

33. Pew 2007, p. 14.

34. Jehu Hanciles has studied this tendency among African immigrants. See Hanciles, *Beyond Christendom: Globalization, African Migration and the Transformation of the West* (Maryknoll, NY: Orbis Books, 2008). I am also currently involved in a research project looking at transnationalism and mission among Latino Pentecostals through the Center for Religion and Civic Culture of the University of Southern California.

35. "Protestantism by Country."

36. See "Demographics of Atheism," *Wikipedia,* http://en.wikipedia.org/wiki/Demographics_of_atheism (last modified February 26, 2011).

37. "Protestantism by Country."

38. "Demographics of Atheism."

39. See Martínez, *Walk with the People: Latino Ministry in the United States* (Nashville: Abingdon, 2008).

40. Juan González, *Harvest of Empire: A History of Latinos in America* (New York: Penguin, 2001).

41. See the U.S. Citizenship and Immigration Services website for more information: http://www.uscis.gov/portal/site/uscis/menuitem.eb1d4c2a3e5b9ac89243c6a7 543f6d1a/?vgnextoid=848f7f2ef0745210VgnVCM100000082ca60aRCRD&vgnext channel=848f7f2ef0745210VgnVCM100000082ca60aRCRD.

42. See the report of the Banco Interamericano de Desarrollo, "Remesas a América Latina y el Caribe 2009," http://www.remesasydesarrollo.org/estadisticas/remesas-a-america-latina-y-el-caribe-2009/.

43. See Andrew Greeley, "Is Ethnicity Unamerican?" *New Catholic World* 219 (June 1976): 106–12.

44. I have published previous versions of this figure in "Aculturación e Iglesia Evangélica Latina en los Estados Unidos" in *Iglesias Peregrinas en Busca de Identidad*, ed. Juan Martínez and Luis Scott (Buenos Aires: Kairós, 2004), pp. 147–64, 157, and in Martínez, *Walk with the People*, p. 19.

45. See Jorge J. E. Gracia, *Hispanic/Latino Identity: A Philosophical Perspective* (Malden, MA: Blackwell, 2000).

46. Pew 2007, p. 75.

47. Trinity study, p. 17.

## Chapter 2

1. The assumed relationship between conversion to Protestantism and assimilation is analyzed more carefully in chapters 5 and 6.

2. Melinda Rankin, *Texas in 1850* (Reprinted by Waco, Texas: Texian Press, 1966), p. 56.

3. See my book *Sea La Luz: The Making of Mexican Protestantism in the American Southwest, 1829–1900* (Denton: University of North Texas Press, 2006), particularly pp. 27–49. The quote is from p. 49.

4. See *Sea La Luz* for a history of these early Latino Protestant churches.

5. Cecil M. Robeck, *The Azusa Street Mission and Revival: The Birth of the Global Pentecostal Movement* (Nashville: Nelson Reference, 2006), p. 88.

6. These leaders formed CLADIC in 1923, and then AIC split from them. Most of the leaders, including Olazábal, eventually returned to the Assemblies of God. CLADIC still exists, though it is a very small denomination today.

7. Clifton Holland, "A Chronology of Significant Protestant Beginnings in Hispanic Ministry in the USA," in *An On-Line Handbook of Hispanic Protestant Denominations, Institutions and Ministries in the USA,* http://www.hispanicchurchesusa.net/ (last modified December 8, 2010).

8. Robert McLean, *The Northern Mexican* (New York: Home Missions Council, 1930).

9. Ibid., p. 43.

10. Samuel Ortegón, "The Religious Status of the Mexican Population of Los Angeles" (MA thesis, University of Southern California, 1932).

11. Leo Grebler, Joan W. Moore, Ralph C. Guzman, et al., *The Mexican-American People: The Nation's Second Largest Minority* (New York: The Free Press, 1970), p. 488.

12. Ibid., p. 487.

13. Ibid.

14. Ibid., p. 488.

15. Frederick L. Whitam, "New York's Spanish Protestants," *The Christian Century,* February 7, 1962.

16. Texas-Mexican Presbytery (PCUS) Records, 1861–1954, http://www.austin seminary.edu/page.cfm?p=574.

17. See Paul Barton, *Hispanic Methodists, Presbyterians and Methodists in Texas* (Austin: University of Texas Press, 2006), for a description of how the three denominations developed in Texas.

18. Harriet Kellogg, *Life of Mrs. Emily J. Harwood* (Albuquerque: El Abogado Press, 1903), p. 304.

19. See my *Sea La Luz,* pp. 89–100.

20. See Whitam, "New York's Spanish Protestants," for a model of this assumption.

21. Various versions of this quote are attributed to different sources. The Samuel Escobar quote, which I have personally heard from him, was "Liberation theology opted for the poor, but the poor opted for Pentecostalism." Another version, attributed to an anonymous nun in Guatemala states that "the Catholic Church opted for the poor, but the poor opted for Pentecostalism." This latter version is quoted by Antonio González in *The Gospel of Faith and Justice* (Maryknoll, NY: Orbis Books, 2005), p. 163.

22. See the Bracero History Archive for complete information on the program: http://braceroarchive.org/about.

23. Pew Research Center, "11.9 Million—Undocumented Immigrants in the U.S.," April 14, 2009, http://pewresearch.org/databank/dailynumber/?NumberID=778.

24. Susan Yohn, *A Contest of Faith: Missionary Women and Pluralism in the American Southwest* (Ithaca, NY: Cornell University Press, 1995), tells the story of the Presbyterian teachers and how they were originally funded by the Women's Missionary Society against the wishes of the Home Missions leadership.

25. Protestant mission boards established specific comity agreements for various countries and regions.

26. "Faith missions" are mission organizations formed outside of denominational structures to address specific needs. They are called faith missions because the missionaries do not have a salary, but have to go by "faith," depending on the offerings of people who believe in the importance of what they are doing. The agencies are usually formed outside of denominational structures.

27. See "Protestantism in Mexico," *Wikipedia,* http://en.wikipedia.org/wiki/Protes tantism_in_Mexico (last modified February 6, 2011).

28. *Foreigners in Their Native Land: Historical Roots of the Mexican Americans* (rev. ed. (Albuquerque: University of New Mexico Press, 2004) is the title David Weber gives the edited work on those Latinos whose roots are in the Southwest, but who became "foreigners" when the U.S. took over the Southwest.

29. Martínez, *Sea la Luz,* pp. 136–40.

30. Ibid., p. 112.

31. *Alelulia* (in Spanish) was meant to be a derogatory term to make fun of those who shouted "hallelujah" in church. Though I was not raised in a Pentecostal church, and we did not shout *alelulia,* we were also called that name.

32. See "Traditionalist Catholics Attack, Expel Christians in Mexico," Persecution. org, August 19, 2009, http://www.persecution.org/2009/08/20/traditionalist-catho lics-attack-expel-christians-in-mexico/.

33. "Hay una senda" was written by Tomás Estrada (copyright 1960 by R. C. Savage, assigned to Singspiration, Inc.).

34. Several presentations during the Aparecida Conference used the term "secta" to refer to the growing Pentecostal movements. The final document refers only to "grupos 'no católicos'" (*V Conferencia General del Episcopado Latinoamericanos y del Caribe Documento Conclusivo,* Aparecida, May 13–31, 2007, pp. 133ff).

35. See "Por un Estado realmente laico en Perú," March 15, 2010, http://www.laicismo.org/detalle.php?pk=2718.

36. For an example, see J. Juan Díaz Vilar, "The Challenge of Proselytism," in *Perspectivas Hispanic Ministry,* ed. Allan Figueroa Deck, Yolanda Tarango, and Timothy M. Matovina (Kansas City, MO: Sheed & Ward, 1995), pp. 83–89.

## Chapter 3

1. See J. Juan Díaz Vilar, "The Challenge of Proselytism," in *Perspectivas: Hispanic Ministry,* ed. Allan Figueroa Deck, Yolanda Tarango, and Timothy M. Matovina (Kansas City, MO: Sheed & Ward, 1995), pp. 83–89.

2. Clifton Holland, *The Religious Dimension in Hispanic Los Angeles: A Protestant Case Study* (Pasadena, CA: William Carey Library 1974), pp. 210–11.

3. Clifton Holland, "A Chronology of Significant Protestant Beginnings in Hispanic Ministry in the USA," in *An On-Line Handbook of Hispanic Protestant Denominations, Institutions and Ministries in the USA,* December 3, 2009, http://www.hispanicchurchesusa.net/.

4. Ibid.

5. Ibid.

6. Andrew M. Greeley, "The Demography of American Catholics: 1965–1990," in *The Sociology of Andrew M. Greeley* (Atlanta: Scholars Press, 1994), pp. 545–64.

7. Larry L. Hunt, "Hispanic Protestantism in the United States: Trends by Decade and Generation," *Social Forces* 77, no. 4 (June 1999): 1601–23. See also Hunt, "The Spirit of Hispanic Protestantism in the United States: National Survey Comparisons of Catholics and Non-Catholics," *Social Science Quarterly* 79, no. 4 (December 1998): 828–45.

8. Greeley, "Demography of American Catholics," p. 562.

9. Hunt, "The Spirit of Hispanic Protestantism," p. 844.

10. Oral report presented in Washington, D.C., when the report *Hispanic Churches in American Public Life* was presented to the public (author's private notes).

11. Clifton Holland, "A Working Table of Statistics on Hispanic Protestant Denominations & Church Associations in the USA, 1993–2009" (unpublished document).

12. "AG Stats Color Handout," 2009 Report (published in 2010), Statistics on the Assemblies of God, USA. http://www.ag.org/top/about/statistics/index.cfm.

13. Based on a personal interview with Jesse Miranda, longtime Latino leader within the Assemblies of God, personal interview, December 6, 2010.

14. Sergio Navarrete, "Los Distritos Latinos de las Assambleas de Dios en los Estados Unidos," in *Iglesias Peregrinas en Busca de Identidad,* ed. Juan F. Martínez and Luis Scott (Buenos Aires: Kairós, 2004), pp. 73–87. The statistical information is on p. 84. Membership totals are not compared because the 2002 report apparently used adherents instead of members.

15. Albert Reyes, "Unification to Integration: A Brief History of the Hispanic Baptist Convention of Texas" (unpublished paper).

16. Based on e-mail exchanges between the author and Albert Reyes. The principal source is the message dated January 16, 2011.

17. Leo Grebler, Joan W. Moore, Ralph C. Guzman, et al., *The Mexican-American People: The Nation's Second Largest Minority* (New York: The Free Press, 1970), p. 488.

18. "Hispanic Ten Year Summary Report (2000–2009)," Annual Church Profile, 2000–2009, compiled by the Center for Missional Research, North American Mission Board, [Southern Baptist Convention], Alpharetta, GA.

19. Pamela R. Durso and Keith E. Durso, *The Story of Baptists in the United States* (Brentwood, TN: Baptist History and Heritage Society, 2006), p. 213.

20. Reyes, "Unification to Integration."

21. Grebler et al., *The Mexican-American People,* p. 488.

22. See Manuel Vásquez, *La Historia Aun No Contada:100 Años de Adventismo Hispano* (Nampa, ID: Pacific Press Publishing Association, 2000).

23. Based on a report by Sharri Davenport of the Multi-lingual Ministries Department of the North American Division of the Seventh Day Adventists, sent by e-mail, February 3, 2011.

24. Johnny Ramírez-Johnson, Edwin I. Hernández, et al., *Avance: A Vision for a New Mañana* (Loma Linda, CA: Loma Linda University Press, 2003), p. xiii.

25. Ibid., pp. 259–79.

26. Carlos Morán, "Breve Reseña de los Latinos de la Iglesia de Dios en los Estados Unidos" (unpublished paper written in 2011 by the National Director of Hispanic Ministries, Church of God).

27. Ismael Martín del Campo, "Assamblea Apostólica de la Fe en Cristo Jesús," in *Iglesias Peregrinas en Busca de Identidad,* ed. Juan F. Martínez and Luis Scott (Buenos Aires: Kairós, 2004), pp. 89–117. The statistical data is on pp. 113–14.

28. See the website of the Iglesia Apostólica de la Fe en Cristo Jesús: http://www.iafcj.org/.

29. Robert McLean, *The Northern Mexican* (New York: Home Missions Council, 1930), p. 43.

30. Grebler et al., *The Mexican-American People,* p. 488.

31. See Justo González, *Each in Our Own Tongue: A History of Hispanics in United Methodism* (Nashville: Abingdon, 1991).

32. The demographic information was provided by Rev. Francisco Canas, the director of the National Plan for Hispanic/Latino Ministry of the United Methodist Church.

33. See the website related to the Office of Hispanic Ministries at http://www.nazarenosusacan.org/.

34. Telephone conversation with Bishop Ismael Martín del Campo of the Apostolic Assembly, January 5, 2011.

35. See the website for Spanish evangelism of the United Pentecostal Church at http://www.spanishevangelism.net/.

36. See the movement's website at http://www.ipul.us/.

37. See the movement's website at http://www.ipuh.us/.

38. "Latino/Hispanic Ministries" on the Episcopal Church USA website: http://www.episcopalchurch.org/109405_ENG_HTM.htm.

39. Juan Martínez, *Sea La Luz: The Making of Mexican Protestantism in the American Southwest, 1829–1900* (Denton: University of North Texas Press, 2006), pp. 68, 69, 164n.14.

40. Grebler et al., *The Mexican-American People*, p. 488.

41. For details on Presbyterian mission work among Latinas, see R. Douglas Brackenridge and Francisco O. García-Treto, *Iglesia Presbiteriana: A History of Presbyterians and Mexican Americans in the Southwest* (San Antonio: Trinity University Press, 1987).

42. Grebler et al., *The Mexican-American People*, p. 488.

43. The document can be found on the Presbyterian Church USA web site: http://www.pcusa.org/resource/hispanic-strategy/.

44. "Iglesia Presbiteriana (U.S.A.) Directorio Ministerios Presbiterianos Hispanos/Latinos," Oficina de Apoyo Congregacional Hispana/Latina, Ministerios Etnico Raciales, Concilio de Misión de la Asamblea General, Louisville, KY, 2010.

45. Grebler et al., *The Mexican-American People*, p. 488.

46. "2008 ABC Total Members by Ethnicity," a spreadsheet sent to the author by Salvador Orellana, National Coordinator for Intercultural Ministries of the American Baptist Home Mission Societies, on January 6, 2011.

47. Information taken from the Foursquare website, www.foursquare.org, specifically four notes: "Foursquare Forms National Hispanic Council" (posted February 2010) and "Foursquare Hispana" parts 1, 2, and 3 (posted in June 2009). The site did not report membership numbers. Much of this same information is available in James C. Scott Jr., *Aimee La Gente Hispana Estaba en su Corzaón* (Seattle: Foursquare Media, 2008).

48. Based on an interview done by Rev. Maribel Zacapa of Bishop José Jiménez, February 2, 2011.

49. According to an e-mail from Bishop José García, state supervisor for California, Church of God of the Prophecy, January 14, 2011.

50. See http://www.clany.org/. The site does not report membership numbers.

51. Pablo Jimenez, "Hispanics in the Movement," in *The Encyclopedia of the Stone-Campbell Movement* (Grand Rapids, MI: Eerdmans, 2004), p. 399.

52. Directory of the Latino Churches of Christ, available at http://www.editorial lapaz.org/directorio_EstadosUnidos.htm.

53. "Directorio del Ministerio de las Iglesias de Cristo e Iglesias Cristianas de habla hispana 2010," Spanish American Evangelistic Ministries, 2010, http://www.saeministries.com.

54. Grebler et al., *The Mexican-American People*, p. 488.

55. Jimenez, "Hispanics in the Movement," pp. 396–99.

56. Ibid.

57. Much of this material was originally presented by this author in a different format in "Types of Latino Pentecostalism in Los Angeles 2009," a white paper for the Center for Religion and Civic Culture of the University of Southern California, 2009.

58. José A. Reyes, *Los Hispanos en los Estados Unidos: Un Reto y una Oportunidad para la Iglesia* (Cleveland, TN: White Wing Publishing House and Press, 1985).

59. Alex D. Montoya, *Hispanic Ministry in North America* (Grand Rapids, MI: Zondervan, 1987).

60. Conversations and e-mail exchange with Dr. Jesse Miranda, last e-mail January 6, 2011.

61. See the Esperanza website for more information: http://www.esperanza.us.

62. See the NHCLC website for more information: http://www.nhclc.org.

63. See the NHCLC mission statement at http://www.nhclc.org/our-mission.

64. See the CONLAMIC website for more information: http://www.conlamic.org/.

## Chapter 4

1. José Míguez Bonino wrote a book from which the title of this section is drawn: *Faces of Latin American Protestantism* (Grand Rapids, MI: Eerdmans, 1997).

2. Jean-Pierre Bastian, *Protestantismos y Modernidad Latinoamericana: Historia de unas Minorías Religiosas Activas en América Latina* (Mexico City: Fondo de Cultura Económica, 1994), pp. 228–32, 279–305.

3. See Samuel Escobar, "A Missiological Approach to Latin American Protestantism," *International Review of Mission* 87, no. 345 (April 1998): 161–73.

4. See "African Initiated Church," *Wikipedia* http://en.wikipedia.org/wiki/African_Initiated_Church (last modified November 28, 2010).

5. Quote by Justo Sierra, *Evolución política del pueblo mexicano* (digitalized for the Internet by Biblioteca Virtual Universal, 2003), p. 228.

6. Larry L. Hunt, "Hispanic Protestantism in the United States: Trends by Decade and Generation," *Social Forces* 77, no. 4 (June 1999): 842.

7. Pew 2007, p. 31.

8. Trinity study, p. 23. At the end of the report the categories are explained, though no explanation is given for the unique categories. This author looked up the research methodology (http://www.americanreligionsurvey-aris.org/reports/methods.html) but could find no explanation for using these categories.

9. Efraín Agosto, "Are U.S. Latino Society & Culture Undergoing Secularization?" (paper presented to the Institute for the Study of Secularization in Society and Culture, Trinity College, March 7, 2006).

10. See the NHCLC website (http://www.nhclc.org) for an example of this broad usage of the term *evangelical.*

11. Many of the ideas in this section were originally developed in "What Happens to Church When We Move *Latinamente* beyond Inherited Ecclesiologies?" in *Building Bridges, Doing Justice: Constructing a Latino/a Ecumenical Theology,* ed. Orlando Espín (Maryknoll, NY: Orbis Books, 2009), pp. 167–82.

12. Miguel A. de la Torre and Edwin David Aponte, *Introducing Latino/a Theologies* (Maryknoll, NY: Orbis Books, 2001).

13. See "Annotated Bibliography of Writings by 19th Century Latino Protestants," appendix F, in Juan Martínez, "Origins and Development of Protestantism among Latinos in the Southwestern United States, 1836–1900" (PhD diss., School of World Mission, Fuller Theological Seminary, 1996), pp. 446–54.

14. Daniel Ramírez, "Alabaré a mi Señor: Cultura e Ideología en la Himnología Protestante Latina," in *Iglesias Peregrinas en Busca de Identidad,* ed. Juan F. Martínez and Luis Scott (Buenos Aires: Kairós, 2004), pp. 207–34, 227.

15. Ramírez, "Alabaré a mi Señor," p. 226.

16. Justo González, *Mañana: Christian Theology from a Hispanic Perspective* (Nashville: Abingdon, 1990), and *Santa Biblia: The Bible through Hispanic Eyes* (Nashville: Abingdon, 1996).

17. González, *Mañana,* pp. 77–78.

18. Orlando E. Costas, *Christ outside the Gate: Mission beyond Christendom* (Maryknoll, NY: Orbis Books, 1982).

19. Orlando E. Costas, *Liberating News: A Theology of Contextual Evangelization* (Eugene, OR: Wipf and Stock, 2002).

20. Ibid., p. 20.

21. Ibid., p. 149.

22. Costas, *Christ outside the Gate,* pp. xiii, xiv.

23. Ibid., p. 194.

24. Ibid., p. 194.

25. Eldin Villafañe, *The Liberating Spirit: Toward an Hispanic American Pentecostal Social Ethic* (Grand Rapids, MI: Eerdmans, 1993).

26. Eldin Villafañe, Douglas Hall, Efraín Agosto, and Bruce W. Jackson, *Seek the Peace of the City: Reflections on Urban Ministry* (Grand Rapids, MI: Eerdmans, 1995).

27. Eldin Villafañe, *Fe, Espiritualidad y Justicia: Teología Posmoderna de un Boricua en la Diáspora* (Rio Piedras: Palabra y más, 2006).

28. Villafañe, *Liberating Spirit,* p. 222.

29. See Villafañe, *Seek the Peace of the City.*

30. For an explanation of the role of *lo cotidiano* in Latina theology, see Ada María Isasi-Díaz, *Mujerista Theology: A Theology for the Twenty-First Century* (Maryknoll, NY: Orbis, 1996).

31. José David Rodríguez and Loida I. Martell-Otero, eds., *Teología en Conjunto: A Collaborative Hispanic Protestant Theology* (Louisville: Westminster John Knox, 1997).

32. David Maldonado Jr., ed., *Protestantes/Protestants: Hispanic Christianity in Mainline Traditions* (Nashville: Abingdon, 1999).

33. Jorge E. Maldonado and Juan F. Martínez, eds., *Vivir y Servir en el Exilio: Lecturas Teológicas de la Experiencia Latina en los Estados Unidos* (Buenos Aires: Kairós, 2008).

34. Benjamín Valentín, ed., *New Horizons in Hispanic/Latino(a) Theology* (Cleveland: The Pilgrim Press, 2003).

35. Benjamín Valentín, "Oy, ¿Y Ahora Qué? / Say, Now What? Prospective Lines of Development for U.S. Hispanic/Latino(a) Theology," in *New Horizons in Hispanic/ Latino(a) Theology,* ed. Benjamín Valentín, pp. 101–18, p. 117.

36. See Jacqueline María Hagan, *Migration Miracle: Faith, Hope, and Meaning on the Undocumented Journey* (Cambridge: Harvard University Press, 2008), in which the author follows the undocumented as they theologize about their experiences.


## Chapter 5

1. There was a bit of overlap among the Methodists in Arizona and Texas, but most denominations did not cross these geographic lines until well into the 20th century.

2. Juan Martínez, *Sea La Luz: The Making of Mexican Protestantism in the American Southwest, 1829–1900* (Denton: University of North Texas Press, 2006), pp. 19–26, 106.

3. Harriet Kellogg, *Life of Mrs. Emily J. Harwood* (Albuquerque: El Abogado Press, 1903), p. 304.

4. Martínez, *Sea La Luz,* pp. 44–45.

5. Ibid., pp. 107–8.

6. See Larry L. Hunt, "The Spirit of Hispanic Protestantism in the United States: National Survey Comparisons of Catholics and Non-Catholics," *Social Science Quarterly* 79, no. 4 (December 1998): 828–45.

7. The book *Pathways to Hope and Faith among Hispanic Teens,* ed. by Ken Johnson-Mondragón (Stockton, CA: Instituto Fe y Vida, 2007), is the first study to look at faith and identity formation among Latina youth.

8. I have published previous versions of this figure in "Aculturación e Iglesia Evangélica Latina en los Estados Unidos" in *Iglesias Peregrinas en Busca de Identidad* (Buenos Aires: Kairós, 2004), pp. 147–164, 159, and *Walk with the People: Latino Ministry in the United States* (Nashville: Abingdon Press, 2008), p. 66.

9. For a study of how and why Americans move between churches or away from them, see Robert Putnam and David E. Campbell, *American Grace: How Religion Divides and Unites Us* (New York: Simon & Schuster, 2010).

10. See Pew study, "English Usage among Hispanics in the United States" (November 29, 2007), at http://pewresearch.org/pubs/644/english-language-usage-hispanics. Nonetheless, Spanish-language media continues to grow in the United States, as seen by the decision of Televisa, the Spanish-language media giant from Mexico, to extend it partnership with Univisión in the United States. See "Univision and Televisa seal deal to extend partnership," *Los Angeles Times,* December 10, 2010, http://latimesblogs.latimes.com/entertainmentnewsbuzz/2010/12/univision-and-televisa-extend-partnership.html.

11. Manuel Ortiz, *The Hispanic Challenge: Opportunities Confronting the Church* (Downers Grove, IL: IVP Academic), pp. 104–5.

12. See the summaries of the Pew 2007 report in the first part of chapter 1.

13. I base this observation on personal experience with family and friends who are third-generation-plus Protestants like me.

14. See Hunt, "The Spirit of Hispanic Protestantism in the United States."

15. Daniel A. Rodríguez, *A Future for the Latino Church: Models for Multilingual, Multigenerational Hispanic Congregations* (Downers Grove, IL: InterVarsity Press, 2011), MS p. 59. (The Rodríguez text had not yet gone to press at the time of writing this book, so the page numbering was still tentative.)

16. Rodríguez, *A Future for the Latino Church,* MS p. 101 (tentative).

17. For models and ideas about how this works in practice, see Mark Lau Branson and Juan F. Martínez, *Churches, Cultures and Leadership: A Practical Theology of Congregations and Ethnicities* (Downers Grove, IL: InterVarsity Press, 2011).

## Chapter 6

1. Juan Martínez, *Sea La Luz: The Making of Mexican Protestantism in the American Southwest, 1829–1900* (Denton: University of North Texas Press, 2006), pp. 45–49.

2. Leo Grebler, Joan W. Moore, Ralph C. Guzman, et al., *The Mexican-American People: The Nation's Second Largest Minority* (New York: The Free Press, 1970), p. 503.

3. Manuel Gamio, *Mexican Migration to the United States: A Study of Human Migration and Adjustment* (New York: Dover Publications, 1971), pp. 114–17. See also Manuel Gamio, *The Life Story of the Mexican Immigrant* (New York: Dover Publications, 1971).

4. For example, Rodolfo Acuña, *Occupied America: A History of Chicanos* (New York: Harper Collins, 1988), and Thomas Sheridan, *Los Tucsonenses The Mexican Community in Tucson 1854–1941* (Tucson: University of Arizona Press, 1986), do not even mention Protestants at all. Arnoldo De León's *The Tejano Community, 1836–1900* (Albuquerque: University of New Mexico Press, 1982) includes two paragraphs that

recognize that there were Protestant preachers in the *tejano* community, but no information about churches in the community.

5. Grebler et al., *The Mexican-American People,* p. 487.

6. Larry L. Hunt, "The Spirit of Hispanic Protestantism in the United States: National Survey Comparisons of Catholics and Non-Catholics," *Social Science Quarterly* 79, no. 4 (December 1998). See the bibliography on pp. 844–45.

7. Ibid., pp. 843–44.

8. See Frederick L. Whitam, "New York's Spanish Protestants," *The Christian Century*, February 7, 1962.

9. See Hunt, "The Spirit of Hispanic Protestantism," and Trinity (2008).

10. See *Sea La Luz*, pp. 44–49, for a description of the American mandate and the role it played in motivating Protestant missionaries in their work among Latinas.

11. The *Penitentes* were a Catholic lay group that formed in northern New Mexico during the Spanish colonial period. For an introduction to this movement, see Alberto López Pulido, *Sacred World of the Penitentes* (Washington, D.C.: Smithsonian Institution Press, 2000).

12. Alexander Darley, *The Passionists of the Southwest, or The Holy Brotherhood: A Revelation of the "Penitentes"* (reprinted by Glorieta, NM: The Rio Grande Press, 1968).

13. Edith Agnew and Ruth K. Barber, "The Unique Presbyterian School System of New Mexico," *Journal of Presbyterian History* 49, no. 3 (1971): 197–221; and Norman J. Bender, "A College Where One Ought to Be," *Colorado Magazine* 49, no. 3 (1972): 196–218.

14. Randi Jones Walker, *Protestantism in the Sangre de Cristos, 1850–1920* (Albuquerque: University of New Mexico Press, 1991); and Martínez, *Sea La Luz.*

15. Paul Barton, *Hispanic Methodists, Presbyterians, and Baptists in Texas* (Austin: University of Texas Press, 2006).

16. Martinez, *Sea La Luz.*

17. Pablo García Verduzco, *Bosquejo Histórico del Metodismo Mexicano* (Nashville: Cokesbury Press, 1933).

18. Douglas R. Brackenridge and Francisco O. García-Treto, *Iglesia Presbiteriana: A History of Presbyterians and Mexican Americans in the Southwest* (San Antonio: Trinity University Press, 1974).

19. Daisy Machado, *Of Borders and Margins: Hispanic Disciples in Texas, 1888–1945* (Oxford: Oxford University Press and the American Academy of Religion, 2003).

20. Justo González, ed., *Each in Our Own Tongue: A History of Hispanics in United Methodism* (Nashville: Abingdon, 1991).

21. Joshua Grijalva, *A History of Mexican Baptists in Texas, 1881–1981* (Office of Language Missions, Baptist General Convention of Texas and Mexican Baptist Convention of Texas, 1982).

22. Rafael Falcón, *The Hispanic Mennonite Church in North America, 1932–1982* (Scottdale, PA: Herald Press, 1986).

23. *50 Aniversario de la Asamblea Apostólica de la Fe en Cristo Jesús 1916–1966* (reprinted by Rancho Cucamonga, CA: Secretaría de Educación Cristiana, n.d.) and José Ortega, *Mis Memorias en la Iglesia y Asamblea Apostólica de la Fe en Cristo Jesús* (Guadalajara: Imprenta Jalisco, 1998).

24. Manuel Vásquez, *The Untold Story: 100 Years of Hispanic Adventism, 1899–1999* (Nampa, ID: Pacific Press Publishing Association, 2000).

25. For an example of this perspective, see E. C. Orozco, *Republican Protestantism in Aztlán* (Glendale, CA: Petereins Press, 1980).

26. Brackenridge and García-Treto, *Iglesia Presbiteriana*.

27. Some of the HTI scholars mentioned in this book are Paul Barton, Arlene Sánchez-Walsh, Daisy Machado, Elizabeth Conde-Frazier, Daniel Ramírez, and Nora Lozano.

28. Paul Barton and David Maldonado Jr., compilers, *Hispanic Christianity within Mainline Protestant Traditions: A Bibliography* (Decatur, GA: AETH, 1998).

29. Moisés Sandoval, *Fronteras: A History of the Latin American Church in the USA Since 1513* (San Antonio: Mexican American Cultural Center, 1983).

30. Daniel R. Rodríguez-Díaz and David Cortés-Fuentes, eds., *Hidden Stories: Unveiling the History of the Latino Church* (Decatur, GA: AETH, 1994).

31. Rodello Wilson, ed., *Hacia una historia de la iglesia evangélica hispana de California del Sur* (Montebello, CA: AHET, 1993).

32. Juan F. Martínez and Luis Scott, eds., *Iglesias Peregrinas en Busca de Identidad: Cuadros del Protestantismo Latino en los Estados Unidos* (Buenos Aires: Kairós, 2004).

33. Arlene Sánchez-Walsh, *Latino Pentecostal Identity: Evangelical Faith, Self and Society* (New York: Columbia University Press, 2003).

34. Luis D. León, *La Llorona's Children: Religion, Life, and Death in the U.S.-Mexican Borderlands* (Berkeley: University of California Press, 2004). This book contains a chapter on Victory Outreach.

35. Rudy V. Busto, *King Tiger: The Religious Vision of Reies Lopez Tijerina* (Albuquerque: University of New Mexico Press, 2006).

36. The Mennonite theologian Hugo Zorrilla has often stated that if you scratch a Latin American or Latino Protestant, down deep enough you find a Catholic.

37. Hjamil A. Martínez-Vásquez, *Latina/o y Musulman: The Construction of Latina/o Identity among Latina/o Muslims in the United States* (Eugene, OR: Pickwick Publications, 2010).

38. PhD student Tim Halls (Fuller Theological Seminary) is studying the "missionary" encounter between Muslim and Latina Protestant immigrants in several U.S. urban areas. Both believe they have a responsibility to "evangelize" the other, even as both are culturally adapting to life in the United States.

39. All the names have been changed, as have other identifying markers. This author knows most of the people or stories from personal experience. A couple of the stories are based on information from colleagues. A couple of stories are composites, so as to make it more difficult to clearly identify the people.

## Chapter 7

1. Justo González, *Mañana: Christian Theology from a Hispanic Perspective* (Nashville: Abingdon, 1990), p. 164.

2. U.S. Census Bureau, "Percent Change in Resident Population for the 50 States, the District of Columbia, and Puerto Rico: 2000 to 2010," Available at: http://2010.census.gov/news/press-kits/apportionment/apport.html.

3. See "Univision and Televisa seal deal to extend partnership," *Los Angeles Times,* December 10, 2010, http://latimesblogs.latimes.com/entertainmentnewsbuzz/2010/12/univision-and-televisa-extend-partnership.html.

4. Ken Johnson-Mondragón, ed., *Pathways to Hope and Faith among Hispanic Teens* (Stockton, CA: Instituto Fe y Vida, 2007).

# Bibliography

## Works Cited in This Volume

Acuña, Rodolfo. *Occupied America: A History of Chicanos*. New York: Harper Collins, 1988.

"African Initiated Church." *Wikipedia*.http://en.wikipedia.org/wiki/African_Initiated_Church.

"AG Stats Color Handout." 2009 Report (published in 2010), Statistics on the Assemblies of God, USA. http://www.ag.org/top/about/statistics/index.cfm.

Agnew, Edith, and Ruth K. Barber. "The Unique Presbyterian School System of New Mexico." *Journal of Presbyterian History* 49, no. 3 (1971): 197–221.

Agosto, Efraín. "Are U.S. Latino Society & Culture Undergoing Secularization?" Paper presented to the Institute for the Study of Secularization in Society and Culture, Trinity College, March 7, 2006.

Banco Interamericano de Desarrollo. "Remesas a América Latina y el Caribe 2009." http://www.iadb.org/mif/remesas_map.cfm?language=Spanish.

Barton, Paul. *Hispanic Methodists, Presbyterians and Methodists in Texas*. Austin: University of Texas Press, 2006.

Barton, Paul, and David Maldonado Jr., compilers. *Hispanic Christianity within Mainline Protestant Traditions: A Bibliography*. Decatur, GA: AETH, 1998.

Bastian, Jean-Pierre. *Protestantismos y modernidad latinoamericana: Historia de unas minorías religiosas activas en América Latina*. México: Fondo de Cultura Económica, 1994.

Bender, Norman J. "A College Where One Ought to Be." *The Colorado Magazine* 49, no. 3 (1972): 196–212.

Bonino, José. *Faces of Latin American Protestantism*. Grand Rapids, MI: Eerdmans, 1997.

"Bracero History Archive." http://braceroarchive.org/about.

Brackenridge, R. Douglas, and Francisco O. García-Treto. *Iglesia Presbiteriana: A History of Presbyterians and Mexican Americans in the Southwest*. San Antonio: Trinity University Press, 1987.

Branson, Mark Lau, and Juan F. Martínez. *Churches, Cultures and Leadership: A Practical Theology of Congregations and Ethnicities.* Downers Grove, IL: InterVarsity Press, 2011.

Busto, Rudy V. *King Tiger: The Religious Vision of Reies Lopez Tijerina.* Albuquerque: University of New Mexico Press, 2006.

*Changing Faiths: Latinos and the Transformation of American Religion* (2007). http://pewhispanic.org/reports/report.php?ReportID=75.

CONLAMIC. http://www.conlamic.org/.

Costas, Orlando E. *Christ outside the Gate: Mission beyond Christendom.* Maryknoll, NY: Orbis, 1982.

Costas, Orlando E. *Liberating News: A Theology of Contextual Evangelization.* Eugene, OR: Wipf and Stock, 2002.

Darley, Alexander. *The Passionists of the Southwest, or The Holy Brotherhood: A Revelation of the "Penitentes."* Glorieta, NM: The Rio Grande Press, 1968.

Deck, Allan Figueroa, Yolanda Tarango, and Timothy M. Matovina, eds. *Perspectivas Hispanic Ministry: The Challenge of Proselytism.* Kansas City, MO: Sheed & Ward, 1995.

De la Torre, Miguel A., and Edwin David Aponte. *Introducing Latino/a Theologies.* Maryknoll, NY: Orbis, 2001.

De León, Arnoldo. *The Tejano Community, 1836–1900.* Albuquerque: University of New Mexico Press, 1982.

"Demographics of Atheism." *Wikipedia.* http://en.wikipedia.org/wiki/Demographics_of_atheism.

Directory of the Latino Churches of Christ. http://www.editoriallapaz.org/directorio_EstadosUnidos.htm.

Durso, Pamela R., and Keith E. Durso. *The Story of Baptists in the United States.* Brentwood, TN: Baptist History and Heritage Society, 2006.

"English Usage among Hispanics in the United States." http://pewresearch.org/pubs/644/english-language-usage-hispanics.

Episcopal Church USA. "Latino/Hispanic Ministries." http://www.episcopalchurch.org/109405_ENG_HTM.htm.

Escobar, Samuel. "A Missiological Approach to Latin American Protestantism." *International Review of Mission* 87, no. 345 (April 1998): 161–73.

Esperanza. http://www.esperanza.us.

Espín, Orlando. *Building Bridges, Doing Justice: Constructing a Latino/a Ecumenical Theology.* Maryknoll, NY: Orbis, 2009.

Estrada, Tomás. "Hay una senda." Copyright 1960 by R.C. Savage, assigned to Singspiration, Inc.

Falcón, Rafael. *The Hispanic Mennonite Church in North America, 1932–1982.* Scottdale, PA: Herald Press, 1986.

*50 Aniversario de la Asamblea Apostólica de la Fe en Cristo Jesús 1916–1966.* Reprinted by Rancho Cucamonga, CA: Secretaría de Educación Cristiana, n.d.

Gamio, Manuel. *The Life Story of the Mexican Immigrant.* New York: Dover Publications, 1971.

Gamio, Manuel. *Mexican Immigration to the United States: A Study of Human Migration and Adjustment.* New York: Dover Publications, 1971.

García Verduzco, Pablo. *Bosquejo Histórico del Metodismo Mexicano.* Nashville: Cokesbury Press, 1933.

González, Antonio. *The Gospel of Faith and Justice*. Maryknoll, NY: Orbis Books, 2005.

González, Juan. *Harvest of Empire: A History of Latinos in America*. New York: Penguin, 2000.

González, Justo, ed. *Each in Our Own Tongue: A History of Hispanics in United Methodism*. Nashville: Abingdon Press, 1991.

González, Justo. *Mañana: Christian Theology from a Hispanic Perspective*. Nashville: Abingdon, 1990.

González, Justo. *Santa Biblia: The Bible through Hispanic Eyes*. Nashville: Abingdon, 1996.

Gracia, Jorge J. E. *Hispanic/Latino Identity: A Philosophical Perspective*. Malden, MA: Blackwell, 2000.

Grebler, Leo, Joan W. Moore, Ralph C. Guzman, et al. *The Mexican-American People: The Nation's Second Largest Minority*. New York: The Free Press, 1970.

Greeley, Andrew M. "The Demography of American Catholics: 1965–1990." In *The Sociology of Andrew M. Greeley*. Atlanta: Scholars Press, 1994.

Greeley, Andrew. "Is Ethnicity Unamerican?" *New Catholic World* 219 (June 1976): 106–12.

Grijalva, Joshua. *A History of Mexican Baptists in Texas, 1881–1981*. n.p: Office of Language Missions. Baptist General Convention of Texas and Mexican Baptist Convention of Texas, 1982.

Hagan, Jacqueline M. *Migration Miracle: Faith, Hope, and Meaning on the Undocumented Journey*. Cambridge: Harvard University Press, 2008.

Hanciles, Jehu J. *Beyond Christendom: Globalization, African Migration and the Transformation of the West*. Maryknoll, NY: Orbis, 2008.

"Hispanic Heritage Month 2010: Sept. 15–Oct. 15," Facts for Features, CB10-FF.17. U.S. Census Bureau, July 15, 2010.

Hispanic Ministries in the Southwest: Directions for the Future. http://www.pcusa.org/resource/hispanic-strategy/.

"Hispanic Ten Year Summary Report (2000–2009)." Annual Church Profile, 2000–2009, compiled by the Center for Missional Research, North American Mission Board, [Southern Baptist Convention], Alpharetta, GA.

Holland, Clifton. "A Chronology of Significant Protestant Beginnings in Hispanic Ministry in the USA." On-Line Handbook of Hispanic Protestant Denominations, Institutions and Ministries in the USA. http://www.hispanicchurchesusa.net/.

Holland, Clifton. *The Religious Dimension in Hispanic Los Angeles: A Protestant Case Study*. Los Angeles: William Carey Library, 1974.

Holland, Clifton. "A Working Table of Statistics on Hispanic Protestant Denominations & Church Associations in the USA, 1993–2009." Unpublished document.

Hunt, Larry L. "Hispanic Protestantism in the United States: Trends by Decade and Generation." *Social Forces* 77, no. 4 (June 1999): 1601–23.

Hunt, Larry L. "The Spirit of Hispanic Protestantism in the United States: National Survey Comparisons of Catholics and Non-Catholics." *Social Science Quarterly* 79, no. 4 (December 1998): 828–45.

Huntington, Samuel. *Who Are We? The Challenges to America's National Identity*. New York: Simon & Schuster, 2005.

Espinosa, Gastón, Virgilio Elizondo, and Jesse Miranda. "Hispanic Churches in American Public Life: Summary of Findings" [from HCAPL project funded by Pew Charitable Trusts]. Institute for Latino Studies at the University of Notre Dame. *Interim Reports* 2 (2003), http://latinostudies.nd.edu/pubs/pubs/ HispChurchesEnglishWEB.pdf.

Isasi-Díaz, Ada María. *Mujerista Theology: A Theology for the Twenty-First Century.* Maryknoll, NY: Orbis, 1996.

Jimenez, Pablo. "Hispanics in the Movement." In *The Encyclopedia of the Stone-Campbell Movement,* ed. Douglas A. Foster, Paul M. Blowers, Anthony L. Dunnavant, and D. Newell Williams. Grand Rapids, MI: Eerdmans, 2004.

Johnson-Mondragón, Ken, ed. *Pathways to Hope and Faith among Hispanic Teens.* Stockton, CA: Instituto Fe y Vida, 2007.

Kellogg, Harriet S. *Life of Mrs. Emily J. Harwood.* Albuquerque: El Abogado Press, 1903.

León, Luis D. *La Llorona's Children: Religion, Life, and Death in the U.S.-Mexican Borderlands.* Berkeley: University of California Press, 2004.

Machado, Daisy. *Of Borders and Margins: Hispanic Disciples in Texas, 1888–1945.* Oxford: Oxford University Press and the American Academy of Religion, 2003.

Maldonado, David, Jr., ed. *Protestantes/Protestants: Hispanic Christianity in Mainline Traditions.* Nashville: Abingdon, 1999.

Maldonado, Jorge E., and Juan F. Martínez, eds. *Vivir y Servir en el Exilio: Lecturas Teológicas de la Experiencia Latina en los Estados Unidos.* Buenos Aires: Kairós, 2008.

Martínez, Juan F. *Sea la Luz: The Making of Mexican Protestantism in the American Southwest 1829–1900.* Denton: University of North Texas Press, 2006.

Martínez, Juan F., and Luis Scott, eds. *Iglesias Peregrinas en Busca de Identidad: Cuadros del Protestantismo Latino en los Estados Unidos.* Buenos Aires: Kairós, 2004.

Martínez-Vásquez, Hjamil A. *Latina/o y Musulman: The Construction of Latina/o Identity among Latina/o Muslims in the United States.* Eugene, OR: Pickwick, 2010.

McLean, Robert. *The Northern Mexican.* New York: Home Missions Council, 1930.

Montoya, Alex D. *Hispanic Ministry in North America.* Grand Rapids, MI: Zondervan, 1987.

NHCLC. http://www.nhclc.org.

NHCLC. Mission statement. http://www.nhclc.org/our-mission.

Orozco, E. C. *Republican Protestantism in Aztlán: The Encounter between Mexicanism & Anglo-Saxon Secular Humanism in the US Southwest.* Glendale, CA: Petereins, 1980.

Ortega, José. *Mis Memorias en la Iglesia y Asamblea Apostólica de la Fe en Cristo Jesús.* Guadalajara: Imprenta Jalisco, 1998.

Ortegón, Samuel. "The Religious Status of the Mexican Population of Los Angeles." MA thesis, University of Southern California, 1932.

Ortiz, Manuel. *The Hispanic Challenge: Opportunities Confronting the Church.* Downers Grove, IL: InterVarsity Press, 1993.

Pew Research Center. "11.9 Million—Undocumented Immigrants in the U.S." http:// pewresearch.org/databank/dailynumber/?NumberID=778.

"Por un Estado realmente laico en Perú." March 15, 2010. http://www.laicismo.org/detalle.php?pk=2718.

"Protestantism by Country." *Wikipedia.* http://en.wikipedia.org/wiki/Protestantism_by_country.

"Protestantism in Mexico." *Wikipedia.* http://en.wikipedia.org/wiki/Protestantism_in_Mexico.

Pulido, Alberto López. *Sacred World of the Penitentes.* Washington, DC: Smithsonian Institution Press, 2000.

Putnam, Robert and David E. Campbell. *American Grace: How Religion Divides and Unites Us.* New York: Simon & Schuster, 2010.

Ramírez-Johnson, Johnny, and Edwin I. Hernández, et al. *Avance: A Vision for a New Mañana.* Loma Linda, CA: Loma Linda University Press, 2003.

Rankin, Melinda. *Texas in 1850.* Waco, TX: Reprinted by Texian Press, 1966.

Reyes, Albert. "Unification to Integration: A Brief History of the Hispanic Baptist Convention of Texas." Unpublished paper.

Reyes, José A. *Los Hispanos en los Estados Unidos: Un Reto y una Oportunidad para la Iglesia.* Cleveland: White Wing Publishing House and Press, 1985.

Robeck, Cecil M. *The Azusa Street Mission and Revival: The Birth of the Global Pentecostal Movement.* Nashville: Nelson Reference, 2006.

Rodríguez, Daniel A. *A Future for the Latino Church: Models for Multilingual, Multigenerational Hispanic Congregations.* Downers Grove, IL: InterVarsity Press, 2011.

Rodríguez, José David, and Loida I. Martell-Otero, eds. *Teología en Conjunto: A Collaborative Hispanic Protestant Theology.* Louisville: Westminster John Knox, 1997.

Rodríguez-Díaz, Daniel R., and David Cortés-Fuentes, eds. *Hidden Stories: Unveiling the History of the Latino Church.* Atlanta: AETH, 1994.

Sánchez-Walsh, Arlene. *Latino Pentecostal Identity: Evangelical Faith, Self and Society.* New York: Columbia University Press, 2003.

Sandoval, Moisés. *Fronteras: A History of the Latin American Church in the USA since 1513.* Austin: Mexican American Cultural Center, 1983.

Scott, James C., Jr. *Aimee La Gente Hispana Estaba en su Corzaón.* Seattle: Foursquare Media, 2008.

Sheridan, Thomas. *Los Tucsonenses The Mexican Community in Tucson 1854–1941.* Tucson: University of Arizona Press, 1986.

Sierra, Justo. *Evolución política del pueblo mexicano.* Digitalized for the Internet by Biblioteca Virtual Universal, 2003.

Spanish American Evangelistic Ministries. "Directorio del Ministerio de las Iglesias de Cristo e Iglesias Cristianas de habla hispana 2010." http://www.saeministries.com.

"Spanish Evangelism of the United Pentecostal Church." http://www.spanishevangelism.net/.

Texas-Mexican Presbytery (PCUS) Records, 1861–1954. http://www.austinseminary.edu/page.cfm?p=574.

"The Spirit of Hispanic Protestantism in the United States: National Survey Comparisons of Catholics and Non-Catholics." *Social Science Quarterly* 79, no. 4 (December 1998): 828–45.

"Traditionalist Catholics Attack, Expel Christians in Mexico." Persecution.org, August 19, 2009. http://www.persecution.org/2009/08/20/traditionalist-catholics-attack-expel-christians-in-mexico/.

Trinity College. "U.S. Latino Religious Identification, 1990–2008: Growth, Diversity & Transformation." American Religious Identification Survey 2008. http://www.americanreligionsurvey-aris.org/latinos2008.pdf.

"Univision and Televisa seal deal to extend partnership." *Los Angeles Times,* December 10, 2010. http://latimesblogs.latimes.com/entertainmentnewsbuzz/2010/12/univision-and-televisa-extend-partnership.html.

U.S. Census Bureau. "Percent Change in Resident Population for the 50 States, the District of Columbia, and Puerto Rico: 2000 to 2010." http://2010.census.gov/news/press-kits/apportionment/apport.html.

U.S. Citizenship and Immigration Services. http://www.uscis.gov/portal/site/uscis/menuitem.eb1d4c2a3e5b9ac89243c6a7543f6d1a/?vgnextoid=848f7f2ef0745210VgnVCM100000082ca60aRCRD&vgnextchannel=848f7f2ef0745210VgnVCM100000082ca60aRCRD.

Valentín, Benjamín, ed. *New Horizons in Hispanic/Latino(a) Theology.* Cleveland: The Pilgrim Press, 2003.

Vásquez, Manuel. *La Historia Aun No Contada: 100 Años de Adventismo Hispano.* Nampa, ID: Pacific Press Publishing Association, 2000.

Vásquez, Manuel. *The Untold Story: 100 Years of Hispanic Adventism, 1899–1999.* Nampa, ID: Pacific Press Publishing Association, 2000.

Weber, David J., ed. *Foreigners in Their Native Land: Historical Roots of the Mexican Americans,* rev. ed. Albuquerque: University of New Mexico Press, 2004.

Villafañe, Eldin. *Fe, Espiritualidad y Justicia: Teología Posmoderna de un Boricua en la Diáspora.* Rio Piedras: Palabra y más, 2006.

Villafañe, Eldin. *The Liberating Spirit: Toward an Hispanic American Pentecostal Social Ethic.* Grand Rapids, MI: Eerdmans, 1993.

Villafañe, Eldin, Douglas Hall, Efraín Agosto, and Bruce W. Jackson. *Seek the Peace of the City: Reflections on Urban Ministry.* Grand Rapids, MI: Eerdmans, 1995.

Walker, Randi Jones. *Protestantism in the Sangre de Cristos, 1850–1920.* Albuquerque: University of New Mexico Press, 1991.

Ward, Geoffrey C., and Ken Burns. *The War: An Intimate History, 1941–1945.* New York: Knopf, 2007.

Wilson, Rodelo, ed. *Hacia una historia de la iglesia evangélica hispana de California del Sur.* Montebello, CA: AHET, 1993.

Whitam, Frederick L. "New York's Spanish Protestants." *The Christian Century,* February 7, 1962.

Yohn, Susan. *A Contest of Faith: Missionary Women and Pluralism in the American Southwest.* Ithaca, NY: Cornell University Press, 1995.

## Selected Works on Latino Protestantism

In 1998 Paul Barton and David Maldonado published an extensive bibliography of materials on Latino Protestantism in the United States, *Hispanic Christianity with a Mainline Protestant Tradition: A Bibliography* (Decatur, GA: Asociación para la Educación Teológica Hispana, 1998). This updated bibliography includes only materials that have been published since 1998 or that were not included in the Barton/Maldonado bibliography. Clifton L. Holland is also developing a series of resources about Latino Protestantism, *On-Line Handbook of Hispanic Protestant Denominations, Institutions and Ministries in the USA,* at http://www.hispanicchurchesusa.net/. The site has a great deal of historical and demographic resources. None of the specific documents from this website are listed in the bibliography.

Alfaro, Sammy. *Divino Compañero: Toward a Hispanic Pentecostal Christology.* Eugene, OR: Pickwick, 2010.

Barton, Paul. *Hispanic Methodists, Presbyterians, and Baptists in Texas.* Austin: University of Texas Press, 2006.

Bender, Norman J. "A College Where One Ought to Be." *The Colorado Magazine* 49, no. 3 (1972): 196–212.

Busto, Rudy V. *King Tiger: The Religious Vision of Reies Lopez Tijerina.* Albuquerque: University of New Mexico Press, 2006.

CONLAMIC. http://www.conlamic.org/.

Crane, Ken. *Latino Churches: Faith, Family, and Ethnicity in the Second Generation.* New York: LFB Scholarly Publishing LLC, 2003.

Crespo, Orlando. *Being Latino in Christ: Finding Wholeness in your Ethnic Identity.* Downers Grove, IL: Intervarsity Press, 2003.

Directory of the Latino Churches of Christ. http://www.editoriallapaz.org/directorio_EstadosUnidos.htm.

Episcopal Church USA. "Latino/Hispanic Ministries." http://www.episcopalchurch.org/109405_ENG_HTM.htm.

Esperanza. http://www.esperanza.us.

García-Johnson, Oscar. *The Mestizo/a Community of the Spirit: A Postmodern Latino/a Ecclesiology.* Eugene, OR: Pickwick, 2008.

García Verduzco, Pablo. *Bosquejo Histórico del Metodismo Mexicano.* Nashville: Cokesbury Press, 1933.

Hispanic Ministries in the Southwest: Directions for the Future. http://www.pcusa.org/resource/hispanic-strategy/.

Holland, Clifton. *The Religious Dimension in Hispanic Los Angeles: A Protestant Case Study.* Los Angeles: William Carey Library, 1974.

Hunt, Larry L. "Hispanic Protestantism in the United States: Trends by Decade and Generation." *Social Forces* 77, no. 4 (June 1999): 1601–23.

Hunt, Larry L. "The Spirit of Hispanic Protestantism in the United States: National Survey Comparisons of Catholics and Non-Catholics." *Social Science Quarterly* 79, no. 4 (December 1998): 828–45.

Jimenez, Pablo. "Hispanics in the Movement." In *The Encyclopedia of the Stone-Campbell Movement,* ed. Douglas A. Foster, Paul M. Blowers, Anthony L. Dunnavant, and D. Newell Williams. Grand Rapids, MI: Eerdmans, 2004.

León, Luis. "Born Again in East L.A., and Beyond." In *La Llorona's Children: Religion, Life, and Death in the U.S.-Mexican Borderlands,* pp. 201–40. Berkeley: University of California Press, 2004.

López Tijerina, Reies. *They Called Me "King Tiger": My Struggle for the Land and Our Rights.* Houston: Arte Público Press, 2000.

Machado, Daisy. *Of Borders and Margins Hispanic Disciples in Texas, 1888–1945*. Oxford: Oxford University Press, 2003.

Maldonado, David. *Crossing Guadalupe Street: Growing Up Hispanic & Protestant*. Albuquerque: University of New Mexico Press, 2001.

Maldonado, David, ed. *Hispanic Christianity within Mainline Traditions*. Nashville, TN: Abingdon, 1999.

Maldonado, Jorge, and Martínez, Juan, eds. *Vivir y servir en el exilio: Lecturas teológicas de la experiencia latina en los Estados Unidos*. Buenos Aires: Kairós, 2008.

Martínez, Juan. *Caminando entre el pueblo: Ministerio latino en los Estados Unidos (Walk with the People: Latino Ministry in the United States)*. Nashville, TN: Abingdon, 2008. (Published simultaneously by Abingdon in English as *Walk with the People: Latino Ministry in the United States*.)

Martínez, Juan. *Sea la Luz: The Making of Mexican Protestantism in the American Southwest, 1829–1900*. Denton: University of North Texas Press, 2006.

Martínez, Juan. "What Happens to Church When We Move *Latinamente* beyond Inherits Ecclesiologes?." In *Building Bridges, Doing Justice: Constructing a Latino/a Ecumenical Theoly,* ed. Orlando Espín, pp. 167–182. Maryknoll, NY: Orbis, 2009.

Martínez, Juan, and Scott, Luis, eds. *Iglesias peregrinas en busca de identidad*. Barcelona: Kairós, 2004. Published in English as *Los Evangélicos: Portraits of Latino Protestantism in the United States*. Eugene, OR: Wipf & Stock, 2009.

National Hispanic Christian Leadership Conference. http://www.nhclc.org.

Padilla, Alvin, Roberto Goizueta, and Eldin Villafañe, eds. *Hispanic Christian Thought at the Dawn of the 21st Century: Apuntes in Honor of Justo L. González*. Nashville, TN: Abingdon, 2005.

Pedraja, Luis. *Jesus Is My Uncle: Christology from Hispanic Perspective*. Nashville, TN: Abingdon, 1999.

Pedraja, Luis. *Teología: An Introduction to Hispanic Theology*. Nashville, TN: Abingdon, 2003.

Ramírez, Johnny. *Avance: A Vision for a New Mañana*. Loma Linda: Loma Linda University Press, 2003.

Rankin, Melinda. *Texas in 1850*. Waco, TX: Reprinted by Texian Press, 1966.

Rodríguez, Daniel A. *A Future for the Latino Church: Models for Multilingual, Multigenerational Hispanic Congregations*. Downers Grove, IL: InterVarsity Press, 2011.

Sánchez-Walsh, Arlene. *Latino Pentecostal Identity: Evangelical Faith, Self and Society*. New York: Columbia University Press, 2003.

Scott, James C., Jr. *Aimee La Gente Hispana Estaba en su Corzaón*. Seattle: Foursquare Media, 2008.

Spanish American Evangelistic Ministries. "Directorio del Ministerio de las Iglesias de Cristo e Iglesias Cristianas de habla hispana 2010." http://www.saeministries.com.

"Spanish Evangelism of the United Pentecostal Church." http://www.spanishevangelism.net/.

"The Spirit of Hispanic Protestantism in the United States: National Survey Comparisons of Catholics and Non-Catholics." *Social Science Quarterly* 79, no. 4 (December 1998): 828–45.

Vásquez, Manuel. *The Untold Story: 100 Years of Hispanic Adventism 1899–1999*. Nampa, ID: Pacific Press, 2000.

Villafañe, Eldin. *Beyond Cheap Grace: A Call to Radical Discipleship, Incarnation, and Justice*. Grand Rapids, MI: Eerdmans, 2006.

Villafañe, Eldin. *Fe, espiritualidad y justicia: Teología posmoderna de un Boricua en la diáspora*. San Juan, Puerto Rico: Palabra y más, 2006.

Wilson, Rodelo, ed. *Hacia una historia de la iglesia evangélica hispana de California del Sur*. Montebello, CA: AHET, 1993.

# Index

# About the Author

JUAN FRANCISCO MARTÍNEZ is an associate dean, the director of the Center for the Study of Hispanic Church and Community, and associate professor of Hispanic studies and pastoral leadership in the School of Theology of Fuller Theological Seminary. Among other topics, his research focuses on the history of Latino Protestantism, Latino Protestant identity, ministry in Latino Protestant churches, and Latino and Latin American Anabaptists.